D1191895

THE ALLIES AND THE RUSSIAN REVOLUTION

THE ALLIES AND THE RUSSIAN REVOLUTION

FROM THE FALL OF THE MONARCHY TO THE PEACE OF BREST-LITOVSK

ROBERT D. WARTH

DURHAM, N. C. • 1954

DUKE UNIVERSITY PRESS

Copyright, 1954, Duke University Press

CAMBRIDGE UNIVERSITY PRESS, LONDON, N.W. 1, ENGLAND

Library of Congress Catalogue Number 53-8270

PRINTED IN THE UNITED STATES OF AMERICA

BY THE SEEMAN PRINTERY, INC., DURHAM, N. C.

Preface

THIS BOOK IS a pioneer attempt to relate the diplomatic history of the first year of the Russian Revolution in so far as it concerns Russia's relations with the other Allied Powers. However, the theme has not been restricted to diplomatic negotiations alone—a self-imposed restriction which historians of diplomacy have been all too prone to accept in the past. I have sought to make the study definitive, but as long as the British, French, and Russian archives remain closed to scholars, the documentation must remain incomplete. It seems unlikely, however, that further revelations will alter the basic picture in any material way. The events themselves are subject to different interpretation, and it will be only natural that many readers will disagree with my own. Nevertheless, I have conscientiously striven to present the record for its own sake in a clear and impartial manner; and while no consistent attempt has been made to offer a particular thesis or to point up a moral, certain implicit conclusions will become apparent in the context of the narrative. For the sake of convenience perhaps the major conclusion may be summed up as follows: Allied policy and diplomacy in the period concerned was based on an almost total lack of understanding of the forces and events of the Russian Revolution. The Allies—like the Central Powers—were primarily concerned with the efficient conduct of the war, but the idealistic reasons for which they were supposedly fighting were nowhere more glaringly contradicted in practice than by their Russian policy—in regard to both democratic and Bolshevik Russia.

A number of individuals have been kind enough to read and criticize various portions of the manuscript. I wish to thank particularly Professors Louis Gottschalk, S. William Halperin, George V. Bobrinskoy, and J. Fred Rippy, all of the University of Chicago, and Professor Anatole G. Mazour of Stanford University, Dr. Fritz T. Epstein of the Library of Congress, and Dr. Henry Blumenthal, my colleague at Rutgers University, for valuable aid in this respect and in many other ways. This does not imply, of course, that they should share in whatever criticism the book may receive. Its imperfections are mine alone. I wish also to express my appreciation to the many librarians whose patience I have tried and found not wanting in the university libraries of California, Chicago, Columbia, Harvard, Stanford, and Yale, as well as to those of the Hoover Library Institute, and the Newberry Library, the New York Public Library, the Library of Congress, and the National Archives. Finally—and in full accordance with tradition—I wish to thank my wife, Terry Warth, for her unstinting aid in performing the countless necessary but unglamorous tasks involved in writing and preparing a manuscript for publication.

ROBERT D. WARTH

Newark, New Jersey
June, 1953

Contents

THE ALLIES AND THE RUSSIAN REVOLUTION

CHAPTER I

Tsarist Russia and the World War

THE WAR of 1914-18 administered a body blow to the creed of nineteenth-century liberalism—unquestioning faith in free markets, free men, and the perfectibility of mankind. From the war emerged the Russian Revolution, an upheaval of such transcending historical significance that it is scarcely yet understood even by those whose profession is the writing and teaching of history. An examination of textbooks on European history yields the interesting point that with few exceptions more space is devoted to the battles and campaigns of the First World War than to the events of the Russian Revolution.

If the assassination of the heir to the Austrian throne at Sarajevo was only the immediate and not the underlying cause of the war, so the Revolution had its inception long before the exhaustion of the tsarist dynasty in 1917 occasioned its collapse and the subsequent victory of Bolshevism. The crushing power of the German army revealed the rotten social structure upon which the old regime rested and hastened the inevitable day of its dissolution. The adventurous foreign policy which Nicholas II pursued throughout his ill-fated reign has been interpreted by some hostile critics as in large part an effort to divert the revolutionary ferment. The Russo-Japanese conflict of 1904 was perhaps so intended but merely succeeded in bringing on the Revolution of 1905, an upheaval from which the dynasty barely managed to escape by means of a few timely concessions.

The early months of the World War seemed to support the theory that a "little victorious war" was just the thing to restore vitality and prestige to the tsarist regime. If it was to be neither little nor victorious, the first half of 1914 had seen portentous signs of trouble which nothing less than war or drastic reform could have averted. Dormant for nearly a decade, the revolutionary spirit revived on a wave of political strikes. In July troops were called out to suppress an effective general strike. Barricades were thrown up and street fighting took place in the capital. The serious nature of the disturbances somewhat marred a good-will visit of President Raymond Poincaré of the French Republic, anxious to cement the alliance with Russia. Although the unrest was mainly confined to the cities, the situation seemed to be fast approaching that of 1905.

The German declaration of war on August 1, 1914,[1] was followed by a popular outburst of patriotism in Russia from which the Social Democrats were the only outspoken dissenters. Their political beliefs were based upon the principles of Marxian socialism, and since 1903 they had been split into two factions, the Bolsheviks (majoritarians), led by Vladimir Ilych Lenin, and the Mensheviks (minoritarians), led by George Plekhanov and Julius Martov. In 1912 the split had become definite and two distinct political parties emerged, each claiming the heritage of the true socialist faith as revealed in the writings of Karl Marx. Both groups expressed disapproval of the war—in marked contrast to the socialists of the other belligerent countries—by refusing to vote credits at the special session of the Duma on August 8. It soon became evident, however, that only the Bolsheviks were opposed to the war as "capitalist" and "imperialist" and that the Mensheviks intended to follow the path of opportunism by supporting the war as "defensive" in nature. On November 18 the Bolsheviks paid for their uncompromising stand when their five representatives in the Duma were arrested and shortly thereafter exiled to Siberia.

The only other significant group in Russia which might be said to have lacked enthusiasm for the war (they never openly opposed it) was the extreme Right. To these men an alliance

---

[1] July 19, 1914, according to the old style Russian calendar. The new style has been used throughout.

with monarchical Germany had always been preferable to one with republican France. But the exigencies of international politics were more important than those of ideology, and they were forced to become reconciled to the alliance system and to the war as best they might. Nevertheless, rumors of pro-German sentiment in high places began to increase as the war went badly for Russia. Though usually without foundation, such stories gained wide credence and were associated with the more scandalous tales circulating about the Empress and her notorious adviser, the religious charlatan, Gregory Rasputin.

Naturally these rumors were disturbing to Russia's allies and quite as much so to that small portion of Russian society which corresponded most closely to the upper middle class of the Western democracies. Long-time admirers of the parliamentary institutions of England and France, they were the most vociferous of all in their support of the war, combining as it did patriotism and political sentiment in a manner which had been denied to the reactionaries. The acknowledged leader of this group was the noted scholar and historian, Paul N. Milyukov; and its party was that of the Constitutional Democrats (Cadets). To staunch supporters of the dynasty the Cadets were revolutionaries, but their political aspirations scarcely went beyond hopes for a liberalization of the regime, the possibility of which they thought considerably enhanced by partnership with the other Allied Powers in the common war effort. These hopes were to be denied—until it was too late for reform—and then the pace of events swept away the "revolutionary" Cadets along with the last vestiges of the monarchy.

The Russian army was a formidable one in numbers, but in every other respect it was greatly inferior to the armies of Germany, England, and France. Well over fourteen million men were mobilized during the war, a staggering total which could not fail to dislocate the economy of the country. The shortage of rifles, munitions, clothing, and other equipment; the inefficiency of the transportation system; the lack of doctors, nurses, and medical supplies; and the incompetence of a good portion of the military leadership all became apparent in the first few months of the fighting. Had the main strength of the German army been turned against Russia instead of France, the defeats of 1914 would have become devastating routs. But the strategy of the German High Command envisaged a quick knockout blow in the West, a plan which might well have succeeded had not a Russian offensive in East Prussia caused the shift of two German army corps to the Eastern Front. They arrived too late to aid in overwhelming the Russians at Tannenberg (August 30) but weakened the invading force in the West, and the French were as a partial result able to win the critical battle of the Marne (September 6-12) and prevent the capture of Paris.

The Russian offensive had been undertaken only after repeated entreaties by France, whose ambassador at Petrograd, Maurice Paléologue, was to be kept busy with such appeals throughout the war. Large and frequent French loans to her faithful ally were responsible in large part for whatever efficiency the Russian army displayed, and it was not likely that Russia would be allowed to forget it. Her illiterate and normally obedient peasant masses tended to be somewhat cynically regarded by the French generals as splendid cannon-fodder, and their immense numbers gave rise to the legend of the "Russian steam roller." The Russians were not entirely unaware of this, and though they often responded generously to appeals for help, they greatly preferred to collect the revenue while confining their offensive operations to the less formidable Austrian front. Britain was in a position to be more tactful in such matters. Her ambassador, Sir George Buchanan, a polished diplomat of the old school, enjoyed great prestige in Russia and, moreover, was not given as disagreeable tasks as fell to the lot of his French colleague. Buchanan, though very conservative, was also more popular among the Cadet leaders and members of the Duma, while Paléologue tended toward social snobbery, preferring the company of the conservative aristocracy.

The events of 1915 were even more disastrous to the Russian cause than those of the previous year. A successful campaign on the southwestern front against Austria ended abruptly when Germany came to the rescue of her ally. A combined offensive began on May 1, which swept the Russians from Galicia and pushed back the entire eight-hundred-mile front. The retreat continued throughout the summer, as casualties approached the appalling rate of three hundred thousand a month. The slaughter was due as much to lack of war matériel as to any other factor. David Lloyd George, who became the British Prime Minister in 1916, later spoke harshly of the blundering Allied military policy, in which futile infantry attacks consumed quantities of munitions that could have been put to better use on the Russian front. "Had we sent to Russia half the shells subsequently wasted in these ill-conceived battles and one-fifth of the guns that fired them," he charges, "not only would the Russian defeat have been averted, but the Germans would have sustained a repulse by the side of which the capture of a few blood-stained kilometres in France would have seemed a mockery."[2]

Lloyd George's indictment, though written with all the advantages which hindsight confers, is an essentially just picture of the niggardliness of British and French support for their Russian ally. Human flesh was certainly an inadequate substitute for the mechanical sinews of modern warfare. Had the necessary supplies been forthcoming, however, their proper utilization would have depended upon outside help in bolstering the floundering Russian transportation system, so inadequate was it for meeting emergency situations. If material support was lacking, financial aid was forthcoming more generously: Britain extended $2,766,000,000 in loans during the war, while France advanced the relatively small sum of $762,000,000.[3] The United States, Japan, and Italy loaned considerably lesser amounts. Only a part of these loans was spent on imports, but at least Russia was not without the financial resources to pay for whatever material could be purchased abroad. Britain, with her large merchant marine, carried an overwhelming proportion of the supplies furnished by the Allied Powers, although Russian and neutral vessels bore a large share of the trade from the United States. The Turkish Straits being closed, the White Sea ports, of which Archangel was the most important, received

---

[2] David Lloyd George, *War Memoirs* (Boston, 1933-37), I, 413.

[3] Harry E. Fisk, *The Inter-Ally Debts* (New York, 1924), p. 111. The figures in rubles and pounds sterling are given by Paul N. Apostol, "Credit Operations," in Alexander M. Michelson *et al., Russian Public Finance during the War* (New Haven, Conn., 1928), p. 320.

almost all of the European trade in the ice-free months. Vladivostok, whose port facilities were not extensive, was handicapped even more by the limited capacity of the Trans-Siberian Railroad in making the long haul from the Pacific to European Russia. Japanese and American goods began to pour through this Far Eastern port in sizable quantities in 1917 and by mid-summer had begun to pile up on the docks for lack of transport. During the winter of 1916-17 Russia's military needs seemed at long last on the way to fulfilment; but it was already too late because her army, though outwardly still formidable, no longer existed as an effective fighting machine.[4]

Oblivious of the fate which was to overtake his army and his empire and sincerely desirous of promoting the military effectiveness of Russia in the common cause, the Tsar on September 5, 1915, took over the supreme command of the military forces from his uncle, Grand Duke Nicholas—a step which the Empress had repeatedly urged upon him. The military experience of the new commander-in-chief had been largely confined to the parade ground. It was a standing joke that his chief contribution toward insuring victory in the Russo-Japanese War had been the wholesale disbursement of icons to the troops. The step was taken against the all but unanimous advice of his ministers, who realized that the Tsar would take the blame in the eyes of the people for future military defeats, even though he might take no part in formulating actual military strategy. The Allied governments were also dismayed by the news but refrained from active protest. The Duma was dismissed on September 16, another blunder which provoked an immediate political strike in Petrograd. These incidents marked a turning point for the dynasty. Henceforth dissatisfaction rose steadily until the imperial couple became isolated from the rest of the populace.

The year 1915 also saw the completion of the first of a number of secret treaties which were to plague the Allied Powers in the years

---

[4] For details on Russia's war imports and credit operations, see Baron Boris E. Nolde, *Russia in the Economic War* (New Haven, Conn., 1928), pp. 141-51 and C. Ernest Fayle, *Seaborne Trade* (London, 1920-24), II, 119-26, 314-15 and III, 237-40.

to come. The existence of these treaties became generally known only when the Bolsheviks found them in the governmental archives and published them late in 1917. The one which most vitally concerned Russia was that pertaining to Constantinople and the Turkish Straits. Since the eighteenth century Russia had sought this warm-water outlet to the Mediterranean. She had fought several wars with this objective in view but was always blocked by the major powers, most notably in the Crimean War (1854-56), in which she was defeated by England and France. Negotiations between the Russian Foreign Minister and the Allied ambassadors established a basis of agreement at Turkish expense in March, 1915. Russia obtained Constantinople and the coveted Straits, while Britain and France were granted spheres of influence in Persia (now Iran) and other parts of the Near East.[5] In April Italy was induced to enter the war on the Allied side with promises of Austrian territory. Further deals of this kind in which Russia participated, most of them concluded in 1916, involved a territorial bribe for Romania's declaration of war, a partition of Asiatic Turkey, and a Russo-Japanese treaty concerning China. A final agreement, concluded shortly before the Tsar's abdication, gave Russia a free hand in determining her western border in return for support of French ambitions along the Rhine.

The Tsar's departure for the fighting zone increased the opportunities for intrigue on the home front, where the Empress and Rasputin held undisputed sway. Nicholas was never a towering intellect, and what little will power he possessed seemed to crumble beneath the imperious will of his consort. Her daily missives of love and advice embodied the extravagant and uninformed notions of an essentially petty nature, ignorant of all that concerned the welfare of the country as a whole, and relying largely upon the counsel of the uneducated and dissolute Rasputin. His debaucheries were common knowledge, but despite indisputable evidence of his unsavory character, the Empress's faith in him remained unshaken because of his apparent ability to cure the illness of

---

[5] An annotated text of the most important relevant documents may be found in F. Seymour Cocks (ed.), *The Secret Treaties and Understandings* (London, 1918).

her son, Alexis, the hemophilic heir to the throne. She was of a highly neurotic disposition, and her attachment to Rasputin was pathological in its intensity. As one of the prime ministers of the period (I. L. Goremykin) used to say, it was a *"question clinique."*[6] Rasputin's influence became so great that the position of any minister who crossed him became highly insecure, and his anteroom was continually crowded with greedy favor-seekers and sycophants. The "ministerial leapfrog," as the rapid turnover among cabinet members came to be known, saw complete mediocrities placed in posts of high responsibility because of their adherence to the court camarilla. The most flagrant instance, since it involved the premiership, was the elevation of the incompetent reactionary, Boris V. Stürmer, to head the cabinet in February, 1916. He covertly opposed the war and was presumably pro-German, so that the appointment naturally incensed the Allies most of all. Rasputin's opposition to the war was also taken as convincing evidence of his pro-German sympathies—just as his opposite in political extremes, Lenin, was to be accused later—and the more fervent patriots regarded him as a German spy. The despairing French ambassador claims to have pondered the advisability of an Allied effort to bribe him and rejected it as too risky.[7]

However grave politically, the military outlook for Russia in 1916 showed some signs of improvement. German preoccupation in the West and Austrian concern with the Italian army left the Eastern Front relatively quiet. An increase in war matériel and financial assistance from the Allies and a rise in domestic production did much to overcome the chronic shortages which faced the Russian army. An offensive against Austria began in June under the able leadership of General Alexis Brusilov. Some spectacular advances were made at the beginning of the campaign, and steady progress was the general rule throughout the summer. But success was achieved only at the cost of a huge casualty list, and a serious breakdown in morale became apparent when the number

[6] M. V. Rodzianko, *The Reign of Rasputin* (London, 1927), p. 10.
[7] Maurice Paléologue, *An Ambassador's Memoirs* (London, 1923-25), I, 343.

of deserters reached alarming proportions—approximately one million by November. Desertions from the Austrian army also reached a high figure, and it was only by forces bolstered with German units that the advance was halted at all. By autumn the Russians were stopped at all points and pushed back in some sectors. Although they failed to satisfy France by launching a frontal offensive against the Germans—a course which would have almost certainly led to disaster—the Italian army was saved from annihilation by the Russian action and salvaged for the Allied cause. So encouraging was the achievement that a meeting of Allied military strategists in November optimistically called for a full-scale Russian offensive in the spring, timed to coincide with a Franco-British attack on the Western Front.

The revival of Russia's prestige in 1916 was considerable, for its moderate successes on the battlefield concealed the mounting political difficulties. An exchange of good-will missions during the year also helped to disguise the serious state of affairs. In February a mission of six Russian journalists had toured England and France.[8] They were given a cordial reception in both countries, with the accustomed round of speeches, banquets, and inspections. A proposed return visit of English journalists finally gained the reluctant consent of the Russian government, only to fall through when the British ambassador advised against it for political reasons.[9] Had the incident been well publicized, it might have offset the effects of the Russians' visit and lent credence to the rumors and vague reports which were beginning to circulate in the Allied countries about internal conditions in Russia.

Another mission of a more official nature followed in May, since ten Duma members and ten members of the upper house (the Council of the Empire) were included in the invitation. The Duma members accepted with alacrity, but only seven members of the conservative Council could be induced to make the journey.[10] The group first toured England and Scotland, where many receptions were given in their honor and furnished the occasion for

---

[8] Constantin Nabokoff, *The Ordeal of a Diplomat* (London, 1921), p. 43.
[9] *Ibid.*, pp. 45-46.
[10] Baron Rosen, *Forty Years of Diplomacy* (London, 1922), II, 213.

many exaggerated demonstrations of friendship. They received an official welcome at a banquet presided over by the Prime Minister, Herbert Asquith. Baron Roman Rosen, former ambassador to the United States and senior member of the imperial Council, was chosen to reply to Asquith's speech, a selection which aroused the opposition of several members of the delegation. Rosen was so offended by this incident, which included some rather insulting remarks concerning his German name and origin, that he refused to accompany the mission on its subsequent journey to the Continent.[11]

In France the delegates had an opportunity to visit the front and seemed to be properly impressed with the French war effort. They also reviewed a contingent of Russian troops which were in training at Mailly, the vanguard of two brigades which later fought on the Western Front.[12] Several of the Duma members made it a point to criticize Paléologue as a poor representative for France to have in Russia.[13] This was undoubtedly a result of the ambassador's well-known taste for court life in preference to the more plebeian Duma circles. For lack of a good replacement Paléologue was allowed to remain until the Revolution made his recall imperative.[14] After touring the war factories and fighting front in Italy, the group returned to Russia with glowing reports of what they had seen in the Allied countries.

An incident on the return journey, quite unrelated to the activities of the mission, achieved considerable subsequent notoriety when Alexander Protopopov, the vice-president of the Duma, met a prominent German financier in Stockholm and received a proposal from him for a peace settlement between Russia and Germany. This was neither the first nor the last such instance of separate peace "leaks" involving Russia. As early as the spring of 1915 a former confidante of the Empress, Maria Vasilchikova, who had been interned in Austria at the outbreak of the war, wrote the first of a series of letters to the Tsar intended to lay the ground-

[11] Ibid., p. 221; Nabokoff, pp. 49-50.
[12] Russia and Her Allies: Extract from the Verbatim Report of the Imperial Duma. Fourth session, sixteenth sitting (London, 1917), p. 10.
[13] Georges Louis, Carnets (Paris, 1926), II, 242-44.
[14] See below, p. 54.

work for possible peace negotiations. She had been approached previously by individuals close to court circles in Berlin and Vienna and later had an interview with the German Foreign Minister. Despite the lack of response from Russia, she was allowed to go to Petrograd late in the year and was even received by the Tsar; but to quiet the open scandal of her ambitious—yet amateurish— attempts at diplomacy she was banished to her sister's estate in Chernigov. A number of similar proposals coincided with the lengthy Vasilchikova affair, notably the unsuccessful effort of the Empress's brother, the Grand Duke of Hesse, to induce the Tsar to send an emissary to Stockholm and the equally futile attempt of the Danish King's personal representative to interest the Russian government in peace talks. These abortive peace "feelers"— among others—eventually convinced the Central Powers that Russia could not be parted from her allies. But the uneasiness of Britain and France is understandable in the face of periodic and often garbled reports of backstage peace negotiations, coupled as they were with even more distorted versions of treason and political chaos induced by the Rasputin clique.[15]

It was partly to put an end to the uncertainty about the Russian war effort that the great British military hero, Lord Herbert Kitchener, then Secretary of War, met his death on a secret mission to Petrograd in June of 1916. Early in May Kitchener had made known to the Russian ambassador his desire to visit Russia if offered an official invitation.[16] The Tsar agreeably invited him to make a thorough survey of the Russian military situation and promised him a free hand in recommending changes.[17] Kitchener and his party sailed for Archangel on June 5, but that evening the ship struck a mine off the Scottish coast and sank within ten

[15] On the separate peace attempts, see Frank A. Golder (ed.), *Documents of Russian History, 1914-1917* (New York, 1927), pp. 40-51; A. Nekludoff, *Diplomatic Reminiscences* (New York, 1920), pp. 424-28; Victor Chernov, *The Great Russian Revolution* (New Haven, Conn., 1936), pp. 33-35 and 43-47; and Esther Caukin, "The Peace Proposals of Germany and Austria-Hungary, 1914-1918" (Ph.D dissertation, Department of History, Stanford University, 1927), pp. 23-43.

[16] Major-General Sir Alfred Knox, *With the Russian Army, 1914-1917* (London, 1921), II, 419.

[17] Sir George Arthur, *Life of Lord Kitchener* (New York, 1920), III, 349-52.

minutes. The only survivors were a few members of the crew. Kitchener's death was a shock to the British public, and so great was his prestige that many persons later professed to believe that the Revolution could have been averted and the war won in 1917 had he been on hand to persuade the Tsar to make necessary reforms. But such opinions are founded more upon hero worship and a naïve conception of historical causation than upon any understanding of Russian realities. The opposition that he would have met may be judged by Rasputin's remark, which the Empress passed on to her husband: "It is good for us that Kitchener died, as later on he might have done Russia harm."[18] A proposal to send General Sir William Robertson, the Chief of Staff, in Kitchener's place fell through when he pleaded the press of duties at home.[19]

To complete the roll of visiting delegations in the spring of 1916, a French mission arrived in Russia while the Duma delegation was making its visit to the western Allies. The aims of this mission were similar to Kitchener's, but as it was led by two cabinet ministers, René Viviani and Albert Thomas, instead of by a military man, it involved some aspects of a good-will tour. Many of the higher bureaucrats seemed to look upon the latter's coming with undisguised dread. A socialist of patriotic persuasion, with a reputation for ruthless efficiency, Thomas apparently fulfilled their expectations. He found much to criticize and was not slow to say so.[20] "Russia must be very rich to permit the luxury of a government such as yours," said Thomas ironically to one official, "because the prime minister is a disaster and the minister of war a catastrophe."[21]

While the festive aspects of the occasion were not overlooked, the Frenchmen spent a good deal of their energy in trying to fulfil one of the primary aims of the visit: the acquisition of Russian manpower for the depleted French army. A mission of the previous December led by Paul Doumer, a member of the French Senate, had already broached the subject. He asked for four

[18] Quoted in Bernard Pares, *The Fall of the Russian Monarchy* (New York, 1939), p. 335.
[19] Lloyd George, II, 213.
[20] Knox, II, 417-18; Paléologue, II, 237.
[21] Rodzianko, p. 188.

hundred thousand men and was willing to settle for successive relays of forty thousand spread over a ten-month period.[22] The Russians disliked the idea of sending battle replacements instead of separate army units and naturally resented the "cannon-fodder" implications of the proposal.[23] They sought to avoid an outright refusal by the use of delaying tactics, promising one brigade as an experiment. In March, when the brigade was already on its way to France, the subject was reopened through the Russian ambassador in Paris. He passed on a request that four hundred thousand men be sent to Salonika, where the Allies had a foothold in Greece, to replace losses among the French colonial troops and that an additional two hundred thousand be sent to Romania to open an offensive against Bulgaria.[24] Only a brigade for Salonika was offered, a response which the French considered rather unsatisfactory. Viviani and Thomas were charged with the unenviable task of persuading the Russian generals to change their minds. At a conference attended by the Tsar and his military advisers, Viviani made an eloquent plea for the exorbitant figures originally proposed by Doumer. Nicholas finally consented to send five brigades (fifty thousand men) to France between August 15 and December 15, besides the one which had left and another scheduled to leave for Salonika on June 15.[25] While far from the goal which had been set, the concession represented no little achievement for the mission. The two cabinet ministers left the country by the Archangel route on May 17.

In late August the brigade destined for Salonika mutinied at Marseilles, killing the commanding colonel and wounding several officers. French troops were called in to suppress the rebellion, and about twenty of the mutineers were executed.[26] Paléologue

[22] Paléologue, II, 119-20 and 133. On the Doumer mission, see Albert Pingaud, "La Mission de M. Doumer en Russie," *Revue des deux mondes*, IX (1932), 865-73.

[23] Victor A. Yakhontoff, *Over the Divide* (New York, 1939), pp. 139-40.

[24] *Krasny Arkhiv* [*Red Archives*], XV (1926), 224. For footnote references to the *Krasny Arkhiv* made throughout the present study, consult the bibliography below for specific information concerning the title of each documentary collection and its editor.

[25] Paléologue, II, 254.

[26] *Ibid.*, III, 16-17.

was reminded of the warning which Sergé Sazonov, the Foreign Minister, had made: "When the Russian soldier is off his own soil he's worthless; he goes to pieces at once."[27] The incident augured ill for the fate of the remainder of the Russian expeditionary force on French soil.[28]

The exchange of missions in 1916 did nothing to alter the suicidal policies of the dynasty, where, in the popular parlance of the time, the "dark forces" still ruled supreme. Sazonov was forced to resign in July, and his portfolio was taken over by Stürmer, who also retained the premiership. The protest of the British and French ambassadors went unheeded by the Tsar.[29] Discontent among the masses grew steadily, and in court circles could be heard talk of a palace revolution—faint at first but with gradually increasing intensity. Food shortages in the cities became chronic, and it was estimated that the cost of living had risen by October to 300 per cent of its prewar level.[30] Defeatist propaganda became rife in the factories and among the soldiers in the rear. A strike of the Petrograd factory workers on October 29 reached such serious proportions that the police and two regiments of the garrison were called out to suppress it. The troops refused to fire on the strikers, turning their guns on the police instead. Four regiments of Cossacks finally drove the mutineers back to their barracks. The punishment was draconic if Paléologue is to be believed: on November 9 one hundred and fifty soldiers were shot, an action which provoked renewed strikes as soon as the news reached the factory districts.[31]

The Duma reconvened on November 14 and furnished a platform for criticism of the government. The ministers were generally the objects of attack rather than the dynasty, for even the "progressive" bloc had no desire to encourage revolution during the war. During the opening session, however, the Cadet leader, Mil-

---

[27] *Ibid.*, p. 17.

[28] See below, pp. 132-37.

[29] Paléologue, II, 302-4; Sir George Buchanan, *My Mission to Russia* (Boston, 1923), II, 16-17.

[30] A police report quoted in Michael T. Florinsky, *The End of the Russian Empire* (New Haven, Conn., 1931), p. 175.

[31] Paléologue, III, 73-74 and 83.

yukov, hinted broadly at the Empress's activities in a speech largely devoted to the nefarious activities of Stürmer, from which the famous phrase, "Is it stupidity or treason?" gained wide currency as a sententious denunciation of the regime. Vladimir Purishkevich, an ardent monarchist, followed on December 2 with an even bolder speech, openly naming Rasputin as the source of trouble. The Duma greeted the eloquent attack with thunderous applause and to demonstrate its patriotic enthusiasm gave another ovation to the assembled ambassadors from the Allied Powers. The American representative, David R. Francis, was also in the diplomatic box, and understanding no Russian, amused his colleagues by bowing right and left to the upturned faces on the assumption that the demonstration was in honor of the United States. Poor Francis was greatly disconcerted when the British ambassador, turning to him with a poker face, said he would immediately inform the Foreign Office that America had joined the Allied cause.[32]

Purishkevich lost no time in following up his words with action. With the aid of three fellow conspirators, the most important of whom was Prince Felix Yusupov, a prominent figure in court society, he began to plot the murder of Rasputin. The deed was carried out in the early hours of December 30 in a peculiarly cumbersome manner, for poison, bullets, blows on the head, and drowning were successively used to dispatch the hardy court favorite. Except for the narrow camarilla around the Empress, the country greeted the news of his death with every sign of satisfaction. Particularly was this true of the upper classes, where the idea was prevalent that the dynasty, purged of Rasputin, would somehow become strengthened through purity and regain national confidence. Such was hardly the case. To the peasants and soldiers the affair was too remote from their immediate interests to arouse more than passing attention. To the royal couple it was a blow to their authority and prestige, as well as a personal loss, and they were thus even less disposed to make concessions.

The Tsar continually received warnings that his policy was

[32] Sir Samuel Hoare, *The Fourth Seal* (London, 1930), pp. 67-68.

leading to disaster, but however drastic, they seemed to make little or no impression on him. On January 12, 1917, Buchanan, the British ambassador, obtained an audience with Nicholas, determined to lay before him the serious state of affairs, even if it exceeded the bounds of diplomatic etiquette. Instead of receiving the ambassador in the informal atmosphere of his study, as he had always done previously, Nicholas awaited him in the audience chamber. This obvious sign of displeasure nearly swayed Buchanan from his intention, but he stuck firmly to his purpose and spoke frankly of the Tsar's ill-conceived course. He pointed out the incompetence of the administration, the food crisis, the rapid ministerial changes, and the growing danger of revolution. In conclusion he warned that the dynasty had come to the parting of the ways: "You have now to choose between two paths. The one will lead you to victory and a glorious peace—the other to revolution and disaster."[33] Nicholas thanked him, apparently taking the criticism with good grace; but, as in all cases in which unpleasant truths were forced upon him, casting inevitable aspersions on the imperial judgment, resentment rather than gratitude was his overriding sentiment. The Empress, who had probably overheard the whole conversation from her usual vantage point in the adjoining chamber, reacted even more strongly, professing to believe—and seemingly converting Nicholas to her point of view—that the inoffensive ambassador was plotting a coup d'état to place one of the Grand Dukes on the throne.[34] This bizarre suspicion was the basis for later assertions by apologists for the dynasty that Buchanan was responsible for the Revolution, which broke out two months later.[35] The Minister of the Interior recommended that the British embassy be watched, and the Empress suggested that the ambassador be recalled. Nicholas balked at anything so drastic for fear of making public his distrust of an ally's representative.[36]

Late in January the often postponed inter-Allied conference

[33] Buchanan, II, 42-49.
[34] Anna Viroubova, *Memories of the Russian Court* (New York, 1923). pp. 202-3.
[35] See below, pp. 32-33.
[36] Viroubova, p. 203; Pares, p. 423.

met in Petrograd, the largest and most resplendent of such gatherings to be held during the war. Buchanan had spoken of its prospects in a decidedly pessimistic manner during his conversation with the Tsar, and his prophecy proved to be only too accurate. "Rarely in the history of great wars can so many important ministers and generals have left their respective countries on so useless an errand," comments Bruce Lockhart, then British vice-consul in Moscow.[37] The British delegation was led by Lord Alfred Milner, a member of the special war cabinet, with General Sir Henry Wilson and five other generals as military advisers. The French sent Gaston Doumergue, Minister of Colonies, and General Eduard de Castelnau, chief of staff, while Italy and Romania of the lesser powers were also represented. The members of the mission had been chosen with great care, for it was hoped that an impressive delegation would have a better chance of success. At the request of the Russian government, the conference was postponed several times to allow the revolutionary fires to subside. When it could no longer be put off, the Duma, scheduled to meet on January 23, was prorogued to February 27 to avoid the embarrassment of open political controversy.[38]

All the Allied representatives, composing a party of fifty, sailed from England and reached the Russian capital on January 29. After a plenary session on February 1, the conference broke up into several committees to deal with questions of politics, finance, and transportation, in addition to technical matters of military supply, organization, and strategy. The army officers made extensive tours of the front, and the civilians sounded out officials and politicians on the state of the country. An interminable round of banquets, luncheons, and receptions insured a proper ceremonial atmosphere and a means of insulating the guests from any serious discussion of the problems which everyone knew transcended the minor technical details with which the delegates so largely concerned themselves. But even with this handicap, which was largely self-imposed, no one attempted to go beyond the bounds of conventionality and raise disturbing questions. The Tsar gave a

[37] R. H. Bruce Lockhart, *British Agent* (Garden City, N. Y., 1933), p. 159.
[38] Lloyd George, III, 448-51.

formal reception, conducting himself in his usual impeccably courteous manner, but studiously avoiding all but the most banal of expressions.[39] Whether it was apathy with a purpose or simply mental anesthesia indigenous to the Romanov bloodstream is impossible to say. Milner seemed to abandon all hope from the beginning and mechanically fulfilled his duties with evident signs of distaste. "We are wasting time!" was his frequent complaint. At one session he noticeably "kept throwing himself back in his chair and groaned audibly" as the trend of the discussion became more discouraging.[40] Only General Wilson retained an optimistic attitude, thoroughly enjoying the round of festivities.[41]

The French delegation appears to have been less concerned with the prospect of revolution than gaining Russian support for territorial acquisitions at the coming peace conference. Doumergue obtained the necessary guarantees for the left bank of the Rhine in a conversation with the Tsar on February 3, which Paléologue, on instructions from Paris, incorporated in a formal letter to the Russian Foreign Minister.[42] These negotiations were kept secret and were not known to the British government until the Bolsheviks published them the following November. The French were hard pressed for a reasonable explanation of their conduct and offered the lame but always reliable excuse that Doumergue had exceeded his instructions at the time.[43]

The conference broke up on February 21 with little to show for its three weeks of work beyond an estimate of the needs of the Russian army and an exchange of views on a wide variety of topics. A request to remain until the Duma convened was withdrawn when a court official intimated that if they stayed, the opening would be delayed another two weeks.[44] This hint alone should have been sufficient to alarm the delegates as to the dangerous political situation. Yet the most obvious signs of cor-

[39] Paléologue, III, 180.
[40] Rodzianko, p. 258.
[41] Hoare, pp. 205-7; Major-General Sir C. E. Caldwell, *Field-Marshal Sir Henry Wilson: His Life and Diaries* (New York, 1927), I, 320.
[42] Paléologue, III, 182-84 and 192-93.
[43] Lloyd George, III, 477.
[44] *Ibid.*, p. 466.

ruption and disorganization, the unrest and strikes in Petrograd, the warnings of the Duma leaders, and the various schemes to dispose of the imperial couple, which were openly bandied about in society circles, failed to arouse in the members of the mission any realization that a revolution was imminent. A possible exception was Sir Walter Layton, a British munitions expert, who unofficially expressed an opinion at variance with the formal reports. A successful prediction of coming revolution has been claimed for the Italian delegation,[45] but there is no substantiating evidence to indicate that their foresight was superior to that of their colleagues. Milner, despite his consistently gloomy outlook during the conference, concluded in his report to the war cabinet that there was "a great deal of exaggeration in the talk about revolution, and especially about the alleged disloyalty of the army."[46] Doumergue was even more optimistic. "I have brought back an excellent impression from my journey," he told the *Matin*. "It is clear from all the conversations that I had and all that I saw that Russia is filled with a unanimous will to pursue the war to a complete victory."[47]

Two days after the Milner mission left Petrograd the Tsar gave an audience to the president of the Duma, Michael Rodzyanko, and heard what proved to be his last warning. The coldness with which the president was normally received became, on this occasion, positively frigid. Nicholas listened indifferently as Rodzyanko began to read his report on the severity of the political crisis and finally interrupted to remark irritably: "Couldn't you get through with it quicker? The Grand Duke Mikhail Alexandrovitch is expecting me to tea." Rodzyanko hastened on, despite frequent interruptions, and concluded: "I consider it my duty, Sire, to express to you my profound foreboding and my conviction that this will be my last report to you." Nicholas wanted to know why. "Because the Duma will be dissolved," was the reply, "and the course the Government is taking bodes no good . . . . You,

---

[45] L. Aldrovandi Marescotti, *Guerra diplomatica* (Milan, 1936), p. 83.

[46] Lloyd George, III, 468.

[47] Quoted in Georges Michon, *The Franco-Russian Alliance* (London, 1929), p. 299.

your Majesty, disagree with me, and everything will remain as it is. The consequence of this, in my opinion, will be revolution and a state of anarchy which no one will be able to control." Nicholas said nothing other than to bid Rodzyanko a curt farewell.[48]

The Duma met four days later, while striking factory workers crowded the streets of Petrograd in what were for the most part orderly demonstrations. An open political rupture was avoided, but it seemed only a question of time until a sham revolution from above or a genuine revolution from below would settle the quandary of the Duma members. After another week had passed the Tsar appeared willing to discuss the question of a responsible ministry and announced his intention of going to the Duma to make a declaration to that effect. He changed his mind at the last moment and left for headquarters on March 8, after receiving the final assurances of the Minister of the Interior that every precaution had been taken to suppress a possible rebellion in the capital. On the same day bread riots broke out, and approximately ninety thousand workers went on strike. By the ninth the disturbances and strikes became more serious and could not be quelled, because the Cossacks, called out to restore order, began to fraternize with the workers. Still, no one as yet imagined that the long-awaited Revolution, of which millions had dreamed and for which thousands had sacrificed their lives, was at last to become a reality. Buchanan, who had never been one to underestimate the danger of revolution, was inclined to minimize the difficulty in his report to London. He quoted the embassy counsellor as of the opinion that the trouble would blow over "as it has always done before," and spoke of "huge crowds" and the occurrence of "some disorders, but nothing serious."[49] Such was the prevalent view, even in revolutionary circles, but already the power had "slipped into the street" to await the arrival of a new political order.

[48] Rodzianko, pp. 260-61.
[49] Lloyd George, III, 478; Prof. V. N. Storozhev, "Diplomatiya i Revolyutsiya" ["Diplomacy and Revolution"], *Vestnik Narodnovo Komissariata Inostrannikh Del* [*Messenger of the People's Commissariat for Foreign Affairs*], No. 4-5 (June 20, 1920), p. 83.

CHAPTER II

The Allies and the March Revolution

THE ANONYMOUS masses of Petrograd furnished the final push that cast the three-hundred-year-old Romanov dynasty into complete and unmourned oblivion. For five days the populace swarmed in the streets of the capital, until on March 12 the growing insubordination of the troops became wholesale mutiny, and what had been a serious rebellion was thus converted into a successful revolution. Already too late, Rodzyanko frantically telegraphed a second message to the Tsar—his first had been ignored—pleading for immediate action: "Measures should be taken immediately, as tomorrow will be too late. The last hour has struck, when the fate of the country and dynasty is being decided."[1] Nicholas read it and impatiently remarked, "Again that fat-bellied Rodzianko has written me a lot of nonsense, which I won't even bother to answer."[2]

After the twelfth scarcely a hand was raised in defense of the old regime, so thoroughly was it discredited. Troops were sent against the capital, only to "demobilize themselves" and join the Revolution. A contagious aura of good fellowship spread over the noisy, enthusiastic crowds. Class lines were as yet blurred and did not become crystallized until the intoxication of victory had worn off. Speakers were greeted with equal fervor, whether

[1] Golder, p. 278.
[2] Leon Trotsky, *History of the Russian Revolution* (New York, 1932-33), I, 79.

the reddest of revolutionaries or conservative nationalists like Rodzyanko. The jails were emptied of prisoners, political and otherwise. Little blood was shed because only the police remained loyal to the monarchy. When found in uniform, which most of them had prudently discarded, they were often lynched without ceremony, but considering the magnitude of the upheaval, such excesses were few.

The pace of events was so swift that a considerable time lag separated the Duma from the revolutionary masses and the Duma from the Tsar. By the time Nicholas decided that a responsible ministry headed by Rodzyanko was necessary, it was already too late for the Duma leaders to carry out their plan to save the monarchy by placing one of the Grand Dukes on the throne. Faced with the desertion of the army, Nicholas abdicated on the fifteenth in favor of his twelve-year-old son, Alexis, naming his brother, the Grand Duke Michael, as regent. Milyukov announced the change to the crowd assembled outside the Duma, and in trying to justify it, was almost shouted down for his pains. Because of his son's chronic ill health, Nicholas later decided to exclude Alexis from the throne, and in his formal abdication manifesto conferred his inheritance upon the Grand Duke.

On the sixteenth a Duma committee sought to persuade Michael to accept the throne. Since neither Milyukov nor Rodzyanko could guarantee his personal safety, Michael prudently declined the offer unless chosen by a popular assembly: an acceptance in view of the prevailing mood of the common people would have been tantamount to suicide. The fiasco of constitutional monarchy now apparent, the Duma leaders still groped for some formula whereby the Revolution could be "disciplined" and become the exclusive property of the Duma. The French ambassador, called upon by Rodzyanko for any advice or suggestions he might have, said that his main concern was the war and that the effects of the Revolution should be minimized and order restored as soon as possible.[3] Basil Shulgin, a conservative deputy, expressed the feelings of his colleagues when he warned that "if we don't take power, others

___
[3] Paléologue, III, 228.

will . . . those who have already elected some kind of scoundrels in the factories."[4] The "scoundrels in the factories" to whom he referred were representatives of the Soviet of Workers' and Soldiers' Deputies, a unique form of revolutionary democracy which had made its first appearance in the Revolution of 1905. The Soviets (or councils) were local bodies composed of deputies elected from among the workers, soldiers, and peasants. The Petrograd Soviet, because of its location in the capital, wielded far more influence and power throughout the Revolution than did the outlying Soviets. These bodies reflected the actual state of public opinion to a much greater extent than the Provisional Government, which took office following the Grand Duke's withdrawal. Already the phenomenon of "dual power" was noticeable, an unbridgeable dichotomy of interest separating the legal government and the *de facto* authority of the Soviet, a gap which was narrow at first but gradually widened until the Bolsheviks were enabled to seize power in November.

The new Provisional Government was handpicked by the Duma leaders. It was headed by Prince George E. Lvov, an honest but colorless right-wing Cadet. That he was chosen in place of the most logical candidate, Rodzyanko, was a tribute to the influence of Milyukov, whose personal unpopularity prevented him from assuming the premiership himself. Milyukov dominated the new government but remained content with the Foreign Affairs portfolio. The cabinet as a whole was controlled by Cadets and conservative nationalists (Octobrists), the only exception being the post of Minister of Justice, which was given to Alexander F. Kerensky, a lawyer of moderate leftist sympathies and shortly to become the leading figure in the government. Nicholas Chkheidze, a Menshevik and the newly elected president of the Petrograd Soviet, was offered the Ministry of Labor but turned it down in compliance with a resolution of the Soviet executive committee against participation in the government. Kerensky, who was also a member of the Soviet, declined to obey the edict and yet managed to retain a foothold in both camps. As Lenin put it, the government

[4] V. V. Shulgin, *Dni* [*Days*] (Leningrad, 1926), p. 111.

was formed with "ten capitalist ministers and Kerensky as hostage of the democracy."[5]

The revolutionary upheaval was naturally followed with avid interest throughout the world. Because of severe censorship by the tsarist authorities, several days elapsed before the news reached the outside world. It was even more startling to observers abroad than to the Russians, for in spite of a large crop of wild rumors and a few sound dispatches which found their way into the foreign press, public opinion and the leaders of public opinion were nowhere prepared for the unexpected trend of events. It was the Allied Powers, of course, who greeted the Revolution with the most fervor. Yet the Central Powers professed optimism, foreseeing a weakened Russian war effort, while at the same time admitting the injury to monarchical prestige. The Allies saw in a democratic Russia purged of tsarist tyranny a revitalized nation capable of renewed sacrifices and were remarkably oblivious of the causes of the upheaval.

Obviously the Revolution could not be beneficial to both sides at the same time. Only a few weeks were to pass before the halfhearted contentions of the Central Powers were amply borne out, although the Allies continued the process of self-delusion until the peace of Brest-Litovsk a year later ended all hope of Russia's ability to render effective military assistance. Britain and France were to a large extent victims of their own propaganda, which portrayed the war as a fight for freedom against autocratic oppression. The presence of tsarist Russia in the democratic camp was always a serious handicap in this ideological warfare, and it was only natural that the Revolution should be hailed as a blow to the Hohenzollern and Hapsburg absolutisms. In this belief they came nearer the truth, since the subsequent collapse of these dynasties is perhaps not unrelated to the moral effect of the Russian example. It should be pointed out, however, that Allied military opinion was more pessimistic in its appraisal of the Revolution. While these conclusions may have been molded almost as much by the traditional distrust of the military mind toward a change in the

---

[5] John Maynard, *Russia in Flux* (London, 1946), p. 278.

status quo as by strict military considerations, in this case, at least, it was less swayed than civilian opinion by political sentiment.

The timeliness of the Revolution was especially marked in the case of the United States, then preparing to embark upon its crusade to "make the world safe for democracy." Though American intervention in the war was hardly a product of the overthrow of tsarism, its influence was incalculable in creating a united public opinion and a more effective propaganda for German consumption. American newspapers and magazines hailed the new Russia with scarcely a reservation and continued to do so long after a few carping notes had begun to creep into the French and British press. To the Boston *Transcript* the Revolution was a "nightmare taken from the breast of the liberal world," while the Dallas *News* typified the nation's sentiment by observing that it "gives a political and spiritual unity to the alliance of Germany's enemies that has heretofore been lacking, for the reason that democracy was in league with autocracy."[6]

While the press reaction in Western Europe was very similar, there was a pronounced tendency to portray the Revolution as a kind of anti-German revolt brought about for patriotic reasons under the auspices of the Duma. A headline in the London *Times*, often regarded as the semi-official organ of the Foreign Office, hailed it as a "win the war movement," and an editorial commented that "the army and people have joined hands to overthrow the forces of reaction which were stifling the national aspirations and strangling the national efforts."[7] Yet as early as the twentieth the *Times* discovered the existence of the Soviet, the members of which it described as "anarchists" and "demagogues" who were "holding wild meetings . . . terrorizing the workers . . . and circulating false and malicious rumors designed to weaken the Provisional Government and to wean the nation from war." The *Nation*, a liberal British weekly, devoted most of its March 24 issue to the Revolution and scolded the press for its "caricature of the glorious rising of Russia from her crucifixion and burial as

[6] Quoted in the *Literary Digest*, LIV (March 31, 1917), 885-86.
[7] March 16 and 19, 1917.

an act of mere chauvinism." But it generously conceded that, "save for the *Times*," the treatment was due more to ignorance than to malice.[8] The same tendency for which the *Nation* spanked the British press was just as noticeable in France, where the *Petite république*, for instance, acclaimed the "triumph of liberalism" as opening the decisive phase of the struggle against "German barbarism."[9] A writer in the *Revue bleue* asserted that the Revolution originated in an "explosion of the Slav soul against its external enemies and those from within who were trying to stifle it."[10] At the same time there were many warm tributes from the more liberal papers. Certainly there were no lack of analogies to the great French Revolution, in addition to those of 1830 and 1848. But as the military bankruptcy of her ally became more apparent, a moral was usually attached to the effect that France, in contrast to Russia's pitiful showing, had stood off the whole of Europe to protect her revolution, a facile comparison of the two situations that will not stand close analysis because of differing circumstances.

For a regime presumably so hated in democratic countries as that of tsarist Russia, there was also a curiously favorable attitude toward Nicholas II in the Allied press that had no counterpart in the United States. It was, in a way, a residue from the "little Father" concept of the Tsar which had so long retained its hold on the Russian peasantry. The *Temps*, the French counterpart of its English namesake, expressed this sympathetic attitude very strongly. His abdication was treated as the generous sacrifice of a patriot anxious to avoid civil war and his downfall ascribed to bad advice and the machinations of an evil bureaucracy which had driven a wedge between the Tsar and his people.[11] Nicholas's florid and rather commonplace manifesto of abdication aroused particular admiration in the conservative Parisian dailies. "Can one conceive of language more noble and eloquent in its simplicity, more marked with sincerity and patriotism?" asked the *Gaulois,* a Catholic paper with royalist leanings.[12]

[8] XX, 882.
[9] March 17 and 18, 1917.
[10] Paul Gaultier, "Le Mysticisme Russe," LV (1917), 510.
[11] *Temps,* March 15, 17, and 24, 1917.
[12] Quoted in *Figaro,* March 18, 1917.

Messages from the Allied countries gave the new regime prompt moral support, followed quickly by official recognition. The leaders of the British Labor party sent a note of congratulation as early as the seventeenth to Kerensky and Chkheidze, which expressed the hope that they would impress upon the Soviet "that any remission of effort means disaster to comrades in the trenches and to our common hopes for social regeneration."[13] The House of Commons and the Prime Minister followed somewhat belatedly with similar messages.[14] The Parliamentary note, interestingly enough, was addressed to the Duma instead of to the Provisional Government, an oversight illustrating the misconception prevalent abroad that the Duma had not only made the Revolution but assumed the functions of government also. The socialists of the French Chamber of Deputies addressed the Soviet a sincere, if platitudinous, telegram, and the three socialist ministers in the French cabinet sent a note to Kerensky. He was selected by the ministers in preference to the government or the Soviet at the suggestion of Paléologue, because, as the ambassador observed, "he alone is capable of making the Soviet realize the necessity of continuing the war and maintaining the alliance."[15] Alexander Ribot became the new French premier on March 21 and paid his respects to the Revolution in a note to Milyukov.[16] These official greetings did not entirely wipe out the rather unfortunate impression created in Russia by statements which Ribot and Bonar Law, the British Chancellor of the Exchequer, made in their respective parliaments praising the Tsar for his faithfulness to the Allied cause. The lesser Allied Powers also sent messages of greeting, as did many unofficial groups and organizations in all parts of the world. Among these was the American Federation of Labor, whose president, Samuel Gompers, was persuaded to send a cablegram to Chkheidze. It was transmitted through State Department channels and apparently lost, so it was not until early April that a second and longer version was sent.[17]

[13] Times (London), March 17, 1917.   [14] Lloyd George, III, 505-8.
[15] Paléologue, III, 234.   [16] Temps, March 27, 1917.
[17] U. S. Department of State, Papers Relating to the Foreign Relations of the United States: Russia, 1918 (Washington, 1931-32), I, 18. Hereinafter cited as Foreign Relations.

The United States, still a neutral power, tendered no official word of congratulation but was the first nation to grant recognition to the new government, an achievement of which the American ambassador, Francis, was always inordinately proud. He asked for the necessary authority on March 18, and it was granted two days later by the Secretary of State, Robert Lansing, after consultation with the President.[18] Francis received the dispatch on March 22 and immediately called on Milyukov to inform him of the favorable reply. That afternoon the ambassador, accompanied by his entire staff of secretaries and attachés in full regalia, was received by the Council of Ministers, and with the proper oratorical ritual, formal recognition was conferred upon the Provisional Government.[19]

Compared with the Allied ambassadors, Francis had necessarily played a minor role in the social and political intrigues of Petrograd. The American embassy was unpretentious, and the elite of Russian society regarded its frequently changing occupants as deficient in the necessary social graces.[20] Francis was Babbittry personified and hardly the man to change the prevailing view. Anecdotes are legion as to his philistine nature. His prowess at poker was legendary, and his unerring ability to hit a spittoon at ten paces was considered a remarkable feat. His background was that of a typical "rugged individualist" of the business world who had gone on to become a success in the political arena. A wealthy banker and grain merchant of St. Louis, Francis had been mayor of that city in 1885, governor of Missouri in 1889, and a member of President Grover Cleveland's cabinet in 1896. His appointment to the Russian ambassadorship in March, 1916, was the result of continued loyalty to the Democratic party and not a reward for exceptional knowledge of Russian affairs or unusual skill in diplomacy. He was above the level of mediocrity only in his overly developed "scent for commerce," a trait which might have been useful in carrying out his instructions to negotiate a new commercial treaty with Russia had the March Revolution not inter-

[18] *Ibid.*, pp. 5-6 and 12.
[19] David R. Francis, *Russia from the American Embassy* (New York, 1921), pp. 93-94.
[20] Meriel Buchanan, *Diplomacy and Foreign Courts* (London, n.d.), p. 145.

fered.[21] The fall of the autocracy and American intervention in the war were events fully in accord with the ambassador's political sympathies. For the most part he shared the conservative views of his colleagues but lacked the experience and knowledge which went along with their conservatism. One of his acquaintances observed at the time, "Old Francis doesn't know a Left Social Revolutionary from a potato."[22] A critic less aware of those genial traits which compensated to some extent for the ambassador's glaring intellectual deficiencies has commented with considerably more asperity: "Ambassador Francis, one of the accidents of Missouri politics, chiefly remarkable for an impervious shell of complacency, went through the greatest upheaval in more than a century without a single mark upon the shining blankness of his mind."[23] Quite apart from his intellectual limitations—or possibly because of them—Francis persisted in retaining the services as embassy "housekeeper" one Mme Matilda de Cram, who was regarded with considerable suspicion by British and French intelligence officers as a possible German agent. Numerous reports reached Washington of the ambassador's indiscretion—as well as suggestions that he be recalled—but aside from a personal warning the State Department apparently did not take the matter as seriously as its informants.[24]

The Allied ambassadors had been authorized to recognize the new regime even before Francis broached the subject to Lansing. On the eighteenth Milyukov approached Buchanan on the matter and was told that assurances were necessary as to Russia's willingness to restore discipline in the army and fight the war to a finish. Though he gave them without hesitation, Milyukov pointed out that the "extremists" suspected him and that he would have to make some concessions or resign. Rather than lose Britain's best friend in the cabinet, Buchanan unhesitatingly recommended

[21] Francis, p. 25; Francis to Frank L. Polk, May 9, 1916, Polk Papers, Yale University Library.

[22] Lockhart, p. 279.

[23] David Loth, *Woodrow Wilson: The Fifteenth Point* (Philadelphia and New York, 1941), p. 185.

[24] Tredwell to Lansing, Dec. 5, 1917 (861.00/851½), National Archives, and material in the Judson, House, Lansing, and Thompson Papers.

concessions.[25] In view of the controversy which attended Milyu-kov's subsequent resignation, it is impossible to perceive wherein these concessions lay.

Buchanan became ill for a few days, so it was not until the twenty-fourth that he and the French and Italian ambassadors called on the Council of Ministers. With the various embassy coun-selors and the military and naval attachés present in full uniform, it was a "weird-looking crew," in the words of one participant,[26] which assembled for the formal ceremony of recognition. The speechmaking went somewhat beyond the conventionalities of Francis's reception. Buchanan, as dean of the diplomatic corps, be-gan by reiterating the desires he had expressed to Milyukov con-cerning the Russian war effort. The Italian ambassador seconded Buchanan's words and proceeded to bore the whole company by reading an interminable report of the Italian Chamber of Deputies debate on Russia. Milyukov, in replying for the Russians, supplied the desired expressions of patriotism in support of an unrelenting prosecution of the war. He vowed that Russia would fight to the last drop of blood, a statement which moved the British military attaché to note in his diary the pertinent query: "I have no doubt that Milyukov would, but can he answer for Russia?"[27]

The tremendous prestige which England and France enjoyed in the councils of the Provisional Government allowed the perpet-uation in royalist circles and in German propaganda of the legend that the Allies were responsible for the Revolution. Even Lenin, at the opposite end of the political spectrum, seems to have been laboring under this misconception.[28] Since Paléologue's monarch-ist views were well known and the Italian ambassador's influence slight in any case, these vague charges narrowed down by a pro-cess of elimination to direct accusations against Buchanan. He was known to have been friendly with many Duma leaders prior to the Revolution, and among the misinformed, especially those of

[25] G. Buchanan, II, 90-91.
[26] Knox, II, 584.
[27] Ibid., p. 585.
[28] See his statement in Pravda [The Truth], No. 14, April 3, 1917. All dates of Russian newspapers cited throughout the present study refer to the new style calendar.

conservative views, it was axiomatic that the Duma and the Revolution were one and the same. One accusation had it that he had sworn vengeance against the Tsar because he had been kept standing at their last audience.[29] But the most fantastic story which found its way into circulation was one to the effect that he had "attended revolutionary meetings with a false nose and a false beard."[30] In reality the ambassador—a firm Tory by conviction—had been "horrified at the idea of meeting men whom he regarded as revolutionaries" and finally consented to liberal contacts with the utmost reluctance; even then it was only at the insistent promptings of his friend, Harold Williams, an influential British correspondent and authority on Russia.[31] Because of his intense patriotism, Buchanan was gradually forced to the conviction that the Duma leaders, especially the Cadets, offered the only bulwark against reaction and a separate peace. Far from being a revolutionary, he did what he could to stave revolution off; and when that proved impossible, he supported the fruitless efforts of the Duma to make it a limited one. After receiving word that the Grand Duke had declined to become the new sovereign, the ambassador exclaimed: "It is the end of everything. The Russian army will never fight without an emperor to inspire them."[32] Milyukov, under pressure from the left-wing press, had to warn him more than once to cease visiting relatives of the former Tsar, and it was only the threat of requesting his recall which forced him to comply.[33]

That a man in Buchanan's position could have brought about the overthrow of the dynasty, even had he so desired, is absurd on the face of it, but legends are not meant for close examination. Its logical continuation is to be found in the tales concerning his alleged responsibility for the breakdown in negotiations by which the royal family was to be given a haven in England. Nicholas had signed his abdication at Pskov and returned to army headquarters. At the insistence of the Soviet he was escorted to his estate at Tsarskoe Selo and placed under arrest there with the rest

---

[29] Princess Paley in the *Revue de Paris,* as quoted in G. Buchanan, II, 94-95.
[30] G. Buchanan, II, 94.
[31] Hoare, pp. 241-42.
[32] M. Buchanan, *Diplomacy and Foreign Courts,* p. 206.
[33] G. Buchanan, II, 101.

of his family. A request was made by the heads of the Allied military missions that they be allowed to accompany Nicholas, to which the chief of staff replied that it was "inexpedient" and might delay the Tsar's departure because the government's consent would first have to be obtained.[34] That the Allied generals had in mind effecting his escape to England is highly probable.[35] The government, in direct contrast to the bitterness of popular feeling, was sympathetic toward the Romanov family and even refused to admit that they were under arrest. Nicholas had been merely "deprived of his liberty," it was explained to the British ambassador, who was understandably not able to grasp the distinction.[36] Kerensky loudly asserted his unwillingness to become the "Marat of the Russian Revolution" and blurted out his intention of escorting the family to Murmansk on the coast.[37] The Petrograd Soviet replied with an order to the railroad workers to stop the train if necessary.

Meanwhile Milyukov had asked Buchanan if his government would grant the royal family asylum, a request which was at once telegraphed to the Foreign Office in London. The war cabinet discussed the question on the following day, and it was decided to extend an invitation with the understanding that they would not leave the country during the war.[38] Milyukov was informed on March 23 and promised that a liberal allowance would be granted for their needs. It was agreed that a British cruiser should pick them up at Murmansk. Through a neutral emissary, Germany gave assurances that the vessel would be allowed a safe passage.[39] But Milyukov begged for secrecy: a hint in the press that the Provisional Government had taken the initiative in the arrangements might make the journey impossible on political grounds alone. An epidemic of measles within the family—all five children had been stricken successively—prevented immediate departure in any

[34] *Krasny Arkhiv*, XVI (1926), 48.
[35] See I Gelis (introduction), *ibid.*, p. 45.
[36] G. Buchanan, II, 104.
[37] Alexander Kerensky, *The Crucifixion of Liberty* (New York, 1934), p. 161.
[38] Lloyd George, III, 510.
[39] Alexander Kerensky, "The Road to the Tragedy," in Kerensky and Captain Paul Bulygin, *The Murder of the Romanovs* (London, 1935), p. 118.

case, and the government procrastinated in the vain hope that Soviet opposition would die down.[40]

King George V of England, a first cousin of the deposed sovereign, sent him a friendly message, purposely avoiding all reference to politics or to the possibility of his coming to England. It was sent through the British military attaché at headquarters under the impression that Nicholas was still there and finally reached Buchanan. The ambassador, having no access to Tsarskoe Selo, asked Milyukov to pass it on to Nicholas. He agreed to do so, but the next day (the twenty-fifth) he thought better of it because of the political repercussions which a misinterpretation of the telegram's contents might entail. Its delivery was "postponed" and the message presumably never reached its proper destination. The ambassador soon received instructions from London to take no further action in the matter.[41] It was this innocuous message which royalist commentators later accused Buchanan of withholding—and thus of a kind of "guilt by default" for the subsequent murder of the imperial family.[42]

The problem of what to do with "Citizen Romanov" and his family had already passed beyond the whims of an ambassador, whatever his personal wishes might be, and indeed, beyond the decision of the Russian or British governments. The Soviet was determined that the family should remain in Russia, and to insure that they did so, a committee was appointed to supervise their detention and guards were placed on duty at Tsarskoe Selo.[43] The reputation of the fallen sovereigns was just as low in certain quarters in England as it was in Russia. In France it was perhaps even lower, where, according to the British ambassador in Paris, the ex-Empress was regarded as a "criminal or a criminal lunatic and the ex-Emperor as a criminal from his weakness and submission to her promptings." The ambassador made no secret of his satis-

[40] G. Buchanan, II, 105; Meriel Buchanan, The Dissolution of an Empire (London, 1932), p. 195.
[41] G. Buchanan, II, 103.
[42] Notably by Princess Paley in her Memories of Russia (London, 1924), pp. 85-86.
[43] Paléologue, III, 268 and 272.

faction that the plan to bring the couple to England had not materialized.[44]

Growing agitation among the workers and within the leadership of the Labor party made it advisable for the government to reconsider its invitation. Foreseeing a political outburst in both Russia and England should any further action be attempted, it was decided not to force the issue. Instead of making an outright refusal, the government sought to "discourage" the projected journey until after the war. Buchanan received a telegram on April 10 informing him that because of internal unrest in England which might lead to strikes in the shipyards and munitions factories it would be wiser to cancel all arrangements for the present. The wording was diplomatic—the offer was no longer "insisted upon"—but the ambassador realized at once that the invitation had been all but withdrawn.[45] A second telegram in June put the matter even more definitely, and Buchanan, who took it almost as a personal blow, called upon the Foreign Minister with "tears in his eyes" to inform him of the news.[46]

While writing his memoirs, Buchanan was faced with the difficult task of defending himself against charges of having prevented the Tsar's escape and at the same time of defending his government's policy. The former was easily done, but the latter was accomplished only by the doubtful expedient of claiming that the "offer remained open and was never withdrawn,"[47] a technicality of which he must have been painfully aware. King George was likewise hurt by England's rebuff to the Tsar. "Those damn politicians," he would say in later years, "if it had been one of their kind, they would have acted fast enough. But merely because the poor man was royal. . . ."[48]

King George put the matter more succinctly than he knew, for Nicholas, as ex-Tsar, was not just another ex-politician. The

[44] Lloyd George, III, 514.

[45] M. Buchanan, *Dissolution of an Empire*, pp. 196-97. See also Meriel Buchanan, " 'The Foulest Crime in History'—The Truth," *Saturday Review*, CLIX (May 18, 1935), 616.

[46] Kerensky, "Road to the Tragedy," *loc. cit.*, p. 118.

[47] G. Buchanan, II, 106.

[48] Edward, Duke of Windsor, "A Prince at War," *Life*, XXIII (Dec. 22, 1947), 93.

unpleasant truth is that the continued existence of a deposed ruler is always an unavoidable threat to a successful revolution. His residence abroad may only increase the danger of counter-revolution and may involve the country which harbors him in unforeseen diplomatic complications. That the royal family survived as long as it did is possibly as much due to the passivity of the Tsar as to the forbearance of the Provisional Government. He accepted his lot with hardly a protest and had neither the inclination nor the opportunity for intrigue. The family was moved secretly to Tobolsk, a remote Siberian hamlet, in August, 1917, and to Ekaterinburg in the Urals in April, 1918. The outbreak of civil war sealed their fate. When approaching anti-Bolshevik forces threatened the town, the Soviet of the Ural territory decided to execute the prisoners to avoid their capture by the Whites. During the night of July 16 the entire family, including their physician and three servants, were herded into the basement of the house where they had been confined. A sentence of execution was hastily read, and the victims were shot down without further ceremony. The bodies were taken to an abandoned mine some miles distant and thoroughly destroyed.

The imprisonment of the Romanovs after the March Revolution and their subsequent fate aroused little interest or sympathy among the Russian people. The martyrs to tsarist absolutism far outweighed in number the relatively few supporters of the old regime who were arrested by the Provisional Government. Thousands of political prisoners returned from Siberia to receive an enthusiastic welcome in Moscow and Petrograd. From abroad came thousands more, especially from the Allied countries. The new government was very generous in providing for their repatriation. The Russian chargé d'affaires in London, Constantine Nabokov, has estimated that more than a million dollars was spent for this purpose. A sum of two hundred and fifty thousand dollars which Nabokov received for their needs just before the Bolshevik Revolution was confiscated by the British government soon afterward and never returned.[49]

Most of the exiles were moderate revolutionaries and loyal

[49] Nabokoff, p. 108.

supporters of the Allied cause. After years of residence outside of Russia, many had become Europeanized and had lost their revolutionary fervor in all but theory. Typical of this group, though far more prominent than the average émigré, was the right-wing Menshevik leader, Plekhanov, and the famous anarchist, Prince Peter Kropotkin. Both had lived in Western Europe for many years and returned to Russia with a minimum of difficulty, eloquent testimony in itself as to the mildness of their views. War-time conditions made traveling a problem of some complication, and the obstacles became almost insurmountable for the émigrés whose lack of patriotism was a matter of record. London was the focal point for the exiles in Western Europe, and since the British navy controlled the sea lanes, a selective veto operated to exclude the more radical from returning to their homeland by this route. Nevertheless, the lesser known managed to slip through before the net became tight, and some were allowed to proceed without interference—thanks to Soviet pressure on the Provisional Government, whose requests, as a friendly ally, could not be lightly disregarded. Nabokov wired home that something would have to be done to stop the influx of Bolsheviks: "You will cut the branch upon which you are sitting," he warned.[50] Such advice was superfluous. Milyukov had not neglected to inform all the Russian embassies and missions that "in the event of any doubt arising as to the character of the political emigrants . . . you are requested to form, in connection with the foreign branch of the ministry under your charge, a committee consisting of representatives of the political emigrants to clear up all doubts that may arise on this question."[51] A later message cautioned that "when issuing passports to emigrants, you may be guided by testimony as to their military reliability furnished by other trustworthy emigrants or by committees formed in accordance with our telegram."[52] The government was thus well aware of the situation but could do nothing so long as the Soviet refused to acquiesce in this political discrimination.

[50] Ibid., pp. 102-3.
[51] March 31, 1917, Krasny Arkhiv, XX (1927), 4-5.
[52] April 14, 1917, ibid., p. 5.

Among the more important figures who failed to obtain passage to Russia were George Chicherin and Maxim Litvinov, both of whom succeeded to the ministry of foreign affairs under the Soviet regime. Chicherin was arrested in August, 1917, ostensibly for making an antiwar speech, and lodged in a London prison until the Soviet government later secured his release. Litvinov managed to retain his freedom, and was about to be deported to Russia after Kerensky's fall, when he was appointed ambassador by the Bolsheviks. Victor Chernov, a leader of the Socialist Revolutionary party and of "defeatist" sentiment, was allowed to return, but not without misgivings.[53]

The many exiles in the United States were, with few exceptions, able to secure passports. Among the most notable of those who returned—though known to but few Americans—were Nicholas Bukharin, Michael Borodin, Bill Shatov, Alexandra Kollontai, and Leon Trotsky. Hundreds of others whose names were unknown then and later streamed back during the spring and summer months, usually by the long Pacific-Siberian route. The American government took no steps to halt this emigration until Ambassador Francis reported demonstrations before the embassy to protest the imprisonment of Alexander Berkman and Emma Goldmann, two anarchists who had been sentenced for antidraft agitation, and Thomas Mooney, imprisoned for his supposed participation in the bombing of a San Francisco Preparedness Day parade in July, 1916. Francis had never heard of these individuals and was forced to ask the State Department for information. He assumed, perhaps correctly, that the leaders of these demonstrations were émigrés from the United States. He also assumed, certainly incorrectly, that the "deplorable conditions in Russia were mainly attributable to returned exiles, majority from America, Trotsky being the most troublesome."[54] On several occasions Lansing sought unsuccessfully to have Francis intercede with the Provisional Government to prevent the issuance of passports by Russian consuls in the United States. "Political agitators and dangerous persons," he charged, were "grossly misrepresenting attitude and

---

[53] Nabokoff, pp. 99 and 104-7.
[54] Francis to Lansing, Oct. 4, 1917, *Foreign Relations,* p. 203.

intentions of American people with regard to the war."[55] But by the time the United States became aroused as to the "menace" of its Russian emigrants, most of those who wished to return had already done so.

The "most troublesome" of the exiles from the United States, Leon Trotsky, whose fame was to become second only to Lenin's, had been expelled from the European continent only shortly before the March Revolution. While in France he had contributed to a small Russian daily newspaper published for the benefit of Russian émigrés in Paris. Under the pretext that copies of the paper were found on the Russian troops who had mutinied at Marseilles, it was suppressed, and Trotsky was forced to go to Spain, whence he came to the United States early in 1917.[56] He settled in New York and with Bukharin and others helped to edit a radical Russian language newspaper, *Novy Mir* [*New World*]. Trotsky had never tired of carrying on long polemical battles with Lenin since his split with the Bolsheviks in 1903 and was nominally associated with the Menshevik wing of the party. It would be more accurate to describe him as a "Trotskyite," however, even though the term came to have a different meaning and is still almost synonymous with "traitor" in the Soviet Union. A brilliant writer and speaker, he seemed temperamentally incapable of adapting his views to fit any program which he had not originated himself and, with but limited success, continually sought to build up a personal following.

Immediately after the outbreak of the Revolution, Trotsky secured passage on a Norwegian liner and sailed on March 27, accompanied by his wife and two sons. At Halifax, Nova Scotia, British naval authorities detained the vessel and closely questioned all the Russian émigrés aboard, placing special emphasis on their plans and political convictions. On April 5 British officers and seamen came aboard and demanded that Trotsky, his family, and five other revolutionaries leave the ship. They refused to go voluntarily, despite assurances that the incident would be cleared up in Halifax, and armed sailors carried them off bodily to a waiting cutter. Trotsky's family was left in Halifax, and the rest

---

[55] Lansing to Francis, Oct. 13, 1917 (861.00/581a), National Archives.
[56] Leon Trotsky, *My Life* (New York, 1930), pp. 252-69.

were taken by train to Amherst, a camp for German prisoners of war. The camp commander refused to forward their telegrams to Petrograd and held up a similar protest to Lloyd George. Trotsky once again proved his ability as an agitator by spreading revolutionary propaganda among the war prisoners. So effective was he that the conservative German officers complained to the British colonel in charge. The colonel sided with the Hohenzollern patriots and forbade any more speeches.[57]

When the news of Trotsky's arrest reached Petrograd, it served to increase the barrage of anti-British propaganda in the left-wing press, already aroused by the detention of many political refugees in London. Buchanan's explanation that the fault lay in a lack of transport only exposed him to fresh attack.[58] The added excuse that the Russians were interned because they had been "traveling under a subsidy from the German embassy to overthrow the Provisional Government" was likewise greeted with derision, *Pravda*, the Bolshevik organ, denouncing it as "a patent, unheard-of, malicious slander on a revolutionary!"[59]

The widespread anti-British sentiment caused the ambassador some uneasiness as to the fate of the British factory owners in Petrograd, whose lives he thought might be endangered by unruly workmen, and, as was his custom when in difficulty, he sought out Milyukov. The Foreign Minister had, of course, been informed of the Halifax affair and requested that the prisoners be allowed to proceed to Russia. But on April 10 he had reconsidered and asked that they be held until further notice. Buchanan, no longer willing to have his government play the scapegoat for the policy of the Russian government, threatened to reveal the true story. Milyukov placated him by promising a public statement absolving the British of blame.[60] In the end the Provisional Government was forced to bow to the demands of the Soviet, and on April 29 the prisoners were released and escorted to a Danish vessel. They arrived in Petrograd on May 18 without further incident. Trotsky immediately began to co-operate with the Bolsheviks and formally joined the party in July. He did not soon forget his experiences.

[57] *Ibid.*, pp. 279-82.
[58] G. Buchanan, II, 120.
[59] No. 34, April 29, 1917.
[60] G. Buchanan, II, 120-21.

England—temporarily at least—became his pet hate among the capitalist powers, and every Sunday he harangued large crowds on the evils of British imperialism.[61]

Other leading revolutionaries, of whom Lenin was the most notable, were living in Switzerland when the Revolution broke out. Transit visas across Allied territory being out of the question, wild schemes were hatched and as quickly discarded in a frantic effort to get back to Russia. As a last resort negotiations were opened with the German government through the mediation of a Swiss socialist, and it was arranged that they should cross German territory to neutral Sweden in a "sealed" railway car—that is, with extraterritorial rights.[62] About thirty persons, most of them Bolsheviks, including Lenin and his wife, Gregory Zinoviev, and Karl Radek, took advantage of the opportunity. The Allies searched for some way of stopping the party with the help of the Swedish authorities but were forced to abandon the project for lack of a feasible plan and in the conviction that it would seriously alienate Russian opinion.[63] To the German general staff Bolshevism was an enemy of Germany's enemy—the Russian government —and therefore a legitimate war weapon in the struggle for military supremacy. Lenin realized that the charge of "pro-Germanism" would inevitably be raised by his political opponents but preferred to take the risk rather than to remain isolated in Switzerland. Yet he could scarcely have foreseen the tremendous campaign of vilification which began soon after his arrival. It became an article of faith among Kerensky's supporters, especially in the Allied countries, that Lenin and Trotsky were German agents. That prominent Bolsheviks had passed through Germany on their way to Russia was "evidence" of treasonable activity only to those who had already become convinced for a different reason. That reason, though it was never publicly admitted, was the unpopular stand which Lenin and Trotsky took in opposition to the war— unpopular, that is, with those patriots bent upon its vigorous prose-

[61] Bernard Pares, My Russian Memoirs (London, 1931), p. 428; Lockhart, p. 225.

[62] For the details of Lenin's return, see Nadezhda K. Krupskaya, Memories of Lenin (New York, n.d.), II, 200-12.

[63] Lord Howard of Penrith, Theatre of Life (London, 1936), II, 264.

cution by the Provisional Government, a policy which had little basis of mass support among the Russian people and was soon to find its adherents largely confined to the Western Allies. Some two hundred Mensheviks, their leader, Martov, among them, followed Lenin over the same route a month later.[64] But as supporters of the Provisional Government, the sincerity of their motives was never called into question.

On April 16 Lenin and his followers were greeted at the Finland station in Petrograd by a huge throng of workers, soldiers, and sailors. Chkheidze, on behalf of the Soviet, gave a short welcoming speech, cautiously suggesting that Lenin join the "revolutionary democracy . . . to defend our Revolution from attempts against it both from within and from without." Coolly ignoring these remarks, Lenin turned to the assembled crowd and spoke briefly: "Dear comrades, soldiers, sailors, and workers! I am happy to greet in your persons the victorious Russian Revolution, to greet you as the vanguard of the world proletarian army . . . . The predatory imperialist war is the beginning of a civil war all over Europe. . . . Tomorrow, any day now, European imperialism may completely collapse. The Russian Revolution you have made marks the beginning of this and has started a new epoch. Long live the world socialist revolution!"[65]

The Allied ambassadors were understandably perturbed by Lenin's arrival, though they had never heard of him until then. His views were considered so bizarre, however, that at first they were inclined to dismiss him as a harmless lunatic. Buchanan spoke of Lenin as an "anarchist," and Francis cabled Washington that "extreme socialist or anarchist named Lenin making violent speeches and thereby strengthening government; designedly giving him leeway and will deport opportunely."[66] To Paléologue, whose "diary" shows evidence of later retouching, Lenin was a "utopian dreamer and fanatic, prophet and metaphysician, blind to any idea of the impossible or the absurd, a stranger to all feel-

[64] Krupskaya, II, 209; Angelica Balabanoff, My Life as a Rebel (New York and London, 1938), pp. 144-46.

[65] Nikolai Sukhanov, Zapiski o Revolyutsii [Notes on the Revolution] (Berlin, St. Petersburg, and Moscow, 1922-23), III, 14-15.

[66] April 21, 1917, Foreign Relations, I, 27.

ings of justice or mercy, violent, machiavellian and crazy with vanity."[67] Buchanan later complained to Milyukov that Russia would never win the war if Lenin were allowed to continue "inciting soldiers to desert, to seize the land, and to murder." The Foreign Minister explained that the government was waiting for the psychological moment to arrest him, which, he thought, was not far distant.[68]

The ambassador might well be disturbed. Before Lenin's coming the Bolsheviks had floundered aimlessly, their position hardly distinguishable from the Menshevik and Socialist Revolutionary policy of support for the Provisional Government. In Switzerland Lenin had denounced the government in one of his milder expressions as "bound hand and foot by Anglo-French imperialist capital."[69] From April 16 on the Bolsheviks, under capable leadership for the first time, called incessantly for an immediate general peace, an appeal all the more effective because it expressed the growing desire of the workers, soldiers, and peasants for an end to the bloody slaughter. The Foreign Minister, whose nicknames, "Milyukov Dardanelsky" and "Paul Dardanelovich," reflected his conception of Russia's war aims in regard to the Turkish Straits, blundered from one crisis to another under the delusion that a foreign policy suited to the tsarist regime was good enough for the Revolution. In that, as will be seen, he was profoundly mistaken.

[67] Paléologue, III, 304.
[68] G. Buchanan, II, 119.
[69] V. I. Lenin, *Collected Works* (New York, 1927-29), Vol. XX, Bk. I, p. 34.

CHAPTER III

Milyukov and the Crisis in Foreign Policy

IN THE thick of the street rioting of the March days, Kerensky had suddenly entered the meeting place of the Duma committee, thrown a package on the table, and said cryptically, "Our secret treaties with the Allies . . . hide them," and disappeared as dramatically as he had come. Not a drawer or closet was to be found, so they were quickly shoved under the table for temporary concealment.[1] "What unconscious symbolism!" writes the former Socialist Revolutionary leader, Chernov. "The confused heritage of old Tsarist diplomacy, burdened with overdrawn notes, and now bequeathed to the new Russia, was hastily hidden under the table."[2]

The political bankruptcy which the Duma leaders revealed in their abortive attempt to divert the Revolution into "safe" channels was, as Chernov suggests, nowhere more apparent than in the realm of foreign policy. Rodzyanko typified their air of complacent optimism when he assured Colonel Alfred Knox, the British military attaché, that the Revolution would make no difference in the Russian war effort. "Russia is a big country, and can wage a war and manage a revolution at the same time," he told the worried officer.[3]

The Allies lost no time in asking for assurances of Russia's devotion to the alliance. As early as March 18 the heads of the

[1] Shulgin, pp. 127-29. [2] Chernov, p. 193.
[3] Knox, II, 569.

military missions sent telegrams to the army commanders on the various fronts calling for a statement of confidence in the "sacred union" to insure the "triumph of the principles of liberty." The replies were as meaningless as the original message, but this semantic soothing syrup enabled the Allied military representatives to convince themselves that the alliance was as firm as ever.[4]

On the same day Paléologue called at the Foreign Office. Milyukov told him that the ministers had been trying to work out a declaration on the prosecution of the war which would satisfy both the Allies and the Soviet and that he hoped to secure the adoption of the proper wording. Paléologue irritably replied that he wanted a certainty, not a hope.[5] The ambassador might have been more charitable in his attitude, because, as far as the personal wishes of the Foreign Minister went, the Allied cause had no more devoted champion in Russia. It must be said, however, that his motives were not purely altruistic. His note of the eighteenth to all the Russian diplomats abroad, a copy of which was forwarded to each of Russia's allies (including the United States, not yet a belligerent), left nothing to be desired in that respect. It summarized recent events and declared that the government would "remain mindful of the international engagements entered into by the fallen régime, and will honor Russia's word."[6] In return Milyukov asked that similar guarantees be furnished by the Allies concerning the secret treaties, assurances which were quickly supplied.[7]

When the Provisional Government's manifesto was published on the twentieth, it was more discreet than Milyukov's candid statement and aroused the French ambassador to anger. Although the government promised to "do its utmost to provide the Army with everything necessary to bring the war to a victorious conclusion" and to "faithfully observe all alliances uniting us to other

[4] Major-General Sir John Hanbury-Williams, *The Emperor Nicholas II as I Knew Him* (London, 1922), pp. 160-63.

[5] Paléologue, III, 248.

[6] C. K. Cumming and Walter W. Pettit (eds.), *Russian-American Relations: Documents and Papers* (New York, 1920), pp. 2-4.

[7] For the exchange of correspondence, see E. A. Adamov (ed.), *Konstantinopl i Prolivi* [*Constantinople and the Straits*] (Moscow, 1925-26), I, 466-76.

powers and all agreements made in the past,"[8] this was not strong enough for Paléologue, who rushed to the Foreign Office to register his resentment in the most scathing terms. At heart in full agreement with the irate ambassador, Milyukov lamely defended himself and promised to remedy the declaration at the next opportunity.[9]

The Soviet took note of Milyukov's activities in a very different manner. On March 27 it announced to the "peoples of the world" the determination of the Soviet to "resist the policy of conquest of its ruling classes," and the "peoples of Europe" were called upon "for concerted, decisive action in favor of peace." The manifesto was above all an appeal to the German proletariat to emulate the Russian example and "refuse to serve as an instrument of conquest and violence in the hands of kings, landowners, and bankers."[10] It was followed by vigorous editorials in *Izvestia*, the official Soviet organ, against "secret diplomacy" and the "poisonous fog of chauvinism" generated in the bourgeois press.[11] These pleas met a hearty response in Russia but could hardly have been read by the peoples of the belligerent countries to whom they were ostensibly addressed. Milyukov ignored the chorus of protest and spoke constantly in favor of acquiring the Straits, explaining to his audiences the numerous distinctions to be made between the various kinds of imperialism.[12] He naturally represented his own kind to be of the utmost beneficence. In defending his foreign policy from the standpoint of a historian rather than as a cabinet minister, Milyukov has said that "in all his declarations he vigorously emphasized the pacifist aims of the war of liberation but always presented them in close connection with the national problems and interests of Russia.[13] The transparent camouflage of "pacifist aims" never concealed for a moment the "problems and interests" which lay embarrassingly exposed to view. Kerensky advised him to "change entirely the language of all our diplomatic notes and

---

[8] Cumming and Pettit, pp. 4-6. [9] Paléologue, III, 254-55.
[10] Golder, pp. 325-26.
[11] March 31, 1917; text in Golder, pp. 326-29.
[12] Pares, *Russian Memoirs*, p. 435.
[13] P. N. Milyukov, *Istoria Vtoroy Russkoy Revolyutsii* [*The History of the Second Russian Revolution*] (Sofia, 1921), Vol. I, Pt. I, p. 84. Hereinafter cited as *Istoria*.

declarations."[14]   But more than verbal juggling was needed to achieve a basic change in foreign policy. Milyukov refused to go even that far. His presence within the Provisional Government was fast becoming a liability—it was certainly no longer an asset.

On April 2 President Wilson addressed a special joint session of the United States Congress and called for war against Germany, "this natural foe to liberty." A paragraph of his speech was devoted to the "heartening things that have been happening within the last few weeks in Russia." With more than his accustomed moral fervor, he spoke of the forbidding autocracy which for so long "crowned the summit of her political structure." "Now it has been shaken off," he went on to say, "and the great, generous Russian people have been added in all their naïve majesty and might to the forces that are fighting for freedom in the world, for justice, and for peace. Here is a fit partner for a League of Honor."[15] Four days later war was officially declared, news which the Russian government received with thanksgiving as additional incentive toward continuing its own war effort. In a message to the President Milyukov congratulated him for bringing the "great democracy of the new world" to the side of "justice . . . against . . . theocratic and paternal autocracy and of aggressive militarism."[16] The Russian Foreign Minister also took the occasion to grant an interview to the press, in which he adroitly embraced Wilson's idealism concerning war aims as though it were his own unique contribution to a better world. At the same time he associated the formula of "peace without annexations or indemnities" with German propaganda and repudiated a "stalemate peace based upon the status quo." The Dardanelles he seemed to assume were as good as under Russian jurisdiction already, while the fate of Romania and Armenia was only slightly disguised: "The Rumanians will be amalgamated to our own Ukraine," and the Armenians, since

[14] Alexander F. Kerensky, *The Catastrophe* (New York and London, 1927), p. 130.

[15] Ray Stannard Baker and William E. Dodd (eds.), *The Public Papers of Woodrow Wilson* (New York and London, 1925-27), V, 6-16.

[16] Milyukov to Wilson (received April 10, 1917), Woodrow Wilson Papers, Library of Congress.

they could not remain under the Ottoman yoke, "must be placed under the protection of Russia."[17]

In an attempt to calm the ferment from below, where the masses were beginning to question the advisability of continuing the war on any terms, let alone those which Milyukov was advocating, the Provisional Government published an appeal for support on April 9. "The purpose of free Russia," it maintained, "is not domination over other nations, or seizure of their national possessions, or forcible occupation of foreign territories, but the establishment of stable peace on the basis of the self-determination of peoples." This sounded almost like the tone of the Soviet proclamation, but then came the core of the message: "These principles will be made the basis of the foreign policy of the Provisional Government, which is unswervingly executing the will of the people and defending the rights of our fatherland, fully observing at the same time all obligations assumed towards our Allies."[18] This was unmistakably a reference to the secret treaties, though, strangely enough, the Soviet executive committee approved the statement before it was released for publication.[19] Milyukov had consented to the declaration only after being overruled by his colleagues and even then only as an appeal to the citizens rather than in a diplomatic note. Should it be interpreted by the Soviet as a concession to its conception of a proper foreign policy, he "reserved his right, in case the compromise should be interpreted one-sidedly, to explain it in his own sense and to elucidate its vague terms in accord with his former policy, the policy of the Allies, and the national interests of Russia."[20] In his usual forthright and blundering manner, he made no attempt to conceal his attitude from the public at large, the result of which "produced the impression of a bomb explosion" and an "outburst of hatred against Milyukov in the Soviet," which, as Kerensky admits, "revealed the entire deep psychological crisis of the government, the crisis of lack of confidence, which began brewing on the very first day of the Revolution."[21] At the time,

[17] New York *Times,* April 8, 1917.
[18] Golder, pp. 329-31.
[19] E. H. Wilcox, *Russia's Ruin* (London, 1919), p. 169.
[20] Milyukov, *Istoria,* Vol. I, Pt. I, p. 87.
[21] Kerensky, *The Catastrophe,* pp. 132-33.

however, Kerensky could make no display of wisdom after the event and was telling Buchanan that the Soviet would die a natural death.[22]

The first All-Russian Congress of Soviets began in Petrograd on April 11 and proved to be still very much alive. After an interminable debate, in which all shades of Left opinion had an opportunity of presenting their views before the delegates, a resolution was passed supporting the "defensist" conception of the war. It was sponsored by Heracles Tsereteli, a Menshevik leader of the Petrograd Soviet, and passed by a vote of 325 to 57, with 20 abstentions. One clause spoke of "preserving the capacity of the army for active operations," a policy which few soldiers were in a mood to implement by practical deeds.[23] Discipline had relaxed enormously since the Revolution, and the Germans adopted an attitude of "wait and see." The front was relatively quiet, fraternization was common, and the army resembled a gigantic debating society more than a trained body of troops. Desertions were again on the increase, and before long thousands of soldiers thronged the railroads in a mad rush to get back to the land before it could be expropriated and divided up in their absence. General Knox, who had been promoted from his colonelcy in April, and other Russian-speaking officers of the British military mission made some attempt to propagandize the soldiers in and around the capital. They were always received politely, but the effect was fleeting, for, as Knox frankly admits, "any impression we may have made was wiped out in a few minutes by the next agitator."[24] In brief, the Russian soldier and the Russian people were heartily sick of the war. Any attempt to make them go on with it was doomed to failure and merely reacted to the further discredit of those who advocated such a policy. That Lenin and the Bolsheviks had the political sagacity to grasp the obvious and to campaign for peace is more a reflection on the sterility of bourgeois leadership than a credit to the mystic properties of Marxist dogma in the service of professional revolutionaries.

[22] G. Buchanan, II, 111.
[23] William Henry Chamberlin, *The Russian Revolution* (New York, 1935). ¡ 112.
[24] Knox, II, 579.

Despite its support of a defensive war, the Soviet continued to agitate for a democratic peace "without annexations or indemnities" and based upon the "free development of all peoples." Alexander Ribot, the French Premier and Foreign Minister, became increasingly suspicious of the Russian government's intentions and telegraphed London and Rome in order to gain support for the dispatch of a stiff note to end their ally's equivocation in the matter of war aims. The Italian Foreign Minister expressed his willingness, but the British reply suggested that the Allied socialist mission which had recently arrived in Petrograd should first be allowed to try to win over their Russian comrades to a more aggressively prowar position.[25]

The mission in question had reached the Russian capital on April 13 for the purpose of dissipating, in the words of the French Premier, the "extravagant dreams with which the minds of the Russian revolutionaries were haunted."[26] The French representatives were Marcel Cachin, Ernest Lafont, and Marius Moutet, all socialist members of the Chamber of Deputies. Cachin later became one of the leading communists of France. Their presence in Russia was something of a paradox. As Paléologue remarked in his diary: "For the last five-and-twenty years the Socialist Party has never ceased in its attacks on the Franco-Russian alliance. And now we see three socialist deputies coming to defend it—against Russia!"[27] The Frenchmen had been chosen for the mission shortly after the Revolution broke out, and when word of their coming reached London, Arthur Henderson, a Labor member of the special war cabinet, was charged with securing an appropriate British delegation.[28] The men chosen were Will Thorne, James O'Grady, and William Sanders, all prominent in the Labor party. The first two were also members of Parliament, while Sanders was a leader of the Fabian Society. A number of attacks on the mission appeared in the Russian press, partly the result of a telegram which the British Independent Labor party (an antiwar group) sent to Russia declaring that the delegates were paid emissaries of

[25] Alexandre Ribot, *Lettres à un ami* (Paris, 1924), p. 230.
[26] *Ibid.*, p. 231.
[27] Paléologue, III, 298.
[28] Lloyd George, IV, 135-36.

the government and not representative of British labor.[29] Henry Hyndman, the leader of the British Socialist party, telegraphed Kerensky in some heat to "contradict most emphatically lying statement of the I.L.P."[30] Philip Snowden, an I.L.P. leader, criticized the mission severely in the House of Commons on two separate occasions on the grounds that it had been sent "by the Government to carry out the Government's policy." Another member inquired sarcastically whether the government had considered "the desirability of inviting representatives of free Russia to come over and consider the government of Ireland."[31]

The delegation was received by the Soviet on April 15, where the assembly listened politely but coldly to their views. They were considered "agents of Anglo-French capital and imperialism"[32] even by the more moderate elements and were cross-examined with such persistence that Cachin, anxious to conciliate his audience, decided to "throw out ballast" by offering to make the restoration of Alsace-Lorraine—lost to France as a result of the Franco-Prussian War of 1870—contingent upon a plebiscite. Paléologue did not take kindly to the proposal and was chided about it by Milyukov, who asked how he could be expected to resist the demands of the extremists when the French socialists themselves were abandoning the struggle.[33]

The members of the Provisional Government received them in a much more friendly fashion on the eighteenth. Sanders, representing his English colleagues, spoke in the customary terms of the common struggle, in which, he declared, "democratic England goes hand in hand with democratic France, Russia, and America." Moutet followed him with a few words of like sentiment. Milyukov, speaking in reply, claimed that "free Russia" had become "twice as strong." "We can say with assurance," he continued, "that the Provisional Government will redouble its efforts to destroy German militarism." Kerensky, whose peculiar grandiloquence seemed especially suited to such occasions, spoke at some length

---

[29] *Ibid.,* p. 136.   [30] G. Buchanan, II, 121.

[31] Great Britain, House of Commons, *Parliamentary Debates* (fifth series), XCII (April 23, 1917), 2035.

[32] Sukhanov, II, 404.   [33] Paléologue, III, 299-300.

on the democratic nature of the war. He concluded naïvely, "We expect you to exert . . . the same decisive influence in your country that we in Russia have exerted on our bourgeois classes, which have now renounced their imperialistic ambitions."[34]

The delegation attended a session of the Soviet executive committee the next day and addressed its members at considerable length. A Bolshevik, Alexander Shlyapnikov, answered them with some vigorous criticism, accusing them of representing the bourgeoisie rather than the workers. The Frenchmen were taxed about their colonial policy in Africa and the Englishmen about their rule in India and Ireland—vulnerable points which the delegates were obliged to defend.[35] After several more of these fruitless verbal tilts in Petrograd, the mission moved on to Moscow, visited the front, and made innumerable patriotic speeches through their interpreter. Upon their appearance before the Moscow Soviet, they were submitted to another searching cross-examination. The Soviet formula of "peace without annexations or indemnities," they declared to be too vague and in part contradictory. When a member of the Soviet complained about the secret treaties, especially about the Constantinople agreement, one of the British delegates jovially burst out: "If you don't want Constantinople, then, damn it, we'll take it!" A correspondent present recalls how the remark was greeted by a painful silence, perfunctory handshaking, and the withdrawal of the Allied socialists.[36] Another observer—by no means a radical—claims that the British Laborites summed up their view of the situation with the remark: "My Gawd, if this is democracy we don't want any of the bloody thing in our country."[37]

Closely upon the heels of the socialist deputation came Albert Thomas on his second mission to Russia. He arrived in Petrograd on April 22, accompanied by an impressive escort of officers

---

[34] Speeches in *Krasny Arkhiv*, XV (1926), 62-63.

[35] See Shlyapnikov's account of the session in *ibid.*, pp. 63-69; for a contrary interpretation see Claude Anet, *La Révolution russe* (Paris, 1918-19), I, 179-81.

[36] M. Philips Price, *My Reminiscences of the Russian Revolution* (London, 1921), pp. 19-20.

[37] Russell diary, June 14, 1917, Charles Edward Russell Papers, Library of Congress.

and secretaries and carrying with him a letter from Ribot recalling the French ambassador.[38] Paléologue's recall had been impending for some time, so he took the news calmly and promised his full co-operation. Thomas held a long conversation with Kerensky on the twenty-fifth, and they both agreed that a revision of war aims was necessary. Paléologue, as was to be expected, vigorously opposed such a step. Kerensky, he told Thomas in the presence of the British and Italian ambassadors, "implies the sure and certain triumph of the Soviet, which means giving the rein to all the passions of the mob, the destruction of the army, the rupture of national ties, and the end of the Russian State."[39] Paléologue became so convinced of the foolhardiness of making concessions to the Soviet that he dispatched a telegram to Ribot on the twenty-sixth warning against any relaxation in the agreements concluded with tsarist Russia. Irked by the ambassador's action, which amounted to a usurpation of authority, Thomas countered with his own telegram the next day. He explained the situation from a contrary point of view, proposing to arbitrate between the government and the Soviet in order to arrive at some kind of stopgap solution.[40]

Milyukov, meanwhile, was the target for a constantly increasing number of attacks from the left-wing press. His complaints to Paléologue about the attitude of Thomas and his fellow socialists were frequent but unavailing. The Foreign Minister refused to budge from his previous position. So far from reality had his flights of fancy soared that he contemplated with all seriousness a Russian descent upon Constantinople and the Straits and was still engaged with the general staff in plans for the operation on the eve of his fall.[41] On April 22, while in Moscow for a short visit, he was interviewed by the Manchester *Guardian's* correspondent there and talked freely of Russia's future policy toward the Dardanelles. Although conceding the right of free trade

---

[38] Paléologue, III, 311 n.   [39] *Ibid.*, pp. 312-13.
[40] Telegram in *ibid.*, pp. 314-17. See also Ribot, pp. 233-34.
[41] See the letters of N. A. Bazili (head of the diplomatic staff at headquarters) to Milyukov, April 3 and April 21, 1917, in Adamov, II, 393-96; General A. I. Denikin, *Ocherki Russkoy Smuty* [*Sketches of the Russian Turmoil*] (Paris, n.d.), Vol. I, Pt. I, p. 182.

through the Straits, Russia must, he declared, "insist on the right to close the Straits to foreign warships," a policy hardly feasible unless "she possesses the Straits and fortifies them." When asked if he thought the United States might raise any objection to such a settlement, he asserted that Wilson's speeches showed no objection in principle to Russia's acquisition of Constantinople in accordance with the agreement already reached on that subject.[42] A Soviet spokesman promptly replied that "Russian democracy has nothing in common with the aims proclaimed by Milyukov."[43]

Three days after the Milyukov interview, the Soviet congress renewed its stand on democratic war aims. Though repeating its determination to protect the Revolution from external aggression, the resolution tacitly warned the government to stand by its statement of April 9 and urged a discussion with England and France to bring about peace "on the basis of the brotherhood and equality of free nations." "An official renunciation of all ideas of conquest by all the governments," it declared, "would be a most powerful means to bring the war to an end on these terms."[44]

That evening Kerensky informed the press that the government was considering the dispatch of a note to the Allies informing them of Russia's new war aims as formulated in the April 9 manifesto.[45] It was reported in the newspapers the next morning as though the note were actually in the process of being drafted, and when Milyukov, who had remained in ignorance of Kerensky's sudden decision, saw the report, he indignantly demanded an official denial. Kerensky admitted the justice of the demand, since the minister most vitally concerned had not been consulted. A denial was published on the twenty-seventh and immediately "provoked a veritable storm."[46] The Soviet insisted that the government send the April 9 manifesto to the Allies or face the prospect of nonsupport for its forthcoming "liberty loan." The rest of the cabinet accepted the demand, and Milyukov had no choice but to agree. His acceptance was conditioned, however, upon the addition of

[42] Manchester *Guardian*, April 26, 1917.

[43] Edward Alsworth Ross, *The Russian Bolshevik Revolution* (New York, 1921), p. 117.

[44] Golder, pp. 331-33.   [45] Kerensky, *The Catastrophe*, p. 134.

[46] *Ibid.*, p. 135.

an "explanatory" note to the Allies along with the text of the manifesto. All of the ministers, including Kerensky, the most outspoken of Milyukov's critics within the cabinet, spent the night composing such a document. Their intention was to follow the principle which Albert Thomas had laid down. "I know my Socialists," he had told the Allied ambassadors. "They will shed their blood for a formula. You must accept it and alter its interpretation."[47] But the finished product did little credit to their ability to follow such astute advice, although Milyukov later blamed Thomas for the notorious "guarantees and sanctions" phrase.[48]

On the morning of May 1 the carefully edited statement was transmitted to the Allied capitals in the name of the Foreign Minister. Although Kerensky afterwards insisted that the "contents of the note should have satisfied the most violent critics of Milyukov's 'imperialism,' "[49] its sonorous phraseology offered but scanty covering for the meaning it was intended to convey. Quite falsely it asserted that the "aspiration of the entire nation to carry the world war to a decisive victory has grown more powerful" and reiterated Russia's duty to "observe the obligations assumed toward our Allies." The note concluded by saying that "the leading democracies, inspired by identical desires, will find the means to obtain those guarantees and sanctions [annexations and indemnities?] which are indispensable for the prevention of sanguinary conflicts in the future."[50]

Only after the message had been sent abroad was it released for publication at home. Without exception the attitude of the left-wing press was one of indignation. The Bolshevik central committee called for the assumption of power by the Soviet and repeated its previous declaration that the Provisional Government was completely imperialist and "tied hand and foot by Franco-British and Russian capitalism."[51] The Soviet executive committee met in a special session, lasting until the early morning hours of

[47] Lockhart, p. 182.
[48] Milyukov, *Istoria*, Vol. I, Pt. I, p. 93.
[49] Kerensky, *The Catastrophe*, p. 135.
[50] Golder, pp. 333-34.
[51] W. Astrov *et al.* (eds.), *An Illustrated History of the Russian Revolution* (New York, 1931), I, 148.

the third, in a futile attempt to decide upon a course of action. They recessed until the forenoon and again convened, but the working-class districts, inclined to regard the note as a deliberate provocation, were in no mood for further compromise. In the afternoon the Finland regiment marched to the Marinsky Palace, the site of the Provisional Government, carrying banners calling for Milyukov's resignation and various anti-imperialist and anti-government slogans. They were soon joined by factory workers, sailors, and additional regiments of the garrison, until the number of armed demonstrators reached an estimated twenty-five or thirty thousand.[52] No ministers were present, but frightened officials of the permanent staff telephoned for help. General Lavr Kornilov, the commander of the Petrograd military district, offered to put down the demonstration with armed force, a proposal more difficult of execution than he realized but which the ministers sensibly rejected in any case. Soviet leaders arrived on the scene and quickly persuaded the soldiers to disperse; most of them returned peacefully to their barracks. Others joined with the civilian population to argue and agitate on street corners. Bolshevik orators sought to enlarge the scope of the general indignation by turning it against the government as a whole, while Cadet partisans directed a counterattack against Lenin, who they asserted was a German agent trying to overthrow the patriotic Milyukov. This was the explanation adopted by the American ambassador, who reported to his government: "This opposition is by Lenin and his followers who I think are inspired and possibly paid by Germany."[53] Actually Lenin tried to restrain the more zealous party workers. He later severely criticized them for their premature action in calling for the overthrow of the government, for the Bolsheviks were as yet too weak for such precipitate tactics.

In the evening a plenary session of the Soviet convened. The prevailing mood of the members was one of bitter hostility to the government, and it was all that the moderate leaders could do to calm the crowd and entice it away from the popular suggestion of a Bolshevik speaker that the Soviet should seize power imme-

[52] Chamberlin, I, 143; Trotsky, *History of the Russian Revolution,* I, 340.
[53] Francis to Lansing, May 4, 1917, *Foreign Relations,* I, 40.

diately.[54] Directly after the meeting the executive committee went to the Marinsky Palace to consult with the government's ministers. The latter pictured the country as on the brink of imminent disaster and intimated that it behooved every man of good will to forget petty quarrels, such as the wording of notes and declarations, and to rally to the defense of the fatherland and the Revolution. Lvov made a half-threat to resign and offered to confer the reins of government upon them if they thought they could do better, knowing full well that the Soviet leaders wanted nothing so much as to avoid the responsibilities of power. On the question of foreign policy the executive committee made a show of firmness. Chernov criticized the Foreign Minister's conduct and proposed that he be shifted to the ministry of education. Tsereteli held out for a new note. Milyukov would agree to neither solution. He had already been warned orally by the American ambassador than an unstable government might not be extended aid from the United States.[55] But for more convincing evidence that the Allies were in favor of "stable government" (that is, with Milyukov as Foreign Minister), he showed Chkheidze a letter from Ribot indicating that France was not going to abandon her war aims and that, while she sympathized with the Revolution, unless Russia steadfastly maintained the alliance, French economic support might be withdrawn.[56] The Soviet president was not cowed by the threat, and a compromise solution was finally worked out whereby the government agreed to "explain" certain ambiguous points in the original note.[57]

Popular unrest had flared up anew in the meantime, with the difference that a progovernment demonstration was arranged by the Cadets to counteract the overwhelmingly anti-Milyukov sentiment of the workers and soldiers. There were isolated clashes between the two groups but no serious street fighting. Shortly after ten o'clock in the evening an enormous crowd of Milyukov's

[54] Sukhanov, III, 274.

[55] Francis to Lansing, May 8, 1917 (763.72/4675½), National Archives; Francis, p. 110.

[56] Price, pp. 30-31.

[57] Sukhanov, III, 280-81 and 283-88; Chernov, pp. 201-2.

partisans massed outside the Marinsky Palace. The Foreign Minister left the meeting with the Soviet leaders in response to the insistent clamor for his appearance and spoke to the throng from the balcony of the palace. "Seeing those inscriptions 'Down with Milyukov,'" he said, "I did not fear for Milyukov—I feared for Russia."[58] Thus he cleverly identified his policy with that of the country as a whole and ended his brief remarks by emphasizing the determination of the government never to betray her Allies by signing a separate peace.

The disturbances of May 3 proved to be only a prologue to those of the fourth. The working-class districts, hearing of the progovernment demonstration of the night before, gathered for a march to the center of the city and could not be dissuaded from their purpose even by the exhortations of a special Soviet delegation headed by Chkheidze. Clashes with Cadet sympathizers brought firearms into play, and mysterious shots from near-by buildings, for which each side blamed the other, resulted in several deaths and a larger number of wounded. Smaller crowds gathered in front of the Allied embassies. Buchanan, with the aid of an interpreter, spoke from the balcony of the British embassy on three different occasions. He succeeded in pacifying the more obstreperous elements, although during one of his speeches a free-for-all fight developed between the two hostile factions.[59] General Kornilov ordered troops and artillery to the palace square. The soldiers turned instead to the Soviet for instructions, and Kornilov, faced with the disapproval of that body, rescinded his order. The executive committee, anxious to avoid civil war, then decreed that no military detachment should come out on the streets without the permission of at least two of the committee's members.[60] To Kornilov's chagrin, this measure immediately and effectively restored order. He had made no secret of his desire to crush the "revolutionary riff-raff." Appalled at the helplessness of the government and unable to endure such affronts to his authority, the general resigned his post soon afterward and was transferred to

[58] Milyukov, Istoria, Vol. I, Pt. I, p. 97; Sukhanov, III, 282.
[59] G. Buchanan, II, 124; Pares, Russian Memoirs, p. 437.
[60] Golder, pp. 335-36.

the southwestern front, whence he was to emerge later as a widely publicized, if no more potent, hero of the propertied classes.

In the evening the Soviet executive committee resolved by a 34 to 19 vote to recommend that the government's explanation of the Milyukov note be accepted by the full membership. The Bolsheviks and the Menshevik Internationalists (the antiwar left wing of the party) voted with the minority against the resolution.[61] It stated that the "whole-hearted protest of the Workers and Soldiers of Petrograd have [sic] made it clear to the Provisional Government and to the nations of the world that the revolutionary democracy of Russia will never agree to a return of the tsarist foreign policy and that it is working and will continue to work for international peace." The government's explanation, it assured the Soviet, "puts an end to the possibility of interpreting the note of May 1 in a spirit foreign to the demand and interests of the revolutionary democracy."[62] Whether or not the explanation actually did what was claimed for it, the government's statement, which was made public the next day, avoided the ambiguities of its previous pronouncements. The most questionable phrase in the Milyukov note, that concerning "guarantees and sanctions," really meant, it was asserted, "the limitation of armaments, an international tribunal, etc." Another doubtful point, the "decisive victory" over the enemy, was clarified by the expedient of quoting the declaration of April 9 as evidence of the government's purity of motive in its desire for victory. The statement concluded by saying that the "above explanation will be handed to the diplomatic representatives of the Allies by the Minister of Foreign Affairs."[63] There is no record to indicate that this part of the bargain was ever actually carried out. Rather than send another note to the Allies, "a step which would menace the country with very serious consequences," Lvov said the whole cabinet was prepared to resign and was confirmed in his stand by Milyukov.[64] Rather prematurely, the latter declared to an American correspondent: "The government has

---

[61] Wilcox, p. 179.
[62] Golder, pp. 336-37.
[63] Ibid., p. 336.
[64] Current History, Vol. VI, Pt. I (June, 1917), p. 481.

won a great victory. Our policy remains unchanged. We have conceded nothing."[65]

Despite the prevailing distrust of the government, the members of the Soviet upheld the recommendation of its leaders by an overwhelming majority. Outwardly the crisis was resolved; inwardly it was just beginning as a delayed reaction from the turbulent events of the preceding days. Only then did the ministers seem to realize that the government was isolated from the popular mood and that some liberalization of its personnel was a minimum concession if it were to survive on any firmer basis than the disdainful tolerance of the Soviet. The obvious answer lay in the incorporation of some of the popular Soviet leaders in the cabinet. Kerensky was strongly in favor of this move, the more so as his prestige, heretofore very high as the only "socialist" member of the government, had been seriously, if not irreparably, damaged by the recent events. Kerensky's pretense that the embarrassing statements of the Foreign Minister were only his "personal opinion" was no longer tenable. Milyukov and Alexander Guchkov, the Minister of War, vigorously opposed bringing socialists into the government, and to force the issue, Kerensky himself offered his resignation—under no apprehension, however, that it would be accepted. After several days of bickering and unseemly squabbling, the latter won out. Lvov announced on the eighth the government's intention to extend its basis, for, as he put it, "the frightful specter of civil war and anarchy hovers over Russia, threatening its freedom."[66] On the following day the Soviet was formally invited to appoint representatives to join the cabinet. The executive committee balked unexpectedly, and by a vote of 23 to 22 decided to stand by its earlier resolution against joining the government.

Kornilov's resignation took effect on the thirteenth, and Guchkov, depressed by the breakdown of the army and unwilling to "share responsibility for the grave sin being committed against the country,"[67] gave up the war ministry on the same day. Faced with the choice of coalition or complete military and economic disorganiza-

---

[65] New York *Times*, May 8, 1917.
[66] *Current History*, Vol. VI, Pt. I, p. 481.
[67] *Ibid.*, p. 483.

tion, the reality of which Kerensky painted for them in the blackest of colors, the Soviet leaders were induced to reverse their position and voted 44 to 19 to enter the government. Their foremost demand was that Milyukov be replaced as a prelude to a change in foreign policy, a policy which they declared should be "vigorous" and aimed at "the speediest possible attainment of a general peace, on the principle of the self-determination of nationalities, without annexations or indemnities; and, in particular, the preparation of negotiations with the Allies, with the object of securing a revision of treaties on the basis of the Provisional Government's declaration of April 9."[68] An appeal to the "socialists of all countries" was published the next day, in which the Soviet declared the war to be "a monstrous crime on the part of the imperialists of all countries," but at the same time—somewhat paradoxically—argued against a separate peace as a "betrayal of the cause of the workers' democracy of all countries."[69]

Surprisingly enough, the Bolsheviks adopted a position similar to that of the Soviet. At their party conference which ended on May 12, a resolution was passed declaring it impossible to end the war "by the simple cessation of hostilities by one of the belligerent parties." But Bolshevik propaganda and practice followed a course from which there could be no other result than a separate peace once they themselves were faced with the obligations of power. Since the resolution can hardly be considered an attempt to sabotage their own agitators, perhaps the explanation lies in the need of at least a verbal alteration in strategy to avoid the charge of pro-Germanism—then a weapon of considerable potency in combating the Bolshevik heresy. Thus the resolution continued: "The Conference once more protests against the vile slander spread by the capitalists against our Party that we are sympathetic towards a separate peace with Germany. We consider the German capitalists the same sort of bandits as the Russian, British and French capitalists, and Kaiser Wilhelm as much a crowned bandit as Nicholas II and the British, Italian, Rumanian and all other monarchs."[70]

[68] Wilcox, p. 183.   [69] Golder, pp. 340-43.
[70] M. Gorky et al. (eds.), The History of the Civil War in the U.S.S.R., Vol. I: The Prelude of the Great Proletarian Revolution (New York, n.d.), p. 185.

However violent their denunciation of the war as imperialist, the Bolsheviks, like the Menshevik and Socialist Revolutionary leaders of the Soviet, were as yet unwilling to support publicly the logical conclusion which their premise demanded.

Chernov's idea of shifting Milyukov to the ministry of education was seized upon as the best means of easing him out of a key position without the bluntness of demanding his resignation. Seven cabinet ministers and the executive committee of the Cadet party urged this course upon the Foreign Minister without success. He resigned on the sixteenth, convinced that the new policy was "harmful and dangerous" to Russia's best interests.[71] The "voluntary" nature of his departure did not prevent him from declaring later before a private gathering of Duma members, "I did not withdraw but was put out." There could be no artificial distinction between the "Tsar's diplomacy" and the "Provisional Government's diplomacy," he maintained in a lengthy defense of his foreign policy. "We agreed with our Allies that if our common efforts were crowned by a common victory we should receive a common reward for our vital needs." Thus belligerently did Milyukov's public career come to an end.[72]

On the same day that Milyukov left his post another man who had once headed the foreign ministry—Sazonov—prepared to leave for London to take over the embassy there, vacant since the death of Count Alexander Benckendorff the previous January. He had procrastinated for several months after his appointment by the Tsar, and it was only at Milyukov's personal request that he agreed to depart without further delay. At the railroad station he was handed a note from Lvov asking him to "postpone" his departure because of Milyukov's resignation. Paléologue and the Allied socialist delegation, with whom Sazonov was to have made the journey on a British cruiser, left Petrograd without him. The confirmation of his appointment by the Provisional Government had been a blunder in the first place and was now politically impossible, for he had always been known as a spokesman for Russian im-

[71] Wilcox, pp. 182-83.
[72] North Winship (American consul in Petrograd) to Lansing, May 22, 1917. "U. S. Consular Reports," Hoover Library, Stanford University.

perialism. Nabokov, the chargé in London, whose monarchist sympathies had led the British government to request his recall, remained at his post.[73] Three subsequent attempts were made to supplant him, but the candidates proposed, Baron Alexander Meyendorff and Prince Gregory Trubetskoy, two dignitaries of the old regime who were even less calculated to please the Soviet, and M. N. de Giers, the ambassador in Rome, never arrived to take over the embassy.[74] Nabokov stayed on until the advent of the Bolsheviks, at which time his status underwent a change only in that he was no longer recognized by the country from which he had received his credentials. His hosts were by then less inclined to look askance at his conservatism as they watched with fascinated horror the spectacle of radicalism run amuck.

The departure of Milyukov and Guchkov from the cabinet still left unsettled the vital question of a proper foreign policy. The government assailed the Soviet proposition to put pressure on the Allies for a revision of war aims as "absolutely inacceptable" and offered the phrase "without acquisitive policy or punitive indemnities" as a substitute for the more unequivocal formula. It was also proposed that the Soviet help to restore discipline in the army, presumably for future offensive action.[75] Ultimately a compromise was worked out which each faction interpreted in its own way, just as the government's previous declarations resorted to ambiguous phraseology to "solve" a difference in viewpoint. Such a statement of policy was issued on the eighteenth, in which the first point, dealing with foreign policy, rejected a separate peace while promising to work for a general peace settlement and to take "the preliminary steps towards effecting an understanding with the Allies on the basis of the declaration made by the Provisional Government on April 9." But the second point, calling for the strengthening of the army's fighting capacity "for both defensive and offensive operations" as the most important task which the government faced, indicated that a general peace was considered a remote and theoretical possibility, not to be taken too seriously.[76]

[73] Paléologue, III, 342; Nabokoff, pp. 82-84.
[74] Nabokoff, pp. 125, 158, and 169-71.
[75] Wilcox, pp. 183-84.   [76] Cumming and Pettit, pp. 19-21.

The reorganized cabinet included ten "capitalist" and six socialist ministers. The latter included Chernov, Tsereteli, and Michael Skobelev, all well-known members of the Soviet executive committee. Kerensky became the Minister of War and Michael Tereshchenko, a wealthy young sugar manufacturer, took the Foreign Affairs portfolio. Lvov remained as Premier, more a figurehead than ever, for Kerensky, Tereshchenko, and Nicholas Nekrasov, a Left Cadet and the Minister of Communications, formed an unofficial triumvirate which to a large extent determined policy.[77]

The new coalition government furnished an appearance of stability, which the press in the Allied countries, gloomily speculating on the internal strife, greeted with varying degrees of optimism consonant with the political orientation of the newspapers concerned. In general the American press, solidly behind the Wilsonian idealism, was inclined to look upon Milyukov's departure as the removal of an obstacle to internal harmony. The chauvinistic French press, on the other extreme, had been berating the Soviet almost daily and commented with disfavor on the inclusion of six socialists in the cabinet and the resignation of such solid patriots as Milyukov, Guchkov, and Kornilov. The Allied governments, concerned largely with Russia's military efficiency, carefully refrained from any hint of displeasure at the turn of events. The possibility of an offensive effort was naturally pleasing to them, and if one ignored the Provisional Government's talk of a general peace as a mere sop to Soviet opinion—which indeed it probably was—the outlook for inter-Allied co-operation seemed distinctly favorable. But to the Soviet the prospect of a just and democratic peace was not to be so lightly dismissed. It took a practical step to implement its proclamations by calling for a conference of socialists from all countries to explore the ground for a general settlement. When these prospective deliberations were effectively sabotaged by the Allied governments, the consequent loss of prestige which the moderate Russian socialists suffered redounded to the benefit of the Bolsheviks, and the separate peace which the Allies so dreaded came that much closer to reality.

[77] Chamberlin, I, 149.

CHAPTER IV

The Allied Socialists and the Stockholm Conference

THE FERMENT within Russia on the question of peace which gave rise to the Soviet call for an international socialist conference was also reflected to a lesser extent in the other belligerent nations. Two and a half years of stalemated trench warfare had taken its toll in morale as well as in human life. In April labor unrest in Germany flared up into serious strikes, and in May mutiny in the French army left the country virtually defenseless for a time. The Revolution in Russia cannot have been more than an indirect cause of these disturbances, but its effect upon the war-weary peoples of Europe was, if intangible, certainly far from negligible. It caused socialists everywhere and of all shades of opinion to raise their heads with renewed confidence. Various attempts had been made throughout the war to organize a socialist conference, but it was not until the impetus of the Revolution that such a meeting became possible. Two previous international gatherings in the small Swiss towns of Zimmerwald (1915) and Kienthal (1916), though subsequent events gave the proceedings a significance which they lacked at the time, were confined to a small group of Left and Center socialists hardly typical of the conservative majorities in their respective countries.

The preliminary step in preparing for such a conference was taken by the neutral socialists of Holland. Without waiting for a formal decision of the International Socialist Bureau, whose executive committee was scattered, the Dutch members decided to go to Stockholm on their own initiative.[1] Since the only route open between Russia and the West lay through Sweden, Stockholm was the logical choice. The Dutch were soon joined by Swedish, Norwegian, and Danish socialists, and together they issued an invitation on April 22 addressed to all groups affiliated with the International, both majority and minority factions, to send delegates to a conference to be held on May 15 for the "examination of the international situation."[2] The majority socialists in England and France gave the invitation a hostile reception, and it soon became apparent that a meeting on the date set was out of the question.

In order to secure the support of the Allied socialists, the Dutch-Scandinavian committee, which had been set up to make the arrangements, turned its attention toward securing the approval of the Russian socialists. Many Soviet leaders had advocated such a conference since the early days of the Revolution, but as yet no official action had been taken on the matter. Late in April Frederick Borgbjerg, a Danish Social Democrat, arrived in Petrograd with an invitation to the Soviet to participate in the conference. The discussions which followed revealed wide differences of opinion. At one extreme, the Mensheviks telegraphed an unqualified acceptance, while at the other, the Bolsheviks, paradoxically enough, declared their opposition on the grounds that Borgbjerg was "directly or indirectly . . . an agent of the German imperialist government."[3] Agreement was finally reached within the Soviet by in effect ignoring the offer. On May 8, with the Bolsheviks abstaining from voting, the Soviet executive committee carried by a large majority a seven-point resolution in which a direct reply to the invitation was avoided.[4] It assumed complete responsibility for calling the conference—as if the groundwork had not already been laid by the neutral socialists. The latter's efforts were recognized

[1] Emile Vandervelde, *Three Aspects of the Russian Revolution* (London, 1918), p. 211.

[2] Comité Organisateur de la Conférence Socialiste Internationale de Stockholm, *Stockholm* (Stockholm, 1918), p. viii.

[3] *Pravda*, No. 41, May 9, 1917.

[4] *Krasny Arkhiv*, XV (1926), 70.

only indirectly in the seventh point: "A special delegation of the Executive Committee should be sent to neutral and Allied countries to establish contact with the socialists of these countries and with the delegation at Stockholm for the purpose of making preparations for the conference."[5]

Invitations were extended by the Soviet to the various socialist factions of Europe and America to send delegates to confer informally with the Soviet.[6] A message was sent through government channels to London, Paris, and Rome asking that the Allies refrain from preventing the journey of the opposition socialists to Russia.[7] Knowing that a "direct refusal would irritate the Russian extremists and perhaps discourage their moderate colleagues," Lloyd George proposed that France and Italy send a reply similar to the one Britain was sending: "Owing to submarine warfare, the means of communication between Western Europe and Russia are very much restricted, and only those persons can be allowed to travel in that direction who wish to do so for business of National importance."[8]

Without the support of the Allied governments the minority socialists had little chance of accepting this hospitable offer. No such obstacle prevented a further influx of patriotic socialists into Petrograd. By coincidence the same train which brought Trotsky and other Russian exiles from Finland on May 18 also carried two prominent Belgian socialists, Emile Vandervelde and Henri de Man, whose plans included a discussion of the Stockholm conference as well as the usual appeals to Russian patriotism. Trotsky knew the Belgians from his days of exile, and a none too friendly discussion ensued, though it probably did not, as Trotsky suggests in his memoirs, break off abruptly because of his doctrinal refusal to associate with "social patriots."[9]

The Belgian mission was received by Kerensky the next day at the Winter Palace. During a visit to the Soviet they voiced their opposition to the Stockholm conference because of the presence of

[5] Golder, pp. 339-40.   [6] Izvestia [News], No. 52, May 11, 1917.
[7] Lloyd George, IV, 138.   [8] Ibid., pp. 138-39.
[9] Emile Vandervelde, Souvenirs d'un militant socialiste (Paris, 1939), p. 230. See Trotsky, My Life, p. 286, for his version of the encounter.

German socialists.[10] Joined by Louis de Brouckère, a colleague who had arrived somewhat earlier, the Belgians made a five-week tour of Russia. They made countless speeches to soldiers and factory workers in the course of visits to Moscow, Kiev, and the southwestern front. Their total audience approached the one hundred thousand mark,[11] a record which far surpassed that of the other Allied missions. They were invariably given a cordial reception, for the name "Belgium" evoked sympathy even in circles where that of Britain or France aroused only hostility, but the practical effect of such conscientious propaganda work must have been next to nothing. The quality of their "socialism" may be measured by Vandervelde's remark that the Cadet program seemed to him "very radical."[12] Arturo Labriola, a former syndicalist, and three of his comrades undertook a similar mission for the Italian government at the same time with no more success than his predecessors had had.[13]

The hopelessness of such endeavors was not, of course, apparent at the time; so yet another socialist representative of the Allied cause arrived in Petrograd on June 2. The newcomer was the British minister and Labor party secretary, Arthur Henderson, whose assignment was analogous to that of Thomas for the French government. Henderson was to have gone earlier with two other Labor party members, but the war cabinet decided that his presence was necessary in view of the current labor unrest. The possibility that German socialists would soon arrive in Petrograd to subvert Russian opinion, and the assumed success of Thomas's mission, finally changed the Prime Minister's mind.[14] Thomas himself was consulted by telegraph and advised the sending of a delegation headed by Henderson. The addition of six socialists to the Russian government seemed such a radical move that Lloyd George feared —quite unnecessarily it would seem—that Buchanan was no longer

[10] Vandervelde, *Three Aspects of the Revolution*, p. 22.
[11] Henry de Man, *The Remaking of a Mind* (New York, 1919), p. 240. A detailed analysis is given in appendix 4 of the official report ("Rapport sur la mission accomplie en Russie . . . ," National Archives [861.00/563]).
[12] General Winogradsky, *La Guerre sur le front oriental* (Paris, 1926), p. 326.
[13] Balabanoff, p. 154.
[14] Lloyd George, IV, 140-41.

in favor with the new administration. With the example of Paléologue's retirement before it, the war cabinet authorized Henderson, in addition to his duties as a patriotic socialist, to take the ambassador's place if he thought it desirable.[15]

The Foreign Office had informed Buchanan of Henderson's arrival, neglecting to mention the diplomatic exchange which was contemplated. It was delicately suggested, however, that it might be well for him to come to London in a few weeks to give the government the benefit of his personal advice. The implication of this message could not have escaped a seasoned diplomat like Buchanan. He immediately wired that Henderson could depend upon his cordial co-operation and inquired whether his "leave" was to be considered as his definite recall. The reply was scarcely less ambiguous, for the Foreign Office shrank back at the ugly word "recall" and assured the ambassador that his services were highly valued. "So far as can be seen at present," the message concluded, "we shall most certainly wish to have you back in Petrograd in due course."[16] Buchanan was annoyed at the palliatives thus dispensed for his benefit but was cheered by the loyalty of his staff. They hastened to wire their influential friends in London, and some declared their intention of resigning should he be forced to give up his post. Without consulting his superior, one of the embassy officials rushed off to see Sazonov, obtained through him the desired assurance from Tereshchenko, the new Foreign Minister, that he would be sorry to see Buchanan go, and dispatched a long private telegram to an important individual in the Foreign Office to the effect that Henderson's appointment would be a disaster.[17]

Henderson, upon his arrival, turned out to be much less a monster than the embassy staff, and possibly the ambassador, seemed to expect. Both men behaved with impeccable courtesy, though the welcoming dinner at the embassy put a considerable strain upon the ambassador's wife and daughter, whose righteous indignation was barely concealed by the amenities of polite society.[18] Henderson did not resort to subterfuge in talking to Buchanan and made

[15] Ibid., p. 141.
[16] G. Buchanan, II, 144.
[17] Lockhart, p. 183.
[18] M. Buchanan, Dissolution of an Empire, pp. 210-11.

it clear during their first conversation that he would have to go. But the longer Lloyd George's special emissary remained in Russia, the more he came to appreciate the ambassador's abilities and his own unfamiliarity with the political situation. By the standards of English parliamentary life the two men may have been at opposite extremes; by Soviet standards they were both prosperous representatives of a capitalist government, the socialism of the one differing in no essential respect from the conservatism of the other.

Like his predecessors in the futile task of creating enthusiasm for the war where none existed, Henderson met cabinet ministers, Soviet leaders, and diplomats. He addressed Soviet meetings in Petrograd and Moscow, but his contacts with the unruly and unwashed Russian proletariat only distressed and bewildered him. While his geography was a little weak, and he was not always sure where he was, between the heat, the dirt, the black bread, and the crowning insult of the burglarizing of his hotel room, it did not take him long to discover that the locality was unhealthy.[19] He began to have doubts about sending Buchanan home. Lvov, when consulted on the matter, expressed confidence in the ambassador and reported that even the socialist ministers felt as he did. Perhaps aided in his decision by the knowledge that an ambassadorship is seldom if ever equal to ministerial rank, Henderson arrived at the only sensible conclusion possible under the circumstances. He wrote a letter on June 14 to the Prime Minister recommending Buchanan's retention, which Thomas, who was then leaving, conveyed to London. The message noted the absence of the "slightest hint of dissatisfaction" with the ambassador except from "the extremists, who, in their present temper, would probably treat in the same way any representative our country appointed who dared to do his duty."[20]

On the question of Stockholm, Henderson was hesitant. At first he joined Thomas and Vandervelde in formulating a statement of opposition which declared the conference "useless and dangerous"—useless because "such a meeting of contrary views

[19] *Ibid.*, p. 212; Lockhart, p. 184.
[20] Mary Agnes Hamilton, *Arthur Henderson* (London, 1938), p. 127.

could not end in action" and dangerous because "it would give rise to misunderstanding and would lead the working and peasant classes to think that a just and durable peace was possible before aggressive imperialism is destroyed."[21] Unlike Vandervelde, whose views remained the same, Henderson and Thomas were impressed by the fervor and unanimity of Soviet opinion and eventually changed their minds. Even Lloyd George appeared to favor the conference for fear of the bad impression which an absence of Allied socialists would produce in Russia. He told Ribot during a meeting which they had in London near the end of May that he intended allowing British socialists of all shades of opinion to travel freely to Stockholm and Petrograd. The French Premier declined to commit himself.[22] Thomas enthusiastically wired Lloyd George from Petrograd that he had "decided to go to Stockholm at any cost" and had already communicated his views to Ribot and to his French socialist friends.[23] Cachin and Moutet, who had just returned from their mission to Russia, also seemed to have caught the Stockholm contagion. They spoke before a general meeting of the French Socialist party on May 27. So lyrical was their description of revolutionary Russia and so evangelical was their faith in Soviet democracy that the assembled delegates voted to reverse the previous decision against Stockholm.[24] Jean Longuet and Pierre Renaudel, two of the party's most prominent members, were chosen to go to Russia to confer with the Soviet. Only a little more than a week later the Italian Socialist party, which had taken an antiwar position since Italy's entrance in 1915, also declared in favor of the conference.

The majority socialists of England, as represented by the Labor party, still remained aloof, but the minority, represented by the Independent Labor party and the Socialist party, held a highly successful convention at Leeds on June 3. The mood of the delegates and the tenor of the resolutions passed indicated strong sentiment in favor of a general peace and approval of Soviet activities to that

---

[21] Vandervelde, *Three Aspects of the Revolution*, pp. 217-18.

[22] Ribot, p. 260.

[23] Hamilton, p. 132.

[24] Ribot, p. 260; Manchester *Guardian*, June 2, 1917.

end.[25] The assembly called on the government to announce immediately its agreement with the "declared foreign policy and war aims of the democratic government of Russia." Another resolution, quite innocuous in intent, called for the establishment of Soviets on the Russian model for a wide variety of purposes—all of them nonrevolutionary in nature. It nevertheless caused a great outcry in the press and aroused some apprehension among the timorous that revolution had reared its ugly head in England itself.

A few days after the Leeds conference, three of its principal organizers, Ramsay MacDonald and Fred W. Jowett of the I.L.P. and E. C. Fairchild of the Socialist party, prepared to leave for Petrograd to consult with the leaders of the Soviet. George Roberts and William Carter, two Labor party delegates, and Julius West of the Fabian Society, were selected to accompany them. The British government had been in a quandary for some time as to whether to grant them passports. Both Henderson and Buchanan had been asked to give their opinion, and both agreed to the visit for the reason, as the latter has put it, that it "could not possibly do any harm, while the proceedings of the Russian extremists might, we hoped, serve as an object-lesson."[26] Lloyd George accordingly gave the mission his blessing, but already hedging on the liberal attitude he had expressed to Ribot, he made it plain that no communication with German socialists, either at Stockholm or elsewhere, would be tolerated.[27]

The delegates boarded a vessel at Aberdeen, Scotland, for the voyage and were disagreeably surprised to learn that the crew declined to sail with its cargo of "antiwar" passengers. To emphasize the point, their luggage was thrown off onto the quay.[28] It soon developed that the crew was swayed not so much by ideological considerations as by loyalty to "Captain" Tupper, an official of the Seamen's and Firemen's Union. His antipathy to pacifists and pro-Germans—or those whom he regarded as such—was quite pro-

[25] For the text of the resolutions passed, see Viscount Philip Snowden, *An Autobiography* (London, 1934), pp. 453-55. For further details see the *Labour Leader,* June 7, 1917.

[26] G. Buchanan, II, 147. [27] Lloyd George, IV, 144-45.

[28] John Paton, *Never Say Die: An Autobiography* (New York, 1936), p. 305.

nounced, and in this case accentuated by the unfair treatment which he fancied had been his lot at the Leeds convention. In the midst of a debate on Russia and war aims, he had brought up the somewhat irrelevant question of compensation for the families of merchant seamen killed or injured by the Germans and had been shouted down with cries of "Let the shipowners pay."[29] MacDonald vainly sought to placate him by offering an apology and a suitable compensation plan for the seamen. Tupper, seemingly favorable to the agreement at first, backed down at the last moment. Obliged to stay at a local hotel for the time being, the socialists were prevented from slipping out to harangue the seamen about their cause by Tupper's alert pickets, who patrolled the area day and night.[30] Long-distance telephone calls to the Prime Minister and other highly placed officials proved a futile means of facilitating their journey, and they were eventually obliged to return to London. West, who had taken no part in the Leeds convention, went on to Russia, as did Mrs. Emmeline Pankhurst, a prominent suffragette, who had no official connection with the mission other than to "expose" it in Petrograd. In July Snowden took up what was already a lost cause in asking Lloyd George for government aid in getting the MacDonald mission to Russia. A cabinet minister, who was appointed to look into the matter, reported that the seamen's union was still adamant in its stand. To the government this was excuse enough to avoid provoking an already embarrassing situation, for public sentiment was undeniably opposed to the trip. Lloyd George, probably rather pleased with the outcome, refused to take further action.[31] Had the mission been an official venture, similar to those which preceded it, there is every reason to believe that the difficulties might not have proved insurmountable.[32]

The ambiguous attitude which the Allied governments took on the passport issue and the uncertain position of various Allied socialist organizations, mainly the British Labor party, caused repeated postponements of the conference. Delegations from the

[29] Lord Elton, *Life of Ramsay MacDonald* (London, 1939), p. 316.
[30] Fenner Brockway, *Socialism over Sixty Years* (London, 1946), p. 155.
[31] Lloyd George, IV, 146.
[32] Elton, p. 320.

neutral countries began to arrive in Stockholm during the latter part of May and were soon joined by socialists from the Central Powers, whose governments readily granted facilities for the journey.

The United States became the first country to refuse passports to its socialists. On May 22, as a result of the President's directive, Secretary of State Lansing informed all American representatives in Europe that the government would issue no passports to delegates wishing to attend the conference.[33] When Morris Hillquit, Victor Berger, and Algernon Lee, who had been chosen by the American Socialist party to go to Stockholm, applied for passports, the answer was a foregone conclusion. Lansing denied their right to go abroad, terming the conference a "cleverly directed German war move." Hillquit impressed him after a short talk as a "natural intriguer and utterly unreliable."[34] To give the decision an appearance of legality, an old law which had remained unenforced on the statute books for more than a hundred years was resurrected and cited as the reason for the refusal. The wording of the statute—familiarly known as the "Logan Act"—made it a punishable crime for an American citizen to negotiate with a foreign government in a dispute concerning the United States. Hillquit pointed out that the socialist parties of Europe were not governments and in any case not involved in disputes with the United States, an argument which was irrefutable on logical grounds had the decision been a matter of logic alone. Politely but firmly his plea was denied.[35] In vain the Stockholm committee protested to Wilson that the principles underlying the conference were the same as those which he was currently advocating in his speeches.

On June 18 three American socialists, Boris Reinstein and Max Goldfarb of the Socialist Labor party and D. Davidovich of a small Jewish socialist party, turned up in Stockholm claiming to represent the United States in the absence of Hillquit and his comrades.

[33] U. S. Department of State, *Papers Relating to the Foreign Relations of the United States: The World War, 1917, Supplement 2* (Washington, 1932), I, 739.
[34] Lansing to Wilson, May 19, 1917, Wilson Papers.
[35] Morris Hillquit, *Loose Leaves from a Busy Life* (New York, 1934), pp. 156-57.

Berger subsequently disavowed their right to speak for the Socialist party, but they remained as representatives of their own small parties. It is very likely that they were refugees from tsarist Russia and without claim to American citizenship. At any rate their arrival was something of a mystery and remained so, because they evidently lacked passports and refused to gratify the curiosity of the American consular officials on that score.[36] The French government followed the American precedent by only a few days. The sudden action of the French Socialist party in favor of Stockholm made it necessary for Ribot to come to a decision more rapidly than he had anticipated. Immediately after his return from London, he placed the matter before the cabinet. Marshal Henri Pétain was called in to give his opinion and so frightened the ministers with predictions of a collapse of the army's morale should the conference meet with French participation that they unanimously agreed upon a refusal of passports.[37] On June 1 Ribot announced the government's stand in the Chamber of Deputies. Cachin, replying for the socialist minority, called for a secret session to discuss the issue.[38] His request was heeded, and for four days the question was debated—without, however, altering the Premier's policy. The socialists remained unreconciled to the decision, and their efforts to change it continued throughout the remainder of the year.

The Italian government followed the lead of its French and American allies by only a few days, and in Britain alone, where a more powerful labor movement had to be reckoned with, did the passport question remain unresolved. The press, a valuable governmental ally in every country, campaigned with almost unbroken hostility against what it commonly referred to as the "Stockholm plot," or, as the New York *Times* phrased it in the American vernacular, "a strictly German confidence game."[39] The foreign cor-

---

[36] Ira Nelson Morris (American minister to Sweden) to Lansing, June 18, 1917, *Foreign Relations of the U. S.: The World War (suppl. 2, 1917)*, I, 744.

[37] Ribot, p. 261; Alexandre Ribot, *Journal et correspondences inédites* (Paris, 1936), p. 139; and Raymond Poincaré, *Au service de la France* (Paris, 1926-33), IX, 148-49.

[38] France, Chambre des Deputés. *Débats parlementaires* (1917), I, 1323-25. Hereinafter cited as *Débats parlementaires*.

[39] Aug. 5, 1917.

respondents in Stockholm aided in the process of distorting the aims of the conference, and one bragged to his fellow newsmen, with perhaps exaggerated confidence in his own prowess, "I think I have killed it."[40]

The conservative Russian press greeted the action of the Allied governments with enthusiastic praise. The Bolsheviks, too, seemed to welcome the news as a practical application of their theories of bourgeois imperialism.[41] Under Lenin's guidance, they remained aloof to the Stockholm idea but not without dissension, even among the leaders. One of the most prominent, Leo Kamenev, argued that the refusal of passports showed that Stockholm was no longer a blind tool of the imperialist governments. Lenin's sharp rejoinder that any compromise with "social-chauvinists" would be a shameful betrayal of socialist ideals was readily accepted by the party as its official doctrine.[42]

The Provisional Government, without notable success, tried to convey the impression domestically that it was wholly sympathetic to the meeting and abroad that it was hostile. The Soviet continued as the unfaltering champion of the conference, and on June 2 it launched a second appeal concerning Stockholm to all socialist and labor groups. The past efforts of the Soviet to achieve a democratic peace were briefly reviewed and an international socialist conference proposed as the quickest way to bring it about. "Its principal aim," the manifesto stated, "must be an agreement among the representatives of the Socialist proletariat regarding the liquidation of the policy of 'national unity' with the imperialistic governments and classes, which excludes the possibility of a struggle for peace, as well as an agreement regarding the means and methods of the struggle."[43]

Confused and hesitant, the British Labor party awaited the return of Henderson before making a definite commitment for or against the conference. In mid-July he left Petrograd and was accompanied from Aberdeen to London by four Soviet delegates,

---

[40] Robert R. McCormick (publisher of the Chicago *Tribune*) to Lansing, June 12, 1917, *Foreign Relations of the U. S.: The World War (suppl. 2, 1917)*, I, 743.

[41] Price, pp. 67-68.

[42] Balabanoff, p. 163; Lenin, *Collected Works*, Vol. XXI, Bk. I, pp. 94-96.

[43] Cumming and Pettit, pp. 22-23.

Joseph Goldenberg, Henrik Ehrlich, Nicholas Rusanov, and E. Smirnov, who hoped that their presence in Western Europe would stir the lethargic Allied socialists into action. Immediately after his arrival, Henderson went to confer with Labor party leaders. Lloyd George, who was annoyed because his minister thus showed preference for party affiliation over government duty, describes him as having contracted "more than a touch of the revolutionary malaria" in Russia,[44] a characterization which is scarcely an accurate description of Henderson's mood at the time. Yet he did become converted wholeheartedly to the Stockholm cause, not for revolutionary reasons but for the same reason that Lenin so strongly opposed it: as the sole means of placating the Soviet and keeping Russia in the war. At the same time the Prime Minister and his associates became converted to the view that Stockholm was now tainted beyond hope of redemption by the presence of the "Kaiser's hirelings." This despite the advice of Buchanan, whose patriotism was above reproach. "It would be a mistake," he wrote the Foreign Office, "to leave the Germans a clear field at Stockholm, more especially as it would render our attitude open to misconstruction here. As we have no intention of being bound by the conference's decisions, I do not see how the attendance of British Socialists can prejudice our interests."[45] The concern of the Allied governments that Stockholm was a German plot was duplicated by the enemy's general staff, who felt that their government had fallen into an Allied trap by granting passports to the German socialists.[46]

The Soviet delegates made it clear to the Labor party executive committee that the Stockholm plans would not be canceled even if the British socialists declined to go. The committee, with Henderson leading the discussion, voted to call a special party conference to decide the question and to recommend that the assembly accept the Soviet invitation on the understanding that any resolutions adopted would not be binding upon the participants.[47] At

[44] Lloyd George, IV, 148.
[45] G. Buchanan, II, 161.
[46] Erich von Ludendorff, *Ludendorff's Own Story* (New York and London, 1919), II, 54-55.
[47] *Report of the Seventeenth Annual Conference of the Labour Party* (London, 1918), p. 4.

the same meeting a delegation was appointed to go to Paris in answer to the invitation of the French Socialist party. It consisted of Henderson, George Wardle (a Labor member of Parliament), and the unpopular MacDonald, the latter having been chosen to represent the minority viewpoint and to balance the conservatism of Wardle. Lloyd George, then in Paris for a conference, was informed of the trip, but the members of the war cabinet, hearing of it only indirectly, were considerably disturbed. Anxious to avoid involving the government in the Stockholm affair—not to mention the scandal of a cabinet minister publicly associating with the notoriously unpatriotic MacDonald—they asked Henderson to confer with them on the evening of the twenty-sixth. His reception was far from cordial, but in spite of the outspoken disapproval, Henderson stuck by his plans and even offered his resignation rather than change them. In the Prime Minister's absence, the cabinet was hardly in a position to take up the offer or to prevent the trip.[48]

On the following day the three Laborites, together with the four Soviet delegates, departed for Paris. Lloyd George started for London at the same time and left behind one of the war cabinet's secretaries to keep a watchful eye on Henderson and his activities.[49] After several prolonged discussions with the French socialist leaders, the only tangible achievement was the passing of a few general resolutions on the procedures to be followed at the coming conference. Henderson worked hard to convince the French and Russians that the decisions of the conference should not be binding, an attitude which the surprised Soviet delegates regarded as a reversal of his previous position.[50] A final decision was postponed, as was the opening date of the conference—this time to September 9. One of the reasons for further delay was the hope that the American Federation of Labor could yet be persuaded to send representatives. The conservative leaders of the Federation were not to be moved. A barrage of invitations had already been rejected, because, as

[48] Lloyd George, IV, 149-50.
[49] Lady Algernon Gordon Lennox (ed.), *The Diary of Lord Bertie of Thame* (London, 1924), II, 161.
[50] *Krasny Arkhiv*, XVI (1926), 36.

President Gompers vaguely phrased it, the executive committee feared that "such a conference would place obstacles in the way of democratizing institutions of the world and would hazard the opportunities for liberty and freedom of all people."[51] In a less idealistic vein, Gompers had previously denounced Stockholm as a piece of "insidious pro-Kaiser propaganda."[52]

The Soviet mission went on to Rome for a meeting with Italian socialist leaders, while Henderson and his party returned to London to face an unfriendly press, an irascible Prime Minister, and a hostile war cabinet. His future in the government already precarious, Henderson talked with Lloyd George and was asked to come back that afternoon for a cabinet session in which the matter would be more thoroughly discussed. He arrived at the appointed time and, much to his surprise, was asked to wait. After he had been left an hour "waiting on the doormat," as the celebrated incident was always picturesquely described, one of his colleagues was sent out to speak to him. Henderson, whose anger had been mounting by the minute, was, according to Lloyd George's urbane expression, "in a highly resentful frame of mind." He was finally admitted to the meeting and registered a heated protest at such unprecedented treatment. The delay, it was explained, was intended only to spare him personal embarrassment while the other ministers discussed his conduct. Henderson belligerently defended his actions and challenged them to demand his resignation. The proposal, which cannot have lacked appeal to a timorous cabinet already beginning to confuse Stockholm with pro-German machinations, for the moment at least, remained in abeyance.[53]

In the evening Henderson defended himself before an illtempered House of Commons. The members seemed as much or more concerned with the impropriety of a cabinet minister consorting with MacDonald than with the Stockholm affair. Lloyd

[51] Samuel Gompers, Seventy Years of Life and Labor (New York, 1925), II, 396.
[52] Merle Fainsod, International Socialism and the World War (Cambridge, Mass., 1935), p. 145.
[53] Lloyd George, IV, 151-52; Parliamentary Debates, XCVII (Aug. 13, 1917), 913-14; George N. Barnes, From Workshop to War Cabinet (New York, 1924), pp. 157-59; and Snowden, pp. 474-76.

George himself was called upon to state the government's position and in so doing was obliged to defend Henderson, whose dual role in the cabinet and in the Labor party was becoming a jurisdictional conflict of more than academic interest. Yet he made it clear that the government was unalterably opposed to Stockholm and did not "propose to allow any sectional conference to decide or to dictate the terms of peace."[54] "I shall not readily forget the sensation which this speech caused in Russia," a British correspondent has remarked.[55]

The incident seemed to be satisfactorily closed. It was not mentioned in cabinet sessions until, on the eighth, Henderson himself broached the subject. The discussion centered upon the passport question rather than the merits or demerits of Stockholm. There no longer being any doubt as to the government's stand, Henderson suggested that an open declaration of opposition be postponed until after the special Labor party conference met on the tenth. If the Stockholm proposal were voted down, and he seemed to think it would be, the government could remain silent and thereby avoid antagonizing labor. This solution was accepted, and the ministers—quite erroneously, it later developed—gained the distinct impression that Henderson's views had now veered around to an anti-Stockholm position.[56]

Nabokov, the Russian chargé in London, had meanwhile grown more and more uneasy regarding the reports common in Labor party circles that his government not only favored Stockholm but was considering a separate peace in case the Allies refused passports. He telegraphed Tereshchenko on August 3 informing him of the anti-Stockholm sentiment in Parliament and in the press and requesting permission to notify the British Foreign Minister that the conference was regarded by the Provisional Government as purely a party affair which would have no effect upon Russia's relations with her Allies.[57] On the ninth the reply came, giving full authorization for Nabokov to state that "although the Russian

---

[54] *Parliamentary Debates,* XCVI (Aug. 1, 1917), 2181-226.
[55] Price, p. 66.
[56] Lloyd George, IV, 156-57.
[57] Nabokoff, pp. 134-35.

government does not deem it possible to prevent Russian delegates from taking part in the Stockholm conference, they regard the conference as a party concern and its decisions in no wise binding upon the liberty of action of the government.[58] Nabokov hastily dispatched a note to the British Foreign Office quoting the telegram in full. This was the first official word as to the Provisional Government's attitude, and the cabinet, heretofore inclined to believe Henderson's assurance that both the Soviet and the government favored the conference, became not only more anti-Stockholm but anti-Henderson.

The special Labor party conference was held on the tenth as scheduled. During the morning session Henderson gave the principal address, a lengthy and cogent presentation of the case for Stockholm. Only in an indirect way did he refer to the Tereshchenko note: "I admit that such evidence as I have, though it is very slight, suggests that there has been some modification of the position of the new Government [the cabinet had been recently reorganized] as compared with the old on the question of the proposed Conference."[59] Lloyd George, who received a prompt report of the speech, sent the minister another copy of Nabokov's letter with a request that it be read to the assembly, evidently hoping it would induce the delegates to vote against Stockholm in the afternoon session. Henderson thought such a procedure unnecessary in view of the reference to the note in his speech and so informed the Prime Minister. By a large majority, 1,846,000 to 550,000, the delegates accepted the Stockholm invitation, an action which at the same time constituted a vote of confidence in Henderson. Because of a disagreement on minority representation at the future conference, the delegates adjourned until August 21.[60]

The decisive nature of the vote was a surprise to everyone, perhaps to Henderson most of all. He avoided the cabinet meeting that evening, where Lloyd George further solidified the anti-Stockholm sentiment by showing the ministers a telegram from Albert Thomas stating that Kerensky was opposed to the conference.

[58] Ibid., p. 137.
[59] Report of the Seventeenth Conference of the Labour Party, pp. 47-51.
[60] Ibid., p. 5.

Although Kerensky's private opinion was undoubtedly reported with accuracy, he quickly denied the authenticity of the message. His political future was too precarious to allow such loose statements to become public knowledge; and at no time did his objections to the conference envisage a refusal of passports.

Nabokov was invited to the Foreign Office the next morning and informed that Henderson's resignation would be requested because of his failure to reveal the presumed change in the Russian position to the Labor party conference. "I have risked so much in defending him before the country in connection with his trip to Paris, and this is how he repays me," was Lloyd George's bitter lament.[61] As a hedge against inevitable repercussions, he asked permission to release the text of Nabokov's letter. Reluctantly the latter agreed. Had he been in Kerensky's place, his consent might have been a great deal harder to obtain, for the publication of the letter caused resentment and consternation in Soviet ranks. It was indeed fortunate for the Provisional Government that Bolshevik opposition to Stockholm had weakened the issue in the minds of the most militant workers and soldiers; otherwise a repetition of the May demonstration would have been a strong possibility. This must also have occurred to the Soviet leaders, since they chose to take a mild view of the incident. *Izvestia* showed no hesitation in attacking Lloyd George and the Allies in general, but its feeble criticism of Kerensky's conduct was in such glaring contrast that the leading Bolshevik organ jeered, "What is this? Brazen insolence or pitiable confusion?"[62] Tereshchenko, as the government's spokesman and apologist, asserted with doubtful accuracy that Nabokov's note had gone beyond the original meaning of the correspondence.[63]

Henderson's letter of resignation was forthcoming before the cabinet got around to requesting it. Lloyd George replied at some length in a letter intended for public consumption. The press,

[61] Quoted in Nabokov's telegram to Petrograd, Aug. 11, 1917, *Krasny Arkhiv*, XVI (1926), 37.

[62] *Rabochy i Soldat* [*Worker and Soldier*], No. 12, Aug. 18, 1917. (*Pravda* had been suppressed; so the Bolshevik organ came out under a variety of names until the November Revolution).

[63] Text of the statement in *Izvestia*, No. 134, Aug. 16, 1917.

scenting an easy victim, subjected the resigned minister to a vigorous attack not always in the best taste, in which the mildest accusations concerned his alleged duplicity and bad faith. Saving his rebuttal for the House of Commons, Henderson spoke before that body on the thirteenth and became involved with the Prime Minister in some sharp exchanges. His case was not so well presented as it might otherwise have been, because his patriotism was stronger than his devotion to the ideals of international socialism, and he refrained from going into the Stockholm issue in all its ramifications out of regard for the "interests of the nation in this great crisis."[64]

Lloyd George warmly thanked Nabokov for his part in the affair, for the Russian declaration had been secured only through his personal initiative. The Provisional Government was not equally pleased, however. Nabokov was reprimanded and told to confine himself henceforth to transmitting "the exact text of our declarations on political questions of principle" without adding remarks of his own.[65] Both Tereshchenko and Kerensky complained to Buchanan that their message had never been intended for publication. So alarmed was Kerensky over the incident that he urged the ambassador to ask his government not to refuse passports to the British socialists.[66] In a special interview with the Manchester *Guardian's* correspondent, Kerensky authorized the statement that the Provisional Government cordially sympathized with the objects of the conference and had always expressed the wish to the Allied diplomatic representatives that no obstacles should be placed in the way of those delegates who were going to Stockholm.[67] "I have insisted again and again," he said elsewhere, "that any opposition offered to it by the Allied Governments, any difficulties put in the way of delegates, is simply playing into German hands."[68] Perhaps a more candid statement of the Provisional Government's real sentiment was expressed by the Assistant War

[64] *Parliamentary Debates,* XCVII, 923-24.
[65] Nabokoff, pp. 151-56.
[66] G. Buchanan, II, 163-64.
[67] Manchester *Guardian,* Aug. 17, 1917.
[68] Emily Greene Balch, *Approaches to the Great Settlement* (New York, 1918), p. 105.

Minister when he told General Knox that he personally—and he thought that most of the other ministers agreed—thought the Stockholm meeting was favored only because it would get rid of the delegates for a time.[69]

The Labor party conference reconvened on the twenty-first, considerably sobered by the knowledge that the government disapproved of the Stockholm project. Inexplicably Lloyd George and his associates were now firmly convinced—or pretended to be—that it was all a German plot to gain a negotiated peace. The Allies scented victory and, even at the cost of Russian support, were unwilling to revise their war aims to suit their own socialists, let alone those of the enemy. Although the Labor party executive committee gave Henderson a vote of confidence, the affair had only accentuated the dilemma of the delegates; so it was a badly divided conference which met to take a second vote on Stockholm. The four Soviet representatives were present as guests of the convention, and Rusanov replied graciously to the welcoming speech of the chairman. Henderson again made the major address of the occasion and aggressively defended his position. By the narrow vote of 1,234,000 to 1,231,000 the previous decision to attend Stockholm was upheld. The block system of voting, by which the 600,000 votes of the miners' federation were cast against Stockholm, even though it had been decided by only a slight majority, partially accounted for the closeness of the balloting.[70] The actual choice of delegates was postponed until the meeting of an Allied socialist conference which was scheduled for the end of the month. A resolution restricting the minority representation of British labor passed by a huge majority, an action which was contrary to both the letter and spirit of the Stockholm invitation and indicated that the Labor party, though its attitude had alarmed the more conservative members of the government, was still "fundamentally sound." The conference committee at Stockholm, the Russian delegates, and the Independent Labor party all protested against such unjust discrimination.[71]

[69] Knox, II, 675.
[70] R. W. Postgate, *The International during the War* (London, 1918), p. 47.
[71] *Report of the Seventeenth Conference of the Labour Party*, pp. 6-8.

The long-awaited inter-Allied conference of socialists met on August 28 in London, with sixty-eight representatives from eight countries present. The United States was unrepresented, and the Russian delegates participated only after being assured that the discussions would be of a consultative nature. Nothing more substantial was accomplished than the passage of several additional futile resolutions on Stockholm. The assembly went on record by a vote of 48 to 13 in favor of sending delegates, and by a 50 to 2 vote they condemned the policy of their governments in refusing passports. Beyond this there was little agreement because of the strange principle that unanimity was necessary before any action could be taken. The obstructionist tactics of the French majority socialists—now actually a minority—were especially obnoxious to the less conservatively inclined, their sole purpose in coming apparently a desire to prevent any decision that might jeopardize the friendly relations between the French government and the majority socialists. No general statement of policy on Stockholm was accepted, and a similar fate met the various statements of war aims proposed by the different national groups. The conference broke up at the end of the second day, its failure obvious even to the participants.[72]

A few days later the British Trades Union Congress met at Blackpool and gave its overwhelming approval to a resolution which declared that "a Conference at Stockholm at the present moment could not be successful." After this unexpected retreat on labor's part, the blow to Stockholm was softened by a final note of defiance: "No Government has any right to prevent an expression of feeling by the working class of its country, and we regard the action of the Government in this matter as an unwarrantable interference with our rights as citizens."[73]

This attitude of defiance was shared by the French Socialist party. When Ribot's ministry fell on September 7, the new Premier retained his services as Foreign Minister, and the socialists, still smarting over the rebuff they had received at his hands on the pass-

---

[72] *Ibid.*, pp. 8-11; *Labour Leader*, Sept. 6, 1917.
[73] *Report of the Seventeenth Conference of the Labour Party*, p. 11.

port controversy, withdrew from the government. Thus the Stockholm question was responsible for the dissolution of the *union sacré,* the political truce by which all parties had rallied to the defense of their country at the outbreak of the war. The Socialist party congress at Bordeaux in early October upheld this action and reaffirmed its pro-Stockholm stand.[74]

The Stockholm project was, in fact, already dead because of the opposition of the Allied governments, though it was not to be accorded a decent burial for some time. The socialist and labor organizations were too weak and too divided to alter the policy of their governments by any means more effective than moral protest. The four Soviet delegates, whose stay in Western Europe had become a protracted one, sailed for home disappointed but outwardly optimistic. The Stockholm committee declared that the American government was largely to blame for the passport difficulty and was all the more bitter about it because of the liberal pronouncements on war aims which President Wilson had made in the past.[75] The committee issued a more elaborate statement on September 15 announcing a fresh postponement of the conference but refusing to concede defeat. "The Stockholm conference must inaugurate a new era in the struggle of the proletariat against imperialism by the re-establishment of an International capable of common action," proclaimed the manifesto. Despite a brief and unavoidable delay, "for every organized proletariat the watchword is still, 'To Stockholm!' "[76]

The last task which the committee undertook was the drafting of a peace program, a document which was intended as a guide for the delegates when they should at length assemble for the conference. It sought to embody the principle, "No victors, no vanquished," and after heated and prolonged argument, the completed platform was released on October 10.[77] As might have been foreseen, it failed to please the socialist majorities of the belligerent

---

[74] Paul Louis, *Histoire du socialisme en France* (Paris, 1925), pp. 370-71. For the resolutions passed at the Bordeaux conference see *Le parti socialiste, la guerre et la paix* (Paris, 1918), pp. 189-99.

[75] Balch, pp. 211-12.

[76] *Stockholm,* pp. 487-90.

[77] *Ibid.,* pp. 493-521.

powers and offered a preview of the difficulties which a full session of the conference would have faced.

The Allies, by issuing passports and allowing their socialists a free hand, could have more easily avoided the imaginary terrors of the "Stockholm plot" than by refusing them and thereby alienating relatively small but influential segments of public opinion. Not only did the Stockholm fiasco offer a clear insight into the nature of Allied war aims, but it was also a further indication of the bankruptcy of the Second International and the rise of the Third (Communist) International. There can have been no more sharply defined issue for the Bolsheviks to present before the Russian people than the definite refusal of the Allies to allow even their patriotic socialists an opportunity to explore the ground for a general peace settlement. That the Bolsheviks did not so sharply define it, and largely allowed the matter to go by default because they had denounced the whole idea from the very first, hardly served to bolster the waning authority of the moderate Russian socialists. The Mensheviks and Socialist Revolutionaries, who had heretofore dominated the Soviet—and thus the course of the Russian Revolution—suffered an irreparable loss of prestige through the Stockholm failure and were forced to give way to socialists promising action instead of words. The Bolshevik victory in November, though scarcely a result of Stockholm, was due in large part to the peace question, an answer to which the Provisional Government, bound inescapably to the aims of its allies, avoided again and again until the time for decision had passed.

Suggestions that the ill-fated conference be resurrected were frequent but unavailing. Stockholm remained a moral issue long after its practical significance had ceased. The British Labor party, especially, took on a new militancy. The crusade for the formulation of just peace terms continued with added impetus throughout the war. To socialists and many liberals Stockholm was not merely a symbol of their impotence but a constant reminder that their influence, having safely been ignored once, might again be disregarded when the time came to make peace.

CHAPTER V

War Minister Kerensky "Persuader-in-Chief"

THE CABINET shakeup in May which led to the formation of a second coalition government presaged far less change in policy than the turnover in personnel seemed to imply. Milyukov, unhappy though he was at his ouster from power, accounted himself fortunate that his successor could be relied upon to carry out a "proper" foreign policy with only minimum acknowledgment of Soviet demands. "As a matter of fact he continued my line of diplomacy," Milyukov has stated of Tereshchenko. "He could not openly admit it, however."[1] Under his administration "the Allied diplomats knew that the 'democratic' terminology of his dispatches was an involuntary concession to the demands of the moment, and they accepted it with condescension so long as concessions in form meant gains in substance."[2]

This was the spirit in which the Allies received the new Foreign Minister's lengthy statement of policy. "Free Russia, like every other country which has made a great renovating revolution, is moved by two motives profoundly idealistic," declared Tereshchenko. "The first is an aspiration to give a just peace to the entire world, not to injure any nation, not to create after the war a hatred . . . which remains always when one nation comes forth from

[1] Paul Milyukov, "From Nicholas II to Stalin: Half-a-Century of Foreign Politics" (typewritten manuscript, Hoover Library, Stanford University, ca. 1940), p. 11.
[2] Milyukov, Istoria, Vol. I, Bk. I, p. 167.

the struggle enriched . . . [and the other is] obliged to accept humiliating conditions of peace." The second was less vague: "Consciousness of its ties with the Allied democracies" and of the "duty which these ties have imposed on her." "Revolutionary Russia," he continued, "cannot and ought not to break these ties sealed by blood; for her it is a question of revolutionary honor which is so much the more precious to her now." With regard to the secret treaties, Tereshchenko declared that their immediate publication was "equivalent to a rupture with the Allies and will result in the isolation of Russia."[3] The coating of idealism was thick but his meaning plain. Russia's devotion to the alliance was undiminished, whatever ideas to the contrary the Soviet might have.

Milyukov's controversial note to the Allies of May 1, which had precipitated the cabinet crisis, went formally unanswered for almost a month while London and Paris rephrased their replies several times. Acutely conscious of his predecessor's mistakes, Tereshchenko refused to accept the notes until they were properly couched in the new "democratic" phraseology.[4] Henderson and Thomas both worked on the notes until they were deemed presentable to the public at large. The United States made no formal reply. Instead, a typical Wilsonian message, long and circumlocutious, yet undeniably sincere in the sentiments expressed, was dispatched on May 22. It affirmed the just and democratic nature of the war ("We are fighting for the liberty, the self-government, and the undictated development of all peoples") and avoided any mention of the unsavory aspects of the Allied cause with which the Russian people were far more concerned.[5] Despite the carefully phrased generalities, both Ambassador Francis and Tereshchenko took it as a reply to the Milyukov note, and Secretary of State Lansing was forced to explain that the President's remarks were "in no sense a reply to anything but . . . a wholly spontaneous and independent communication."[6] The Russian Foreign Minister

[3] Foreign Relations, I, 75-77.
[4] Francis to Lansing, May 31, 1917, ibid., p. 86.
[5] Cumming and Pettit, pp. 23-25.
[6] Lansing to Francis, June 3, 1917, Foreign Relations, I, 88.

approved heartily of Wilson's idealistic words but asked permission to change a few passages that might be misinterpreted, "considering the state of nervous excitement that prevails in Russia" and the "existence of misinterpreters who are ever ready to do their destructive work."[7] Taken out of context, such phrases as "the day has come to conquer or submit" and "that status [of the German Empire] must be altered" were perhaps capable of exploitation but rather more indicative of Tereshchenko's anxious frame of mind. His request was refused, and the original message was released for publication on June 10.

The British and French notes were published two days later. Both stressed the just nature of the Allied cause and expressed gratification that the Russians also agreed that the war was one of liberation and not of conquest. Britain's reply blandly stated that "the agreements which they have from time to time made with their allies" were, "broadly speaking," in conformity with the liberal war aims expressed by President Wilson and seconded by the Russians. "But if the Russian government so desire," the note concluded, Britain is willing "to examine and, if need be, to revise these agreements."[8] The French communication was much more verbose and ignored the secret treaties. The last sentence—a minor prose masterpiece in the accepted jargon of diplomacy—made subtle hints while saying nothing really definite: "The Russian government may be assured that the French government is desirous of coming to an understanding with it, not only regarding the means for continuing the struggle but also regarding those for ending it, by examining and settling a common agreement as to the conditions in which they may hope to reach a final settlement in accordance with the ideas by which their conduct of the war is directed."[9] The Soviet gave these notes a cool reception. Izvestia, normally friendly toward Wilson, singled out his message for special criticism because of its "nebulous and high-flown phrases," which seemed to imply that the desire for peace and socialist brotherhood was a result of German intrigue. "That is not the

[7] Francis to Lansing, June 4, 1917, ibid., pp. 89-91.
[8] Times (London), June 12, 1917.
[9] Ibid., June 14, 1917.

kind of language with which to speak to democratic Russia," said *Izvestia*.[10]

The evasive response to the Milyukov note only confirmed in a more formal manner the determination of the Allies to resist the obstreperous Soviet in its embarrassing demands for a revision of war aims. Philip Snowden made a sustained attack upon this policy in the House of Commons on May 16 and aroused a full-scale debate on the subject which lasted until nearly midnight. He offered an amendment to a routine financial bill welcoming the Russian declaration on war aims and calling on the British government to issue a similar statement. With that as a point of departure, he went on to eulogize the Revolution and its democratic diplomacy in contrast to the "imperialism and conquest naked and unashamed," which he intimated was the basis of Allied diplomacy.[11] Other members of the House joined in the attack, and Lord Robert Cecil, the Under-Secretary of Foreign Affairs, frankly —and rather defiantly—declared that the agreements made with the tsarist regime were still binding so far as Britain was concerned. Russia, said Cecil, "can release the rest of the Allies from any particular undertaking, but until that is done we are bound in honour to carry out our engagements not only with Russia but with the rest of the Allies."[12] In other words, he would be happy to have Russia renounce the lucrative benefits to be derived from a victorious war, but a mutual renunciation was quite another matter. Snowden's amendment was finally put to a vote and defeated 238 to 32.

A shorter but somewhat similar debate took place in the Chamber of Deputies on May 22. Ribot made some conciliatory remarks in praise of Russia, which seemed to satisfy the Chamber for the time being. The subject was brought up again on June 5 and a resolution on war aims passed, consisting very largely of a denunciation of German aggression. It called for the restoration of Alsace-Lorraine, the liberation of invaded territories, and reparations for war damages. Three minority resolutions, much further

[10] No. 78, June 13, 1917.
[11] *Parliamentary Debates*, XCIII, 1625-33.
[12] *Ibid.*, col. 1668.

in the direction of what the Soviet would have considered acceptable, were proposed by different factions of the Left but rejected by a majority of the deputies.[13]

To the rank and file members of the Soviet the wording of resolutions and diplomatic notes was an abstruse matter of no concern. They were interested in peace, not the by-products of the struggle to obtain it. To the Soviet leaders, especially those who had entered the government, the manipulation of words was a major occupation to which they devoted themselves in all seriousness. Sobered by the responsibilities of power, they were veering to the Right while the masses were veering to the Left. Near the end of May Tsereteli, Chernov, and Skobelev, all acting in their dual capacity of representatives of Soviet democracy and members of the Provisional Government, cornered the British ambassador and proceeded to catechize him for almost two hours on the war, the Revolution, and the secret agreements. Buchanan successfully withstood the ordeal and convinced them of his government's good intentions. Tsereteli reported to the Petrograd Soviet on the twenty-sixth that all was well and that Russia's new democratic foreign policy was on its way to realization.[14]

In such a state of self-delusion, it was only another step for Tsereteli and his fellow socialists to become converted to the view that a successful military offensive would rehabilitate Russian prestige and bring about in a much shorter time that just and honorable peace for which the Allies were presumed to be fighting. An offensive appealed especially to the bourgeois elements of the population, who looked upon it as a cure-all for the radical virus which was unaccountably infecting the masses despite all that had been done to curb the disease. Patriotism, not religion, was to be the opium of the people.

Kerensky was the most vociferous of these self-appointed spokesmen for military resurgence as a means of attaining the ideals of the "revolutionary democracy." A considerably disillusioned Kerensky was to complain in after years that "the tried statesmen

[13] *Débats parlementaires* (1917), I, 1329-30.
[14] Ariadna Tyrkóva-Williams, *From Liberty to Brest-Litovsk* (London, 1919), pp. 91-92; G. Buchanan, II, 132-35.

of the Entente regarded the leaders of revolutionary Russia as pleasant simpletons who were dying to pull the Allied chestnut out of the fire of the World War, quite unselfishly, for the sake of their revolutionary ideals, as it were."[15]   It would have been rather difficult for these statesmen to gain any other impression, so readily did the "pleasant simpletons" of Russia adopt the idea of an offensive without first requiring any guarantees in the way of a revision of war aims. London and Paris, through their ambassadors, applauded the prospect of renewed military activity and urged the Provisional Government on, but the primary incentive came from Russia, not the Allies.[16]

At the same time that Kerensky was so earnestly striving to please the Allies, they were carrying on peace negotiations with Austria behind Russia's back. These plans for a separate peace failed to materialize, largely because of Italy's refusal to give up her claims to certain territory which had been promised as the price of her entrance into the war; but all the while, Russia's interests were freely discussed and disposed of without the knowledge of the Provisional Government.[17]   The Allies planned to present Russia with the accomplished fact. As Ribot told the Austrian representative on May 20, "We need not inform her of our negotiations until they are practically finished."[18]

The Russian army, while it had long since ceased to exist as an effective fighting unit, was still a force to be reckoned with in terms of manpower. Upon assuming his duties as War Minister, Kerensky—"a buffer between the commanding corps and the rank and file," as he has described himself[19]—devoted his full energies and seemingly inexhaustible eloquence to the impossible task of creating a warlike spirit where none existed. As he toured the front trying to convince the troops that Germany constituted the main threat to their Revolution, he earned the jeering title of "persuader-in-chief" from his political enemies of both Left and

[15] Kerensky, *Crucifixion of Liberty*, p. 344.
[16] *Ibid.*, p. 339; Kerensky, *The Catastrophe*, p. 207; Denikin, Vol. I, Pt. I, p. 178.
[17] Kerensky, *Crucifixion of Liberty*, pp. 338-39.
[18] G. de Manteyer (ed.), *Austria's Peace Offer* (London, 1921), p. 162.
[19] Kerensky, *The Catastrophe*, p. 184.

Right but little real support for his anti-German crusade. His flamboyant oratory, often verging on the hysterical, was always good enough to insure him an attentive hearing and some fleeting success. Unfortunately for his cause, however, this shallow radicalism of the "revolutionary phrase" did not permanently convince the unsophisticated peasant soldier that a war which the Soviet denounced on the one hand as imperialist and on the other praised as a defense of the Revolution was a war to be supported at the risk of one's life.

Even more inept as propagandists were the representatives of Russia's allies stationed in the capital with the embassies and military missions. They placed an excessive emphasis upon the restoration of discipline and the continuance of the war. Hugh Walpole, the English novelist, headed a propaganda bureau for the British government. In numerous speeches General Knox, a high Tory by political faith, dutifully paid his respects to the Revolution in his halting Russian; Colonel Thornhill, his aide, made by far the best showing as an orator and was the envy of his less fluent colleagues; Bernard Pares, a British professor and authority on Russia, devoted his full time to speaking and served as interpreter on other occasions. His friend and associate, Professor Samuel Harper of the University of Chicago, has recalled an incident which epitomizes the distrust with which the average Russian soldier held the wealthier classes and explains why even the sincerest spokesmen for the Allied cause met little response. One day Harper noticed a group of soldiers looking at a Petrograd newspaper, the illustrated supplement of which was devoted to America and her entry into the war. Using it as an entering wedge to begin a conversation with them, he pointed to a picture of George Washington and commented that Washington had been the father of the American Revolution. Harper was distinctly embarrassed when one of the soldiers remarked, "Prosperous-looking gentleman."[20] But not all the Allied nationals remained firm patriots like Harper, Pares, and Knox. A few succumbed to the revolutionary atmosphere and shocked their friends by "going Bolshevik." In this

[20] Paul V. Harper (ed.), *The Russia I Believe In: The Memoirs of Samuel N. Harper* (Chicago, 1945), p. 100.

category were several foreign correspondents and the British naval attaché, Captain Harold Grenfell,[21] not to mention many others whose views became so radically altered that they were suspected of harboring Bolshevik sympathies upon returning home.

At the height of the propaganda campaign for the coming offensive, the largest and most elaborate of all the Allied missions arrived in Russia to spur on the war effort and lend the prestige of the United States to the support of the Provisional Government. This was the delegation sent by President Wilson "to convey to the Russian Government the friendship and good will" of the United States and "to express the confident hope that the Russian people, having developed a political system founded on the principle of democracy, will join with the free people of America in resisting with firmness and fortitude the ambitious designs of the German Government, which by force, intrigue, and deception, they are striving to attain."[22] In less idealistic language, Secretary of State Lansing had on April 11 called the President's attention to the need for such a mission in order to "prevent the socialistic element in Russia from carrying out any plan which would destroy the efficiency of the Allied Powers." Wilson agreed that the project was a good one and that similar suggestions had already come from a number of quarters.[23]

Lansing lost no time in drawing up a tentative list of members suitable for the undertaking and cabling Ambassador Francis to find out if the contemplated mission would be welcomed by the Provisional Government. He added that Francis might "discreetly ascertain whether it would be wise to have a prominent Hebrew a member of the commission" and whether the question of his orthodoxy was material or not.[24] The ambassador replied reassuringly that the mission would be welcome; nor would there be any objection to "element mentioned" and that "either kind of such element equally acceptable."[25] Despite the delicate skirmishing on the question, it was decided not to include a member of the

[21] Pares, *Russian Memoirs*, p. 442.
[22] Lansing to Francis, May 1, 1917, *Foreign Relations*, I, 108.
[23] Baker, VII, 16.
[24] April 14, 1917, *Foreign Relations*, I, 107.
[25] April 19, 1917, *ibid*.

Jewish faith because of the widespread anti-Semitism still prevalent in Russia. Eugene Meyer, then a New York businessman, had consented to serve but was tactfully asked to withdraw.[26] It would have been much less embarrassing to the Provisional Government had Meyer been allowed to go, because distorted rumors of the incident caused so much ill-feeling both in Russia and the United States that Prince Lvov felt obliged to deny publicly that he or any other member of the government had opposed including a Jew on the mission.[27]

Although a sincere attempt was made to represent the various interests in American society, the personnel of the nine-man commission was one well calculated to meet with polite interest from the Russian bourgeoisie, apathy from the masses, and active hostility from their revolutionary spokesmen. Yet a thoroughly capitalist America, in which socialist doctrines had scarcely made a dent, could hardly be expected to overload the mission with antiwar radicals even if Wilson and his advisers had somehow become convinced of the unpleasant reality—that only such persons would have been able to influence the Russian populace. Instead the delegation was heavily weighted in favor of the "better element" of the population, of which Charles R. Crane and Cyrus H. McCormick, prominent industrialists, and Samuel R. Bertron, a New York banker, were the chief representatives. John R. Mott, a leader in the Young Men's Christian Association, was chosen in deference to religious sentiment, while seventy-four-year-old James Duncan, an American Federation of Labor vice-president, and Charles Edward Russell, a publicist of socialist convictions, were presumably to represent the American working man. Duncan was suggested by Samuel Gompers, who declined to go himself,[28] and Russell must have seemed a queer sort of socialist indeed to the kind which was shortly to gain ascendancy in Russia. He was an ardent supporter of the war and was later expelled from the Socialist party when he refused to resign his appointment.[29] At the time New York socialist leaders contented themselves with remarks of

[26] Lansing to Wilson, May 3, 1917, Wilson Papers; Baker, VII, 62.
[27] New York *Times*, May 30, 1917.   [28] Gompers, II, 398.
[29] New York *Times*, June 11, 1917.

emphatic disapproval, the party secretary commenting that Wilson would have done better not to send any socialists than one of Russell's type.[30]

To represent the army and navy, Major-General Hugh L. Scott, Chief of Staff, and Rear Admiral James H. Glennon, a naval ordnance expert, were added to the commission. General Scott, beyond the age of real usefulness in such an important position as Chief of Staff, was very possibly sent as an alternative to retirement.[31] To head the mission, perhaps the worst choice of all, the distinguished but uncompromisingly conservative Elihu Root was chosen. Seventy-two years old, a lifelong Republican, an ex-Senator from New York, and former Secretary of State under President Theodore Roosevelt, Root was not the man to arouse any patriotic fervor in Russian hearts. His political sentiments were frankly, if unconsciously, expressed in a remark he made to his companions while visiting a Russian village on the way to Petrograd: "I am a firm believer in democracy, but I do not like filth."[32]

While historical perspective has demonstrated the hopelessness of the mission from the very beginning, a more liberal man would certainly seem to have been preferable. Just why Root was chosen for the difficult task is uncertain. His friends claimed afterward that it was just a plan to get rid of him in order to avoid using his services in a more important capacity, possibly as a member of the cabinet.[33] If Root had similar thoughts, he kept them carefully to himself. But upon one occasion he gave vent to his bitterness over the failure of the mission by accusing Wilson of not wanting to accomplish anything. "It was a grand-stand play," Root complained. "He wanted to show his sympathy for the Russian Revolution. When we delivered his message and made our speeches, he was satisfied; that's all he wanted."[34] Neither commentary upon the President's motives seems warranted. Two cabinet members, Lansing and William G. McAdoo, were apparently instrumental

---

[30] *Ibid.,* May 12, 1917.
[31] Philip C. Jessup, *Elihu Root* (New York, 1938), II, 358.
[32] *Ibid.,* p. 361.
[33] Colonel T. Bentley Mott, *Twenty Years as Military Attaché* (New York, 1937), p. 192; Charles R. Flint, *Memories of an Active Life* (New York, 1923), p. 234.
[34] Jessup, II, 356.

in getting his consent to the appointment.[35] Because of Root's hostility to certain domestic reforms of the "New Freedom," Wilson had spoken harshly of him in the past but became convinced that Root was an "admirable choice" and that he was "genuinely and heartily in sympathy with the revolution in Russia."[36] Josephus Daniels was the only cabinet member who objected to Root, and Wilson upheld McAdoo and Lansing when they rebuked Daniels for pointing out the obvious—namely, that Root's conservatism would be a decided handicap in Russia.[37]

Root accepted the appointment as a duty and without enthusiasm. "You have no idea how I hate it," he wrote to a friend, "but it is just like our boys going into the war; there can be no question about doing it."[38] Writing to his wife while en route to Russia, he commented, "I shall be awfully bored in Petrograd, but only for a little while."[39] Liberal and radical circles alike greeted the President's choice with outspoken criticism. The editor of the *Novy Mir,* the newspaper upon which Trotsky had worked during his brief stay in New York, said that "it would probably be better to send no commission at all than one headed by Mr. Root," and Professor Alexander Petrunkevitch, a Russian scholar teaching at Yale University, declared that American socialists had undoubtedly warned their comrades in Russia against Root. This latter revelation caused some excited talk of examining cables to Russia and the possible prosecution of the socialists allegedly involved in such nefarious practices, but the incident passed without further action.[40] Rabbi Stephen S. Wise went so far as to write to the President requesting him not to appoint Root,[41] and Samuel Untermeyer, a prominent Jewish writer and speaker, accused Root at a public meeting of being "utterly out of sympathy with our race" and "incredibly narrow and provincial in his conception of the Jew."[42] To these attacks, Root offered no reply, but the newspapers and magazines of the country came to his defense with few exceptions.

[35] *Ibid.;* Josephus Daniels, *The Wilson Era: Years of War and After* (Chapel Hill, N. C., 1946), p. 58.

[36] Baker, VII, 42.   [37] Daniels, p. 58.   [38] Jessup, II, 356.   [39] *Ibid.,* p. 359.

[40] New York *Times,* May 2 and 3, 1917.

[41] Wise to Wilson, April 28, 1917, Wilson Papers; Baker, VII, 42.

[42] New York *Times,* May 4, 1917.

Less publicized, though of more practical significance than the Root mission, was the special railroad commission to Russia which left Washington as the controversy over Root was beginning to die down. It was headed by John F. Stevens, who had been chief engineer during the building of the Panama Canal, and included four other prominent engineers and railroad executives. Such a mission had been suggested first by the Council of National Defense and enthusiastically seconded by Ambassador Francis.[43] Originally Stevens was to have been a member of the Root party but was transferred to head the railroad mission. Root was understandably annoyed at this dual authority in dealing with the Provisional Government and wrote to Lansing on May 6 to request that the Stevens group be attached to his mission as technical advisers. The request was politely denied, Root being informed that his mission was essentially political and that no such conflict of authority seemed probable.[44] Some unpleasantness nevertheless did develop in Russia because of Root's interest in transportation matters, and he was informed tartly by Stevens that his mission did not "look with favor" upon the interference of "outside parties."[45]

The Stevens party arrived in Vladivostok late in May and proceeded to inspect the Trans-Siberian Railroad. Although Stevens himself was troubled with ill-health and the internal harmony of the mission left something to be desired, its work continued until the government was overthrown in November, at which time a group of nearly three hundred railroad operating men, engineers, and interpreters had already made plans to leave for Russia to undertake more extensive work. Francis advised them to come ahead anyway, since he had no confidence in the survival of the Bolshevik government and, in any case, expected no separate peace. The party reached Vladivostok on schedule but immediately re-embarked for Japan, where it remained for several months in

[43] Newton D. Baker (Secretary of War) to Lansing, March 31, 1917; and Francis to Lansing, April 9, 1917, Foreign Relations, III, 183-84.

[44] Lansing to Root, May 9, 1917, U. S. Department of State, Papers Relating to the Foreign Relations of the United States: The Lansing Papers, 1914-1920 (Washington, 1939-40), II, 336-37; also in Elihu Root Papers, Library of Congress.

[45] Stevens to Root, July 1, 1917, Root Papers. See also the diary of William L. Darling, p. 20, Hoover Library, Stanford University.

idleness awaiting clarification of the political situation in Russia. It subsequently played a part in the intervention of the Allied Powers in Siberia in 1918 and 1919.[46]

Not until May 18 did the special diplomatic mission finally leave Washington for the long journey to Petrograd by way of the North Pacific and Siberia. The mission was supplemented by a large staff of military aides, secretaries, clerks, and orderlies. These minor posts were filled with men of "political influence and good character," but it was only with the greatest difficulty that a man who spoke Russian was squeezed in at the last minute.[47] There was no one along who could have been called an authority on Russia, though Professor Harper gave the members of the mission his version of the current Russian situation when he boarded their train briefly near Chicago.[48] He was not selected to make the trip himself, presumably because Lansing had been told from several different sources that the professor was not as popular in Russia as he had previously supposed.[49] But Harper went to Russia by the Atlantic route in an unofficial capacity and worked closely with Francis throughout the summer months.

The mission sailed from Seattle on an old converted cruiser, arriving in Vladivostok on June 3. The party was greeted cordially by city officials but quickly hustled on board the former Tsar's special train to forestall a possible demonstration by the city's radical element.[50] The danger was probably quite remote, for an attempt to arouse the population against the mission had elicited little support. The instigators were supposedly New York socialists, exiles under the Tsar, who had recently returned to their homeland.[51] The ten-day trip over the Trans-Siberian Railroad to the Russian capital was largely uneventful. Stops were made at many towns along the way, as local dignitaries beamed their welcome, crowds cheered, and speeches were made. But these brief de-

[46] For details on the railway mission, see the Darling diary and the John F. Stevens Papers, Hoover Library.

[47] Mott, p. 193.   [48] Harper, p. 99.

[49] Lansing to Wilson, April 12, 1917, Wilson Papers; Baker, VII, 18-19.

[50] Mott, p. 196.

[51] Foreign Relations, I, 131; D. Fedotoff White, Survival through War and Revolution in Russia (Philadelphia, 1939), p. 142.

partures from the monotony of the journey were of a purely ceremonial nature, not to be taken as seriously as the orators sometimes
took themselves. In Petrograd the delegation was installed in the
sumptuous Winter Palace, whose well-stocked wine cellar was
put at the disposal of the guests. Root found that his room had
once been occupied by Catherine II, "whose morals," he recalled
in a letter to his wife, "differed from Queen Victoria's."[52]

The following day, June 14, inaugurated the round of official receptions, luncheon conferences, private interviews, and patriotic speeches, which was to be the chief occupation of the
Americans during their stay in Petrograd. The first reception was
held at the Foreign Office, but a more formal affair was arranged
by the Provisional Government on the fifteenth, where Francis
was given an opportunity to unleash his "Fourth of July" oratory
in introducing the members of the mission. His eloquence was
received with solemn courtesy by the audience, save for a "few
furtive grins" when he declared there were no classes in free
America.[53] Root's speech was confined to the customary platitudes
reserved for such occasions, and Tereshchenko replied in kind for
the Russians. Another minister, apparently disgusted at the wordy
flight from reality, exclaimed to the Russian naval aide assigned
to the mission: "Young man, will you please tell these Americans
that we are tired of this war. Explain to them that we are weary
of the long and bloody struggle."[54] The aide was aghast at such
effrontery and refused to translate the remark. If the impression
created by all the contemporary sources is correct, such candor
would have made no impression on Root and his colleagues in
any case, unless that the minister concerned was either a crank
or a Bolshevik, and they probably would have been amazed to
discover that the opponents of the war were not confined to a few
discredited agitators. Their restricted contacts, however, made it
certain that no such discovery would be made. Russell, whose
normal optimism failed him at times, epitomized the situation
quite ably when he noted in his diary on the twenty-first that "if

[52] Jessup, II, 361.
[53] Fedotoff White, p. 143.
[54] Ibid., p. 144.

this commission is to accomplish anything besides looking pleasant and eating copiously, the fact is not yet apparent."[55]

Each member of the mission sought out the Russian equivalent of those elements which he represented in American society. Admiral Glennon visited the Russian fleet on the Baltic and Black seas; General Scott inspected the front and made a side trip to Romania; Mott talked to church officials; Duncan and Russell managed to discover a few genuine "proletarian" groups apart from official functionaries.[56] Conversations with the appropriate ministers indicated the military, naval, and financial needs of Russia. But the chief contacts, especially of Root, Crane, McCormick, and Bertron, were with government officials, diplomats, businessmen, and other middle-class groups which were even then mere figureheads, without support among the masses. The numerous speeches, of which Root's set the theme, concerned the sacred duty of democratic Russia to protect her newly gained freedom from the encroachments of Germany and found a ready response from select audiences already convinced. Yet even in Petrograd the lower classes could scarcely have been aware of the existence of an American mission, to say nothing of the rest of Russia. Except for a few attacks in the left-wing press, its presence was ignored, and in the bourgeois papers the speeches of Root and others were given only perfunctory attention.[57] On the only recorded occasion when a speech was made by a member of the mission before the Petrograd Soviet, it was permitted only as a favor to the American correspondents. The speaker in question—Russell—had been put off repeatedly, and it had been broadly hinted that one of the chief difficulties preventing his appearance was his admitted status as a government delegate rather than as an American socialist. Russell's patriotic remarks received a sharp rejoinder from a Soviet speaker and were so watered down and sugar-coated by the translator, in order not to offend the American, that he went away convinced that the Soviet was solidly behind the Allied cause.[58] That

[55] Russell diary, Russell Papers.
[56] Mott, pp. 197-98; Fedotoff White, pp. 145-65; Basil Mathews, *John R. Mott* (New York, 1934), p. 249.
[57] Robert Crozier Long, *Russian Revolution Aspects* (New York, 1919), p. 285.
[58] *Ibid.;* diary, June 25, 1917, Russell Papers.

instance, as one observer cynically remarked, "was as close as the American mission . . . got to the Russian revolution."[59] Yet most of the members appeared to be aware of the existence of the Soviet, and some of them were even vaguely conscious of its importance in Russian affairs. But only Duncan and Russell made any attempt to meet and converse with the Soviet leaders. No one, however, had any direct contact with the Bolsheviks, whose reputation as German agents was one of the few things known about them. General Scott thought the time propitious "to execute about one hundred of these German agitators like . . . Lenin and Trotsky, or at least to deport them," but failed to receive any satisfaction from Kerensky when he suggested the possibility to him.[60] This merely confirmed the general's opinion that Kerensky was a radical and that "radicalism pervaded the whole government to a dangerous degree."[61]

If Root was unaware of the actual state of public opinion in Russia, he did have the political acumen to recommend to the State Department as early as June 17 the only means by which that opinion could be changed—a large-scale propaganda campaign. He urged the immediate expenditure of one hundred thousand dollars and suggested five million as a nominal sum for the future operation of the plan. In the same message he termed the Russians "an infant class in the art of being free containing one hundred and seventy million people." "They need to be supplied with kindergarten material," he added, and are "sincere, kindly, good people but confused and dazed."[62] This patronizing attitude toward the Russians, though it was devoid of malicious intent, typified the viewpoint of some members of the mission, a viewpoint which a Russian of decidedly anti-Bolshevik orientation has termed "not unlike that of a lot of missionaries descending . . . upon a tribe of benighted savages on some Pacific island to bring to them the blessings of the white man's civilization and deriving a great deal of satisfaction from the flattering notion that the Lord had made them from

[59] Arno Dosch-Fleurot, *Through War to Revolution* (London, 1931), pp. 163-64.
[60] "Russia," undated paper in the Hugh L. Scott Papers, Library of Congress.
[61] "Russian Revolution," undated paper, *ibid.*
[62] Root to Lansing, April 17, 1917, *Foreign Relations,* I, 121-22.

other clay than the poor heathens they were about to proselytize."[63]

It was not until June 27 that Lansing sent a reply to Root's message, only casually mentioning at the end of his cable that the matter was "receiving careful consideration."[64] McCormick, Bertron, and Root meanwhile contributed more than thirty thousand dollars of their own money for initial propaganda expenses. A million copies of Root's speech of June 15 had already been printed at British and French expense, and half a million copies of Wilson's speeches were printed with the additional money. Germany is spending "at least a million dollars monthly to capture the minds of the Russian people," Root warned in another of his appeals for support. Bertron sent a message of his own to McAdoo. These cables elicited a reply that the expense already incurred would be authorized but that the question of a further outlay was still receiving "careful attention."[65] On July 9, before the answer was received, the delegation left Petrograd for the return journey. Root was irked at the delay in answering his messages and convinced that his presence in Washington might stir up some action. Cabling Lansing on the tenth, he expressed satisfaction at what the mission had accomplished. The government's stability was soon to be put to a severe test in the rioting of the "July Days," yet Root concluded that the "situation is certainly much more hopeful and stable than it was when we arrived."[66] On the trip home the group drafted a formal report of their experiences which embodied their joint conclusion that the mission had "succeeded to some degree in bringing to bear upon conditions in Russia the moral force of the hundred million people of the United States . . . and in giving strength and confidence to the elements of Russian life which are struggling towards order and the effective prosecution of the war."[67]

[63] Fedotoff White, p. 146.

[64] Foreign Relations, I, 127.

[65] Frank L. Polk (Acting Secretary of State) to Francis, July 7, 1917, ibid., p. 129.

[66] Foreign Relations, I, 130. Detailed reports by Scott, Glennon, Bertron and McCormick, Mott, and Duncan may be found in the Root and Russell Papers, the latter collection also containing Russell's report.

[67] Foreign Relations, I, 131-46.

The mission reached Washington with the expectation that the President would receive them at once. But he seemed in no hurry, and when the members were finally invited to the White House, he appeared to be ill at ease and avoided mentioning the projected propaganda campaign. Root suspected, he said later, that Wilson had not even read their dispatches.[68] Yet the President appeared to be very well informed on the Russian situation and asked Root to return later for a conference. A supplementary report, analyzing the propaganda campaign in detail, reached Wilson late in August, and a final talk with Root, Mott, and McCormick at the White House on the thirtieth found him still noncomittal as to the plan.[69] The idea, though not the specific details, was resurrected several months later and a modified propaganda campaign attempted in Russia under the jurisdiction of the Committee on Public Information, but the time had already passed—even in August—when it was practicable to think of staving off Bolshevism and a separate peace with the power of the written and spoken word.

While the American mission was visiting Russia, a Russian mission arrived in the United States headed by Professor Boris Bakhmetev, Assistant Minister of Commerce and Industry, who was to take over the ambassadorship in Washington until the appointment of a permanent ambassador. The post had been vacant since the resignation in April of its former occupant, George Bakhmetev (no relation), because of his pro-tsarist sympathies. Nabokov, whose situation in London was analogous, refused to resign his post but apparently felt emancipated enough from his past monarchical ties to criticize the Provisional Government for its failure to take full advantage of the ideological affinity between the two countries. They did nothing, he complained, but replace one Bakhmetev with another at Washington.[70] The judgment is overly harsh, because the mission included not only the new ambassador but a huge assortment of government and military officials, who, if not moved by democratic fervor, at least did their best to give that impression. In fact, the visit was officially stated to be for the purpose of expressing "the gratitude of the Provisional Russian

[68] Jessup, II, 367-68; Mott, p. 209.
[69] Baker, VII, 244.   [70] Nabokoff, p. 118.

Government for the initiative taken by the great Allied Republic in the official recognition of the democratic regime which has been established in Russia."[71] Actually the presence of such a large mission denoted more than an exchange of felicitations. The United States had already granted a credit of one hundred million dollars for the purchase of war matériel, and the approximately forty-five persons who made up the party, though the number was certainly excessive, were purchasing agents, technical and financial experts, representatives of the army and navy, and other specialists concerned with the efficient spending of the money which had already been loaned and that which was confidently expected to be allotted in the future.

The mission reached Seattle on June 15 and proceeded across the country to Washington. The members were greeted by Lansing and other government officials and escorted through the streets of the city to receive the cheers of the populace. Bakhmetev was presented to the President the next day and released a long statement to the press in which he emphasized the common aims of the two countries, expressed confidence in the stability of the Provisional Government, and promised that Russia would fight beside her allies until "the German autocratic principles are destroyed."[72] The delegates were received by the House of Representatives on the twenty-third, where Bakhmetev's address was frequently interrupted by bursts of applause. The House was particularly pleased by his emphatic denials that Russia contemplated a separate peace.[73] A similar reception was accorded them by the Senate on the twenty-sixth. Bakhmetev varied the wording but not the import of his speech and again gave his assurance that "Russia rejects with indignation any idea of separate peace." Both houses of Congress unanimously passed a resolution wishing the new republic well and expressing "the earnest hope of the Congress that democracy and self-government may bring to the people of Russia that large measure of prosperity, progress, and freedom

[71] Foreign Relations, I, 154-55.
[72] A. J. Sack, The Birth of the Russian Democracy (New York, 1918), pp. 394-97.
[73] U. C. Congress, Congressional Record, Vol. LV, Pt. 4, pp. 4136-37.

which they have brought to the people of America."[74] On July 5 Bakhmetev called on the President more formally to present his credentials with the proper diplomatic protocol. He made a short speech of the same tenor as his previous remarks, and Wilson answered with his customary tribute to free institutions, praising the Provisional Government for its efforts to insure that Russia "will assume her rightful place among the great free nations of the world."[75]

The Russians went on to New York to be greeted by enthusiastic crowds and a ticker-tape shower in a parade through the streets. The new ambassador made numerous speeches in the city, all of them exuding patriotism and optimism. The paean of mutual self-congratulation was marred only once when a hostile demonstration interrupted a Madison Square Garden mass meeting at which Bakhmetev spoke. Several of the most vociferous objectors were forcibly removed, and the meeting continued after a ten-minute interruption.[76] After this strenuous round of festivities, the members of the mission settled down to more serious work. The ambassador took charge of the negotiations concerning the war loans and supervised his staff in their extensive purchases. Nearly half a billion dollars in credit was advanced up to the time of the November Revolution, less than half of which was actually spent.[77]

The Root and Bakhmetev missions illustrated much more clearly than the missions of the Allied socialists the controlling assumptions of the liberal bourgeois leaders and their abiding faith in good will, patriotism, and democratic idealism as a means of keeping the Russian people in a war they had come to detest. When Bakhmetev, for instance, assured his listeners that only a small group of pro-German extremists opposed the Provisional Government's policy, he was not deliberately misrepresenting the situation but only echoing, with perfect good faith, the "sound" opinion of every good Allied patriot, whether a "radical" like Kerensky

[74] *Ibid.*, Vol. LV, Pt. 4, pp. 4264-65.   [75] Both speeches in Sack, pp. 390-91.
[76] New York *Times,* July 8, 1917.
[77] Frederick L. Schuman, *American Policy toward Russia since 1917* (New York, 1928), pp. 47-48.

or a conservative like Root. Anyone who ventured to express a contrary opinion—and there were a few such prophets of gloom—immediately came under suspicion of defeatism, if not more sinister beliefs.

A somewhat different kind of mission, for it was accomplished largely without public fanfare, was the Russian naval mission to the United States headed by Admiral Alexander Kolchak, the commander of the Black Sea fleet, who later became the dictator of the White forces during the civil war. During the visit of the Root mission, Admiral Glennon and his staff had journeyed to Sebastopol, where the Black Sea naval base was located, and met Kolchak, who had just resigned his post under pressure from the mutinous sailors. Glennon, a persuasive speaker, helped to pacify the sailors but did not succeed in removing their ban on Kolchak. The Russian admiral returned to Petrograd with the Americans and apparently made a very favorable impression, for Glennon invited him to come to the United States. The offer was mainly a gesture of good will, with some vague idea of utilizing his knowledge and experience in an American naval expedition against the Straits.[78] The Provisional Government was rather cool to the plan at first, but when Root himself approached Kerensky on the matter, permission for a Russian naval mission was reluctantly granted. The rumor got around that Kolchak was to be appointed to command the United States navy, and the American naval attaché in Petrograd was deluged with applications by Russian naval officers anxious to escape the distasteful revolutionary environment for service abroad. Francis and Kolchak both issued denials to help squelch the story.[79]

The admiral and his staff of four officers departed near the end of July and spent some time in England inspecting the naval aviation facilities there. The party sailed for Canada on a British cruiser and from there went to New York and Washington as guests of

[78] Fedotoff White, p. 155; Elena Varneck and H. H. Fisher (eds.), *The Testimony of Kolchak and Other Siberian Materials* (Stanford University, Calif., 1935), p. 85; "Report of Admiral Glennon," Root Papers; Francis to Lansing, June 24, 1917 (861.00/414), National Archives.

[79] Pauline S. Crosley, *Intimate Letters from Petrograd* (New York, 1920), pp. 105-6.

the American government. Kolchak called on Bakhmetev, Lansing, and other officials and found that the proposed naval expedition had been abandoned—if in fact it had ever been seriously considered. He spent several weeks working and sightseeing at the naval war college in Newport and then observed maneuvers in the Atlantic aboard the battleship *Pennsylvania.* Disappointed at the lack of useful activity, Kolchak decided to take his leave and return to Russia. He made his farewell calls and was presented to the President. One officer remained in the United States; the other three sailed with Kolchak from San Francisco on a Japanese steamer shortly after the Bolshevik seizure of power in November.[80] The admiral remained in the Far East until an opportunity presented itself in the fall of 1918 to take an active part in the anti-Bolshevik movement in Siberia.

The internal situation in Russia remained unchanged by the comings and goings of the various missions. Under the effective slogans, "Peace, Land, and Bread" and "All power to the Soviet," the Bolshevik program began to penetrate the mass consciousness, even though the party itself was still regarded with distrust by all but the more politically alert elements of the working class. Kerensky and Tereshchenko half-heartedly carried on their campaign for a revision of war aims on the part of the Allies. Thomas returned to France in mid-June with a message for Ribot asking for an Allied conference "to subject to reconsideration the agreements concerning the ultimate aims of the war," a meeting "which could take place as soon as there are favorable conditions for it."[81] The note was also transmitted to the British government. Since it was sufficiently vague as to the date for such a conference and promised steadfast loyalty to the Allied cause, England and France safely ignored this summons to the mourner's bench to cleanse themselves of sin.

At the same time Kerensky tried by indirect means to get President Wilson to intercede for Russia with its allies on the war aims issue. Lincoln Steffens, a prominent American journalist best known for his "muckraking" exposés of big business, was

---

[80] Varneck and Fisher, pp. 95-101.
[81] Cumming and Pettit, pp. 26-27.

then in Petrograd and was persuaded by Francis and Crane (of the Root mission) to return with Kerensky's message to the President. Steffens made the journey as far as Seattle with the Bakhmetev mission. There the ambassador, who had been warned of the journalist's reputation as a radical, drew him aside and asked him to go on to Washington by a different route. Steffens readily agreed not to compromise the mission's respectability any longer and took his leave. Wilson received him at the White House on June 26 and listened thoughtfully as Steffens relayed Kerensky's plea for an abrogation of the secret treaties. "Kerenski asks you to clear away their suspicion of loot and conquest so conspicuously and so clearly that the sight and the sound of it will reach to the uttermost villages of Russia and be known to every peasant, soldier, sailor, and worker throughout Russia and all over Asia," Steffens reports himself as saying. Wilson's answer was that he knew nothing about the secret treaties, meaning, as Steffens interpreted it, that he knew nothing of them *officially* and therefore could not be expected to ask Britain and France to renounce treaties to which the United States had not been a party.[82] Whether by creating an artificial duality between Wilson the private citizen and Wilson the public official, or by some other rationale, he successfully warded off several such attempts to enlighten him and with an apparently clear conscience maintained before a Senate committee in 1919 that he had first learned of the notorious secret agreements at the peace conference in Paris.

Meanwhile Kerensky's preparations for the offensive were drawing to a close. On the same day that the Wilson-Steffens conversation took place, he left for the sector of the southwestern front where the Russian attack was to begin. The Allied military attachés conferred with him there, and the British representatives promised a supporting action on the part of the British armies in France, aid which was not forthcoming when the time came for the promise to be fulfilled.[83] Much of the war matériel with which the offensive was to be conducted was furnished by England and France, though a large part of it turned out to be of inferior

[82] Lincoln Steffens, *Autobiography* (New York, 1931), pp. 764-72.
[83] Kerensky, *The Catastrophe*, p. 217.

quality. A British armored car squadron under Commander Oliver Locker-Lampson and other small units of British troops took part in the offensive.[84]

Several days of artillery bombardment preceded the attack. The advance began on July 1 under conditions so unpropitious for success that the officers were uncertain whether the troops would obey orders. Only a few units could be relied upon without question, and others were openly mutinous. The advantage of surprise and the poor morale of the opposing Austrian troops made possible some local successes which were inflated into major victories by the official communiques. "Today is the great triumph of the revolution," Kerensky proclaimed. On July 1 "the Russian revolutionary army with colossal enthusiasm assumed the offensive."[85] The Allied press exaggerated with no less bombast the presumably tremendous scope of the Russian advance. When, in a week's time, it became obvious that Russia and not the Central Powers had suffered a serious setback, the Allied censorship permitted only hints as to the real scope of the disaster. The American press was the least restricted in this respect and printed German accounts of the battle, but the French press, tightly bound with restrictions of all kinds, quietly dropped the matter of the "victorious offensive" with no further comment.

The German general staff, which had for so long chafed under political restraint on the question of military operations against revolutionary Russia, gladly rushed up reinforcements for a counterattack. The result was a catastrophic rout. Only a relative handful of troops remained to fight. The rest fled in disorder, as pillaging and outrages of all kinds testified to the breakdown of all semblance of discipline. As early as the fourth General Knox returned to Petrograd in disgust to telegraph London his opinion that the Russian army was "irretrievably ruined as a fighting organisation."[86]

Later in the month and on a much smaller scale, attacks were

[84] Robert Wilton, *Russia's Agony* (New York and London, 1918), pp. 277-81; *Times* (London), July 14, 1917.
[85] Trotsky, *History of the Russian Revolution*, I, 384.
[86] Knox, II, 648.

made on the northern and western fronts. The Russians were thrown back easily without even achieving the dubious advantage of initial success. General Kornilov, whose troops made the most impressive gains before the rout began, wired Kerensky: "I declare that the fatherland is perishing, and hence, unasked by anyone, I demand the immediate cessation of the offensive on all fronts to preserve the army and reorganize it on the basis of strict discipline, in order not to sacrifice the lives of a few heroes who deserve to see better days."[87] The commander-in-chief, General Brusilov, was pessimistic but belligerently spoke of a purge which would presumably restore the army's fighting capacity. He informed Kerensky, "I consider that the purging of the army can be effected only after the purging of the rear and after the propaganda of the Bolsheviks and the Leninists has been proclaimed criminal and punishable as high treason."[88] Brusilov shared the misconception, prevalent among men far more politically astute than he, that agitators are the causes and not the products of social stress. Bolshevism did not become popular in the army because its proponents drugged unsuspecting victims with the heady wine of Marxism but because the Bolshevik party stood alone in its uncompromising stand against continuing the war.

The complete breakdown of the front had its counterpart in the rear, where a semi-revolution in Petrograd, known as the "July Days," threatened the further existence of the Provisional Government. The revolutionary temper of a large portion of the workers and soldiers in the capital had so far outstripped the rest of the population that the Bolsheviks were finding it increasingly difficult to restrain their more hot-headed followers from overt action which might involve the party in revolutionary adventurism more deeply than the prospects for success warranted. The first days of the offensive brought ominous signs of unrest. The resignation of four Cadet ministers on the fifteenth was at least partially responsible for bringing the crisis to a head. That they had become more and more dissatisfied with their lack of influence in the cabinet had been apparent for some time, and the question of Ukrainian auton-

---

[87] Chernov, p. 303.   [88] Gorky *et al.*, I, 242.

omy, the issue upon which they chose to take their departure, was merely the culmination of a long series of grievances against their less conservative colleagues.

On the morning of the sixteenth one of the machine-gun regiments declared for open insurrection. Bolshevik speakers were sent over to calm the soldiers—and with apparent success. But the turbulent machine-gunners, absorbed in a continuous meeting, were dissuaded only temporarily. Joined by other military units and thousands of factory workers, an unorganized mass of armed demonstrators poured into the streets. Taken by surprise, the Bolshevik leaders, since it was too late to curb the outbreak, could only confer a hesitant blessing upon the action of their overly enthusiastic supporters. Automobiles jammed with soldiers careened wildly about the city; crowds surrounded the Tauride Palace demanding that the Soviet assume power whether its timid leaders wished to or not; looting was widespread, and the toll of dead and wounded, mostly the result of indiscriminate firing, mounted to several hundred. That part of the garrison which declined to join the demonstrators also remained aloof from the government. Had a concerted attempt been made, the key ministers and official buildings could have been captured in short order. Only Chernov suffered misadventure and was saved from a possible lynching by Trotsky's quick action in placating a mob of sailors, some of whom were about to carry off the minister in an automobile.

By the eighteenth the tide had clearly turned in favor of the government, not the least of the reasons being the timely publication by the ministry of justice of some very weak evidence purporting to show that Lenin and his associates were German agents. This had the desired effect upon popular feeling, and some of the heretofore neutral regiments declared their support of the government. The insurrectionary forces were weakened by the departure of most of the aggressive pro-Bolshevik sailors from the nearby naval base at Kronstadt. Kshesinskaya Palace, where the Bolsheviks maintained their headquarters, was occupied; and the editorial offices of *Pravda* were raided, the paper closed, and much equipment destroyed. Trotsky, Kamenev, and other party leaders were arrested, while Lenin and Zinoviev went into hiding to escape a similar fate.

The conservative reaction, though pronounced, was not a protracted one; nor was it accomplished with severe repression and bloodshed. Rightist sentiment, not at all averse to a little bloodletting, was disappointed at such leniency. The Allied representatives likewise expressed regret. "Had the Provisional Government at this time arraigned Lenin and Trotzky and the other Bolshevik leaders, tried them for treason and executed them," says Francis, "Russia probably would not have been compelled to go through another revolution, would have been spared the reign of terror, and the loss from famine and murder of millions of her sons and daughters."[89] Knox submitted a draconian program to the government which called for the revival of the death penalty in the army and navy, the punishment of "agitators" responsible for the rioting, a military censorship, the establishment of a militia in Petrograd and other large cities composed of patriotic soldiers, and the creation of labor battalions for all members of the local garrison who did not agree to these conditions. Tereshchenko told Buchanan that he agreed with all but the first point.[90] As it later developed, this was the only one which the government adopted.

Even had the most severe measures been politically feasible, Kerensky was not the man for ruthless action against his opponents. Although Trotsky had called him the "mathematical center of Russian Bonapartism,"[91] he lacked the temperament from which successful dictators are made, and the propertied classes, always on the outlook for a "man on horseback" to champion their interests, were eventually forced to look elsewhere for a candidate.

[89] Francis, p. 141.
[90] Knox, II, 661-62.
[91] Trotsky, *History of the Russian Revolution*, II, 154.

CHAPTER VI

Prime Minister Kerensky: From Kornilov to Lenin

An aftermath of the "July Days" and the collapse of the army—though not directly related—was the second reorganization of the government. Strongly opposed to the radical land program which Chernov was proposing, Lvov submitted his resignation on the twentieth. It was readily accepted, for the time was long overdue when the Provisional Government could afford the luxury of a figurehead in the position of Prime Minister. Kerensky took his place, thus legalizing a situation which had already existed in fact. The Cadets refused to join the cabinet unless it set for itself the "task of saving the country from foreign destruction and internal disintegration." The Soviet insisted no less strongly on land reform, and Kerensky, finding the role of compromiser increasingly difficult, resigned along with a number of his colleagues. As he had foreseen, his resignation had to be rejected for lack of a suitable replacement, and he was allowed a free hand in choosing his cabinet. The new "save the Revolution" government was announced on August 6, with very little change among the more important ministries. In terms of numbers, and despite the departure of Tsereteli, the socialists were now in the majority. Yet such was the quality of their socialism that Milyukov has said, with perfect truthfulness, "The actual predominance in the cabinet unquestionably belonged to the convinced supporters of bourgeois democracy."[1]

[1] Milyukov, *Istoria*, Vol. I, Pt. II, pp. 44-45.

The prolonged cabinet crisis following so close upon the disorders in Petrograd and the German counterattack caused great uneasiness among the Allies. Tereshchenko sought to calm these fears with a note of explanation. "The criminal propaganda of irresponsible elements was used by enemy agents and provoked mutiny in Petrograd," he reported to the Foreign Offices of the West. "At the same time part of the troops on the front, seduced by the same propaganda, forgot their duty to the country and facilitated the enemy's penetration of our front." The Foreign Minister tried to avoid ending the communication on a note of pessimism, however slight, by repeating in endless variation the determination of the Russian people to fight on against its internal and external foes.[2] The spectacle of enemy agents armed with subversive propaganda undermining the social structure of a whole country had a certain appeal to minds unable or unwilling to deal in the realities of a revolutionary crisis, so Tereshchenko's simple explanation of his country's troubles was accepted as obvious and beyond cavil in the diplomatic chancelleries of the Allied Powers.

But agreement as to the causes of Russia's plight did not prevent the onset of what Nabokov has described as a period of "Diffidence Mingled with Irritation" in regard to the Kerensky government.[3] This changed attitude was already apparent at the Allied conference which began in London on August 7. It was well attended by the leading statesmen and soldiers of Britain, France, and Italy. The British hosts "neglected" to invite even a single Russian representative, though Russia, as one of the original members of the Triple Entente, was still a power of far greater prestige than Italy. When Nabokoff tried to obtain an appointment with Arthur Balfour, the Foreign Minister, he was informed that Balfour would be too busy attending the conference to see him. Russia's interim ambassador was not at all backward in telling his informant just what he thought of an excuse of that sort, considering that his country had not even been notified of the conference, and within a few minutes he was tendered an invitation. By dispensing with the proper formal attire, he just had time to reach the meeting

[2] *Foreign Relations*, I, 172-73.　　　[3] Nabokoff, p. 126.

place at Downing Street before Lloyd George opened the session by suggesting a "stern protest" to Kerensky "against the continuation in Russia of disruption and anarchy."[4] Much to his discomfort, Nabokov was asked for his opinion, and after some discussion, Albert Thomas was charged with drafting a suitable message. The latter's skill was such that the element of protest was largely disguised as a greeting to Kerensky and the new ministry. The note expressed "firm confidence in their controlling authority and in the re-establishment of a strict discipline, clearly indispensable to all armies, but above all to the armies of free nations." By discipline alone, the Provisional Government was cautioned, would the Russian army secure "popular liberty, national honor, and the realization of the war aims common to all the Allies."[5] The ambassadors too constantly badgered Kerensky about the need for discipline. He accepted these strictures with steadily increasing irritation, and upon one occasion, after listening to Buchanan, asked what the ambassador would think were he to tell Lloyd George how to govern England.[6]

The Allied press echoed this criticism of the Provisional Government, though only the most reactionary as yet ventured to attack Kerensky openly. The American press continued to praise him for his democratic and idealistic leadership, but in England and France the hope was more and more frequently expressed that the new Premier would take matters into his own hands, and, as the Tory *Saturday Review* put it, "save Russia with a whiff of shrapnel."[7] Similarly, the Paris *Rappel* complained that the ignorance of the Russian masses favored German intrigue as represented by Lenin and other spies working as revolutionaries and thus made necessary "a kind of dictator, a Red Tsarism, to defeat both anarchy and Austro-Germany."[8] The delusion that Kerensky was the man for the job lasted only until an apparently much more able candidate appeared on the scene in the person of General Kornilov, whose comparative success in the disastrous July offensive brought him the supreme command of the army as a reward.

[4] *Ibid.*, p. 128.   [5] French text, *ibid.*, p. 129.
[6] Pares, *Russian Memoirs*, p. 468.   [7] CXXIV (July 28, 1917), 57.
[8] Quoted in the *Petite republique*, July 27, 1917.

For a short time General Michael Alexeyev had been considered for the "strong man" role, largely because of Nabokov's recommendations, and Lloyd George invited him to come to England for a visit.[9] But Alexeyev was soon forgotten in favor of the new commander-in-chief. Kornilov, a slight, sinewy man with Mongolian features, was of plebeian Cossack origin, politically illiterate but intensely patriotic. This "man with a lion's heart and the brain of a sheep," as he was described by General Alexeyev,[10] was not an outspoken reactionary, and yet with a sure instinct, men of conservative sentiment—industrialists, landowners, officers, Cadets, and Allied diplomats—scented the banner of counterrevolution long before the object of their attentions had done so himself and flocked to his support. His declared aim was simply to "bring the people to victory and to a just and honorable peace" by restoring discipline to the front and suppressing "anarchy" in the rear. Unfamiliar with party labels, Kornilov regarded Bolsheviks and moderate socialists alike as subversive influences bent upon blackening the honor and good name of Russia in the eyes of the world. With such views it is not surprising that he was looked upon with mistrust in Soviet circles. A campaign in the conservative press to build him up as a man of the people did little to remedy this lack of popular appeal.

Almost from the beginning Kerensky regarded the new commander-in-chief with misgivings but reconciled his appointment with the need of strong measures for a desperate situation. It was not until the Moscow State Conference in late August, however, that Kornilov's flirtation with the middle classes became too obvious to be ignored with complacency. The conference was one of Kerensky's characteristic creations, essentially an "assembly of good will" in which every strata of Russian society was to be represented for the purpose of finding some common bond of unity in support of the government. It was conceived purely as a prestige-building enterprise and lacked the slightest legal justification for its existence. Its historical significance rests not upon what it

[9] Nabokoff, p. 163.
[10] Trotsky, *History of the Russian Revolution*, II, 145. David Shub ascribes the phrase to General Brusilov in his *Lenin* (Garden City, N. Y., 1948), p. 223.

accomplished—which was precisely nothing—but upon the colorful drama of revolution in microcosm. The element of class conflict, inherent in all revolutionary situations, was constantly present, even if peacefully expressed. The delegates, numbering approximately twenty-five hundred, were carefully proportioned between Right and Left, and the thundering applause which greeted a favorite of one faction was invariably balanced by the conspicuous silence of the opposing faction. In terms of their enormous numerical preponderance, the masses were greatly discriminated against by this kind of "equality," so much so that the Bolsheviks declared it a counter-revolutionary gathering and refused to participate. Their presence was nevertheless keenly felt when, despite disapproval by the Moscow Soviet, the Bolsheviks called an effective general strike of the city's workers on the first day of the session. Even so, this convincing display of their political influence over the working class was lost upon most of the delegates, who regarded the Bolsheviks as a group of fanatic visionaries and thus without practical importance.

The assembly opened on the twenty-fifth in the sumptuous Bolshoy Theater, a brilliant and impressive gathering of liberal Russia's most able men. The delegates were seated in the auditorium from right to left in rough approximation to their political beliefs, while in the precise center of the stage, symbolizing his carefully cultivated nonpartisan role, sat Kerensky. The former imperial boxes were reserved for the diplomatic corps of the Allied and neutral powers. As chairman Kerensky opened the conference with one of his typical speeches, a two-hour oratorical *tour de force,* dazzling in phrase but disturbingly empty in content. Threats against extremists of both Right and Left, complaints and reproaches, meticulously balanced so as to give no undue offense, were interspersed among appeals to unity and gloomy forebodings of disaster. In referring to the Pope's recent peace proposal, he reaffirmed his faith in the Allied cause, and at this point the whole audience, save Martov's Menshevik Internationalist group and a few Bolsheviks present as trade union delegates, rose and faced the diplomatic box to give the Allied ambassadors a rousing ovation.[11]

Kornilov arrived in Moscow the next day and was met at the station with all the pomp of visiting royalty. He was cheered and pelted with flowers as wealthy women fell on their knees before him. A prominent Cadet concluded a speech of welcome with the plea, "Save Russia and the grateful people will crown you." A popular biography in pamphlet form, entitled *Kornilov, the National Hero,* was distributed in the streets of the city. Copies had been printed at the expense of the British military mission and, according to Kerensky, brought to Moscow in General Knox's railway carriage.[12] The "National Hero" later went to pray at the famous shrine of the Iberian Virgin, which the Tsars had customarily visited when in Moscow. In the evening he saw Kerensky, who insisted that the speech which Kornilov was to deliver the following day should be confined wholly to military matters. The general refused, but the text which one of his supporters prepared for him refrained from directly attacking the government. At the opening of the second session of the conference Kornilov took his place so quietly that he remained unnoticed. So he went out and ostentatiously returned to his box some time later to be greeted this time with a mighty ovation by the entire right half of the auditorium, while the left side remained silent and unmoved. The applause was repeated as he rose to speak. He painted a frightening picture of the military situation and hinted that the road to Petrograd lay open to the enemy. To the forces of the Left this remark was the most significant that he made. Was it an honest analysis or a sinister threat? Whichever it was, the representatives of Soviet democracy were already convinced that the general and his followers boded no good for the future of the Revolution.

After Kornilov's short but dramatic appearance, the proceedings lacked interest for most of the Allied observers, and henceforth their special box usually remained empty.[13] Speaker after speaker rose to give his opinion or the opinion of the organization to which

---

[11] Sukhanov, V, 161; E. P. Stebbing, *From Czar to Bolshevik* (London, 1918), p. 156.

[12] Kerensky, *The Catastrophe,* p. 315.

[13] René Marchand, *Why I Support Bolshevism* (London, n. d.), p. 11.

he belonged. During the third session Kerensky read a short message of encouragement from President Wilson: "I venture to take the liberty to send to the members of the great council now meeting in Moscow the cordial greetings of their friends, the people of the United States, to express their confidence in the ultimate triumph of ideals of self-government against all enemies within and without, and to give their renewed assurance of every material and moral assistance they can extend to the Government of Russia in the promotion of the common cause in which the two nations are unselfishly united."[14] Both sides of the assembly joined in applauding these politically harmless sentiments, though it can scarcely be said that they "electrified" the audience, as a United Press correspondent claimed in his dispatch.[15]

The conference came to an end on the twenty-eighth as Kerensky optimistically summed up its achievements in a rambling and, towards the end, often incoherent speech. His voice alternating between high-pitched shrieks and broken whispers, he concluded with such a remarkable display of maudlin hysteria that the alarmed ministers sitting near by feared a nervous attack at any moment. "Let my heart become stone," he wailed; "let all the strings of faith in man perish, let all the flowers and wreaths of man dry up. . . . I shall throw far away the keys of my heart, which loves men; I will think only about the state." The stupefied audience broke into spontaneous applause to bring the Prime Minister out of his self-induced hypnotic state. He absent-mindedly groped his way off the stage and then had to be recalled to bring the conference to a formal end.[16]

Far from the "better understanding" and the "greater respect for each other" which Kerensky read into the proceedings, the aftermath of the Moscow Conference was one of heightened tension, suspicion, and rumor. The forces of counterrevolution began to move from the realm of speculation into that of action. Already several reliable cavalry divisions, composed of Caucasian and Cossack troops, and most notably the "Savage Division" under General

---

[14] *Foreign Relations*, I, 177.
[15] *Literary Digest*, LV (Sept. 8, 1917), 17.
[16] Chamberlin, I, 205; Chernov, pp. 359-60.

Krymov, had been shifted to a vantage point near Petrograd in the guise of reserves for the Finnish front. It was hoped that a Bolshevik uprising would furnish an excuse to march on the capital; but failing this, various "patriotic" societies within the city were prepared to create a fake demonstration so that the government might be "saved" from the Bolsheviks. Kerensky's role during this period was so ambiguous that the Bolsheviks scented treachery and later accused him of being a party to the plot until his own neck became endangered. His actions certainly did not inspire unqualified confidence, but whatever the merits of the charge, he never regained his popularity after the Kornilov affair. Had he acted with firmness and resolution, the conspiracy might never have attained fruition.

The Allied governments had a far more compromising record than Kerensky's in dealing with the Kornilov movement. Officially they maintained an attitude of strict neutrality; unofficially the conduct of their representatives in Russia and the tone of their most influential organs of opinion left no doubt where the sympathies of the ruling groups in Britain and France lay. In their support of Kornilov can be detected the faint pattern of future Allied intervention in Russia—not, it should be noted, directed against the "menace of Bolshevism," as was the case later, but against the democratic government of a friendly ally fully two months before the Bolsheviks took power. The Allied military missions were in particularly close contact with Kornilov and frequently assured him of their moral support.[17] General Knox, indeed, can almost be regarded as a participant in the plot, so suspicious were his activities on behalf of the general. He left for England in late August and while there strongly urged the war cabinet to intervene in Kornilov's favor.[18] It is also very possible that Knox was the go-between in arranging for Locker-Lampson's armored car squadron to join Kornilov's forces, since it is scarcely conceivable that their commander would have done so upon his own initiative and without the knowledge or consent of the British authorities. The squadron in question, which had remained in

---

[17] Denikin, II, 63.
[18] Knox, II, 677-78; Lloyd George, V, 101-2.

Russia after taking part in the July offensive, was furnished with Russian uniforms and proved to be one of the few reliable detachments in the advance against the capital.[19]

Lord Milner, one of the most prominent members of the British war cabinet, personally assured Kornilov of his support in a letter which was conveyed to the general in late August by Fyodor Aladin, a political adventurer who had been a member of the first Duma.[20] Aladin carried with him a large sum of money and soon became known as one of Kornilov's foremost backers, slated for the post of Foreign Minister in the event of success. His mission to Russia, financed by the British government and facilitated by the Royal Navy, had been suggested the previous March by Buchanan in a telegram to the Foreign Office.[21] The ambassador, though he admitted that all his sympathies were with Kornilov, refused to take an active part in the attempted *coup*. On September 5 the director of one of Petrograd's largest banks called on him as the spokesman for an organization backed by several important financiers and industrialists. As active supporters of Kornilov, they proposed that the British armored cars be placed at his disposal and that the ambassador help them to escape should the enterprise fail. Probably neither one was aware that the much sought after armored cars had already been committed, but Buchanan nevertheless rebuffed the banker's overtures and told him that Kornilov would be wiser to let the Bolsheviks make the first move. He kept the details of the plot to himself—contrary, he confesses, to his duties as ambassador to a friendly power—and significantly remarked in his diary some days later: "There is nothing to be done but to await events and to trust that Korniloff will be strong enough to overcome all resistance in the course of a few days."[22]

The press in the Allied countries, except for the few which were socialist or strongly liberal, jumped on the Kornilov bandwagon with alacrity. The olympian London *Times,* which one periodical

[19] Kerensky, *Crucifixion of Liberty,* p. 351; U. S. Congress, Senate, Committee on the Judiciary, *Bolshevik Propaganda* (Washington, 1919), p. 780; Gorky *et al.,* I, 350.
[20] Kerensky, *The Catastrophe,* p. 315; Price, p. 69.
[21] Buchanan to Balfour, March 26, 1917, *Krasny Arkhiv,* XXIV (1927), 119.
[22] G. Buchanan, II, 175-76 and 182.

attacked as the organ of "the enemies of democracy in the war cabinet,"[23] led the campaign in England, justifying its stand by citing the decay of the Russian army. "There must be an end of committees and debates, of councils of sham workmen and loafing soldiers, of talk about Utopia while the enemy are thundering at the gate," it proclaimed.[24] An unnamed traveler from Russia was quoted with approval as saying that the Soviet was a "self-constituted organization of idealists, theorists, anarchists, [and] syndicalists . . . largely of the international Jew type, who have hardly any working men or soldiers among them, and some of whom are known to be in German pay." "By finally throwing in his lot with these garrulous and obstructive bodies," scolded the Times, "Kerensky has made an irrevocable breach with General Kornilov and all who side with him." Not only was Kerensky blamed for the break, but the few papers which ventured to criticize the general to the advantage of the Soviet were severely taken to task.[25] The Saturday Review, pointing to the millions already poured into the "bottomless pit of Russian anarchy," hoped that Kornilov, "who stands for order and discipline, may win for Russia's and the Entente's sake."[26] The Manchester Guardian, perhaps the most influential of England's liberal newspapers, vigorously condemned this point of view: "Kornilov is not the destined military savior of Russia for the benefit of the Allies. Whether he means it or not, he is in rebellion against those who alone can preserve her today and redeem her tomorrow. He is her enemy and our enemy. No good will come for us or for her but by his defeat and submission."[27]

The French press backed Kornilov with even less restraint, though the Temps, more cautious than its contemporaries, refrained from compromising itself without ample room for retreat. The Journal des débats claimed that Kornilov, far from attempting counterrevolution, was only acting "in the interests of public safety"; he merely wishes to "reduce by force the demented objections of the Soviet," while Kerensky "insists on a resort to per-

---

[23] New Age, XXI (Sept. 13, 1917), 417.
[24] Sept. 8, 1917.   [25] Sept. 11 and 13, 1917.
[26] CXXIV (Sept. 15, 1917), 197.   [27] Sept. 12, 1917.

suasion."[28] *Figaro* praised Kornilov as the "most respected and the noblest of all the Russians,"[29] and the weekly journal *Opinion* said bluntly: "A military dictatorship, solidly established, can arrest the dissolving action of the Byzantine politicians . . . and show the utopian rhetoricians the dangers of their tendencies."[30] The Socialist party organ, *Humanité,* was one of the few Parisian dailies to stand staunchly behind Kerensky and the Soviet.

American press opinion, normally more democratic than that of Britain and France, was sharply divided on the Kornilov issue and a good deal less sympathetic toward Kerensky than it had been. The New York *Times,* without aligning itself definitely with either side, indicated that it had little faith in the Prime Minister. Much more frankly, the San Francisco *Chronicle* stated, "Russia needs a dictator, and Kornilov looks to be the man best fitted for the job," and the Portland *Oregonian* justified the venture on the grounds that the general, despairing of hope, had "undertaken to seize the reins from babbling hordes of theorists and politicians at Petrograd."[31] On the other hand, the weekly *New Republic,* representative of more than a negligible amount of liberal opinion, castigated the "bourbons" who were willing enough to support Kerensky as long as he stood against the Bolsheviks and were now deserting him, "relieved of the hard necessity of underwriting socialism anywhere."[32]

It was not until the rattlebrained but well-meaning Vladimir N. Lvov, procurator of the Holy Synod in the preceding cabinet, appointed himself intermediary between Kornilov and Kerensky that the latter became aware of the full implications of the plot against his regime. Lvov—not to be confused with the former Premier, Prince George E. Lvov—was anxious to avoid an open break between the two men in hopes that a military dictatorship could be inaugurated without needless conflict. When he approached Kerensky on the matter in early September, the Prime Minister allowed him to believe that he was authorized to come

[28] Sept. 12 and 18, 1917.   [29] Sept. 12, 1917.
[30] X (Sept. 15, 1917), 168.
[31] Quoted in the New York *Tribune,* Sept. 23, 1917.
[32] XII (Sept. 15, 1917), 168.

to an agreement with Kornilov, when in reality he was but an unwitting scout in the enemy's camp. Lvov sought out the general and received three demands which he conveyed to Kerensky: a declaration of martial law in Petrograd, the resignation of the cabinet, and the transfer of all power to a directorate headed by the commander-in-chief himself. Kerensky pretended to agree to these demands, and Kornilov retired on the evening of the eighth confident that his advance on Petrograd would encounter no opposition from the government. But in the morning he received a curt telegram from Kerensky ordering him to relinquish his command. The final break was at hand. Kornilov refused to comply with the order and issued an appeal for mass support which could have found a ready response only among a limited number of Russians, couched as it was in the pious and patriotic language of a bygone era. It read in part: "The terrible conviction of the inevitable ruin of the country compels me in these frightful times to call upon all Russians to save their dying land. All in whose breast a Russian heart beats, all who believe in God, in the Church, pray to Him for the greatest miracle—the saving of our native land."[33]

Superficially it seemed as if Kornilov had only to give the signal and his troops would occupy the virtually unprotected capital. Most of the generals and probably a majority of the lower-ranking officers gave him their support. All of the ministers resigned, some because they distrusted Kerensky and others because they were for Kornilov. The wildest rumors swept the city in the absence of any reliable information as to the whereabouts of the insurrectionary forces. The diplomatic corps was advised to leave the city for a safer location, but after a meeting at the British embassy the Allied representatives decided to stay. Less assured of gentle treatment in the event of a Kornilov victory, some of the more faint-hearted Soviet leaders made preparations for a hasty departure. For a time Kerensky was a dictator without power—alone in a "terrifying vacuum," as Chernov has phrased it.[34] Even his closest associates urged him to resign in favor of General Alexeyev. On the tenth, at the peak of the crisis, a Soviet delegation appeared, offering as

[33] Golder, pp. 521-22.   [34] Chernov, p. 371.

the price of its support only the relentless suppression of the Kornilov threat. But the workers and soldiers had not waited for the government's permission to prepare for resistance. Political differences were temporarily forgotten as Bolsheviks, Mensheviks, and Socialist Revolutionaries co-operated to form a "Committee for Struggle with Counterrevolution." A workers' militia was formed and largely armed by the military organization of the Bolshevik party. Petrograd and its environs became an armed camp, every factory a fortress, every house a potential blockade. Instead of waiting passively for the enemy to strike the first blow, agitators were dispatched to sap the morale of the approaching troops. Railway workers received instructions to tear up the tracks, to sabotage the engines, to delay the advance in every way. Many arrests were made as the secret Kornilovite societies within the city were crushed before they had time to act.

The Allied ambassadors, fearing widespread civil war, offered to mediate the conflict. This action anticipated the wishes of the British war cabinet, which decided on the twelfth that Kerensky "should be informed that the British Government viewed with the greatest alarm the probabilities of civil war, and urged . . . to come to terms with General Kornilov, not only in the interests of Russia herself, but in that of the Allies."[35] At first Kerensky was inclined to welcome outside intervention, but when the prospects of victory brightened, Tereshchenko was delegated to thank the ambassadors and decline their services.[36] Obviously a government which had any confidence in its stability could not accept an offer which placed the legally constituted power and the rebels on an equal footing. The ambassadors, already under fire in the more radical papers, issued an emphatic denial that they were involved with Kornilov. Yet the declaration was carefully worded so as not to give Kerensky any encouragement and to emphasize that the struggle with Germany was still the issue of paramount importance: "In the interest of humanity and anxious to prevent irreparable calamities, they [the ambassadors] offered their good services with

[35] Lloyd George, V, 103.
[36] Joseph Noulens, *Mon ambassade en Russe soviétique* (Paris, 1933), I, 71; G. Buchanan, II, 183-84.

the sole aim of serving the interests of Russia and the work of the Allies."[37] Joseph Noulens, the new French ambassador, who had arrived in July as a replacement for Paléologue, far from considering his efforts to effect an agreement indiscreet, later attacked the Provisional Government for its "inexcusable collusion" with the "most determined enemies of public order" in its "pitiless" suppression of the revolt.[38]

While the wife and daughter of the British ambassador were engaged in their Red Cross work, a Cossack officer in full uniform approached them with the request that they furnish medicine, bandages, and other supplies to Kornilov's troops when they entered the city. Although quite aware of the compromising nature of their act, both readily consented, because, says Miss Buchanan, "in our hearts we were all on the side of Korniloff, and besides, there was no denying the fact that this young Cossack officer, with his trim waist, his very blue eyes and perfect manners, was very alluring."[39] But even while the alluring officer was assuring his sympathetic admirers that Kornilov would be successful, the general's forces were rapidly disintegrating before the onslaught of Soviet propagandists. Quite apart from this activity, the organization and planning of the *coup* was so inept as to endanger the whole enterprise. Without proper co-ordination from headquarters and against the opposition of the railway workers, the advance was a haphazard and piecemeal affair. Some units were sent in the wrong direction; others were stopped because the tracks were torn up or blockaded. The troops could not proceed on foot because the need for a food supply had not been anticipated. They were flooded with Soviet proclamations, and in vain the officers tried to keep away the horde of persuasive agitators who spread doubt and suspicion in their minds. Insubordination was invariably the result. The soldiers formed their own committees, arrested their officers, and went over to the side of the Provisional Government. Without the firing of a shot, the counterrevolutionary threat collapsed.

[37] *Times* (London), Sept. 13, 1917.   [38] Noulens, I, 71.

[39] M. Buchanan, *Dissolution of an Empire*, p. 239; see also her *Diplomacy and Foreign Courts*, pp. 231-32.

General Krymov, whose dreaded "Savage Division" was left stranded on the sidings and stations of eight different railroads, shot himself when the full extent of the debacle became apparent. Kerensky took over the post of commander-in-chief, appointing General Alexeyev as his chief of staff. The choice was designed to alleviate the lot of the conspirators, whom Kerensky wished to treat with leniency. "Don't speak in such a tone," he snapped at a soldier who talked of merciless punishment for the implicated generals. "Your duty now is to obey your officers; and we shall do ourselves whatever is necessary."[40] On the fourteenth Kornilov and his chief aides were arrested—almost apologetically—and placed under guard by sympathetic Central Asiatic troops. An investigating commission dragged out the preliminary examination, bent upon delaying the trial as long as possible, while the Soviet continued to demand firm and decisive action. After the November Revolution the generals easily escaped from their token confinement and fled to the south, where they devoted their efforts to organizing anti-Bolshevik armies.

The Kornilov fiasco was very embarrassing to the Allies, for not only had they encouraged a counterrevolutionary revolt against the government of a democratic ally, but they had also placed their hopes upon a "strong man" who, upon subsequent trial, proved conspicuously weaker than his opposition—the despised "rabble" of the Petrograd Soviet. The German press, accustomed to frequent attacks upon Hohenzollern autocracy and militarism, was not slow to take advantage of this glaring example of Allied hypocrisy. The *Temps,* replying for the badly compromised Parisian dailies, lamely admitted that while it was "true that a part of the French press supported Kornilov," the German newspapers were grossly exaggerating the extent of the support. The *Temps* maintained its own innocence of the charge and as proof quoted the admission of the *Berliner Tageblatt* that it had not chosen clearly between Kerensky and Kornilov.[41] The Manchester *Guardian,* one of the papers which the *Times* had had in mind when it denounced part of the British press for its anti-Kornilov stand, took note of the

[40] Chamberlin, I, 221.   [41] Sept. 19, 1917.

attack with a polite but crushing reply: "In the course of its long and distinguished career [the *Times*] has committed many indiscretions and many follies, but none so great and so gratuitous as this." Such open praise for Kornilov, continued the *Guardian*, would of itself be of comparatively small consequence were it not for the misunderstanding and resentment which it must necessarily cause in Russia, and the rather deadly use which can, and no doubt will, be made of it by German propaganda. If we were to suppose that the attitude of the *Times* did in truth represent the views of our Foreign Office, let alone of the War Cabinet, the matter would of course be infinitely more serious. It would mean that at the head of affairs in this country we had men without vision, and whose understanding of the most critical events affecting one of our chief allies was warped by narrow and reactionary views.[42]

The *Guardian* correctly, if inadequately, foretold the reaction in Russia. The leftist publications flayed the Allies without restraint. The Bolshevik organ in Petrograd, after citing the damaging evidence point by point, fiercely denounced the foreign and domestic instigators of an "imperialist plot against the Russian Revolution" and the "hack-writers of the banking organs, trying to cover up their work with the noisy, lying phrase, 'the Bolshevik danger.'" "But no one is ignorant of the fact," the paper went on, "that the government circles carrying out the will of the Anglo-French capitalists pharisaically point to the Bolsheviks while they clumsily hide the fleeing criminals and their lying sensationalism about the 'unbalanced situation' in Russia."[43] The ambassadors naturally found these press attacks very offensive. Buchanan, after protesting about a Bolshevik newspaper in Moscow which he found particularly objectionable because of its reference to the illegal use of the British armored cars, received assurances from Tereshchenko that it would be closed.[44] The newly appointed Minister of War, General Alexander Verkhovsky, was given responsibility for the matter and merely instituted legal proceedings against the editor. This complacent attitude greatly incensed Tereshchenko and was the

[42] Sept. 15, 1917.
[43] *Rabochy Put* [*The Workers' Path*], No. 8, Sept. 25, 1917.
[44] Buchanan to Balfour, Oct. 2, 1917, *Krasny Arkhiv*, XXIV (1927), 160.

cause of considerable dissension within the government, much to Buchanan's surprise and regret.[45]

Hardly had these attacks died down before they revived on the strength of the Gurko affair. General Basil Gurko had been chief of staff under Nicholas II and was given a lesser post on his promise of loyalty to the new regime. In early August he was arrested when a letter was discovered which he had written to the former Emperor declaring his continued devotion to the cause of the monarchy. The Provisional Government, apparently at a loss about what to do with him, decided to send him abroad. A British passport was obtained through the embassy, and on September 19 the general left Petrograd for Archangel, where he was received by Admiral Kemp of the British navy. To avoid possible unpleasantries with the local Soviet, Gurko stayed on board the admiral's yacht until the arrival of an English steamship.[46] King George later gave the general a reception at Buckingham Palace, news of which did nothing to endear the Allied cause to Russian hearts. It was thus with good reason that the British naval attaché in Petrograd, referring mainly to the Kornilov affair, commented, "In their wildest flights of imagination [the Bolsheviks] could have prayed for no more useful allies than the Entente embassies."[47]

Only a few days after the Kornilov threat had been disposed of, another Russian insurrection, though of a radically different kind, occurred upon foreign soil. This was the still little-known revolt of the Russian troops in France—or, to be more precise, the suppression of this revolt. If the incident lacked the political significance of the general's *coup,* it had a far more violent denouement. After the severe repression of the mutiny in one of the brigades bound for Salonika in August, 1916,[48] the two brigades on French soil, comprising about sixteen or seventeen thousand men, fought bravely in several campaigns. But their losses were extremely severe, especially from the effects of gas, with which the Russians

---

[45] G. Buchanan, II, 190.

[46] General Basil Gourko, *War and Revolution in Russia* (New York, 1919), p. 398; Francis to Lansing, Aug. 3, 1917 (861.00/460), National Archives.

[47] Harold Grenfell in a letter to the Manchester *Guardian,* Nov. 20, 1919.

[48] See above, p. 15.

had had no previous experience.[49] Isolated from their homeland, they experienced a breakdown of morale even more rapid than that of their comrades in Russia. Not without some basis in fact did they come to regard themselves as cannon-fodder, sold to the French in exchange for munitions.[50] The first brigade was composed largely of workers from the Moscow and Samara districts and showed signs of developing a mutinous spirit much sooner than the third, whose soldiers were predominantly of peasant stock.

The March Revolution, of course, greatly accelerated the decay of discipline. Although the troops swore allegiance to the new regime, only a third of their number, mostly of the third brigade, supported its policy of continuing the war. After suffering heavy casualties in an April offensive, the first brigade, virtually ignoring its officers, organized unit Soviets, elected representatives, and refused to fight any longer.[51] The commanding general resigned and was replaced by General Zankevich, a Russian observer with the French army. Two civilian appointees of the Provisional Government, Eugene Rapp, the representative of the Russian war ministry in Paris, and Serge Svatikov, charged with investigating possible tsarist secret police activity abroad, visited the men and tried to return them to the paths of duty and patriotism. Similar attempts were made by Russian émigrés in France and by the four Soviet delegates who had come to Western Europe on the Stockholm conference mission. These efforts were a conspicuous failure—and for the same reasons that prevented the Allied missions from achieving any better results in Russia. To the French authorities the Russian troops were now a military liability, and to avoid infecting their own troops with a mutinous spirit, they were moved in June to the camp of La Courtine, located about sixty miles southeast of Limoges in central France.[52]

[49] Noulens, II, 137.

[50] Yuri Lissovsky, "Lager Lya-Kurtin" ["The Camp of La Courtine"], *Arkhiv Russkoy Revolyutsia*, XVII (1926), 263.

[51] André Obey, "Camarades rouski," *Revue de Paris*, XXVII (Dec., 1920), 538-39.

[52] Lissovsky, *loc. cit.*, pp. 268-72; Obshchestvo Bivsh. Rossiiskikh Soldati vo Frantsii i na Balkanakh, *Oktyabr za Rubezhom* [*October Abroad*] (Moscow, n. d.), pp. 28 and 39.

In their new camp the Russians, as if suffering from a highly infectious disease, were isolated from outside contacts. Internal dissension sharpened almost to the point of bloodshed, and scarcely a day passed without incidents between the two brigades. Early in July a large part of the third brigade, joined by several hundred patriotic soldiers from the first, withdrew from the camp and went to Felletin, a near-by city. Here they bivouacked on a semi-permanent basis while the French military authorities, not at all pleased with their precipitant action, decided what should be done with them. Svatikov received two delegates from the first brigade in Paris and heard the grievances of the rebel troops. He advised the Russian war ministry to begin their immediate repatriation, and, so as not to furnish a reward for mutinous behavior, the return of the loyal brigade also.[53] The French government heartily concurred in this opinion, and its ambassador in Russia proposed to Tereshchenko that one unit be sent back at the beginning of August and the other in October. The Provisional Government objected, complaining of the transport and supply difficulties, an excuse which Ambassador Noulens—probably correctly—interpreted as a concealment of the true reason. The ministers, he thought, did not wish the returning soldiers to make unfavorable comparisons between the technical level of the two armies, a comparison which could hardly be complimentary to Russia.[54] Such an explanation credits the ambassador's patriotism far more than his common sense. It seems much more plausible that Kerensky still had hopes of restoring the discipline of the army, both at home and abroad, and hated to confess failure on the very doorstep of his French allies. Zankevich was accordingly ordered to institute the most rigorous disciplinary measures, including the restoration of the death penalty.[55]

The troops at La Courtine rejected a later proposal that they be sent to Salonika for service there and in early August were

[53] Pierre Poitevin, *La Mutinerie de La Courtine* (Paris, 1938), pp. 76-79; Yu. N. Danilov, *Russkie Otryady na Frantsuzskom i Makedonskom Frontakh 1916-1918 gg.* [*The Russian Troops on the French and Macedonian Fronts, 1916-1918*] (Paris, 1933), pp. 134-35.
[54] Noulens, II, 140.
[55] Kerensky to Zankevich, July 29, 1917, *Krasny Arkhiv*, XCIX (1940), 58.

presented with a forty-eight-hour ultimatum in which to signify their complete submission by joining the third brigade at Felletin. Foreseeing a rejection of these terms, a strong force of French troops, including machine-gun, artillery, and cavalry units, began to surround the camp before expiration of the ultimatum. About fifteen hundred men gave themselves up, but the remainder, well over eight thousand, refused to leave or to surrender their arms. Since neither the French nor Russian authorities were as yet prepared to use the overwhelming force at their disposal, the situation remained stalemated throughout the month of August. By cutting off their food supply, the authorities could have forced the rebels to submit without the threat of bloodshed, but this solution was not adopted for fear that near-by farms and villages would be plundered. The besiegers were meanwhile reinforced by more French troops and several thousand Russians drawn from the most reliable elements of the third brigade and a special artillery detachment which had just arrived from Salonika.[56]

In early September the civilian population was evacuated from the whole area as a precautionary measure. On the fourteenth Zankevich issued a second ultimatum to the rebels demanding their unconditional surrender by the morning of the sixteenth. Those who chose to remain in the camp, declared the general, would be considered "traitors to the country and the Revolution" and fired upon without further delay.[57] The "traitors" retaliated with an appeal to their Russian comrades not to fire upon their own countrymen. Neither manifesto had any visible effect. No one surrendered, nor did the patriotic troops indicate any distaste for the unpleasant business at hand. Both sides had dug trenches and made their final preparations long before the "zero hour"—ten o'clock. The battle opened with a light artillery bombardment and some small arms fire. The rebels, whose firepower was greatly inferior to that of their opponents, kept up their morale by singing the *Marseillaise* and other songs. The besiegers, despite their preponderance in numbers, attempted no offensive. By dawn of the

[56] Poitevin, pp. 91-116; Lissovsky, *loc. cit.*, pp. 274-75; *Oktyabr za Rubezhom*, p. 45.
[57] Poitevin, pp. 123-25.

next day, about two hundred men had given themselves up, but the remainder gave no indication of surrendering. After a heavy howitzer bombardment later in the morning, however, they allowed seven or eight hundred horses to leave the camp, an indication that they did not expect to hold out much longer. In the afternoon white flags were raised, and the great majority of the mutineers docilely filed out of the camp. About one hundred and fifty men, braver or simply, perhaps, more fanatical than their comrades, chose to defy the inevitable and blockaded themselves in the hospital and the officers' mess. On the eighteenth loyal Russian infantry units advanced against machine-gun fire and occupied strategic positions in the camp. By the following morning, with the aid of a constant artillery barrage, resistance ceased completely and all but a few soldiers hidden in the woods were quickly rounded up.[58]

Considering the heavy expenditure of ammunition, the casualties were surprisingly light, although, if one were to believe local tales, the victims numbered into the hundreds and even thousands. The losses of the mutineers totaled nine killed and forty-nine wounded, while the opposing troops suffered only three casualties, two of them fatal.[59] The prisoners were divided into three categories according to their degree of guilt. Those regarded as the ringleaders of the mutiny, about eighty in number, were imprisoned. Another group of five hundred was sent under guard to a near-by camp, and the remainder stayed at La Courtine under severe military discipline to repair and clean up the buildings. A week later two companies refused to obey orders and submitted only when threatened with the immediate intervention of French troops.[60] Three soldiers were arrested, and, like that of the other prisoners, their ultimate fate is obscure. Some were certainly executed, though the exact number is unknown.[61]

[58] Ibid., pp. 134-52.
[59] Ibid., p. 160; Danilov, p. 147, gives the rebel casualties as eight killed and forty-four wounded.
[60] Poitevin, p. 165.
[61] John Reed puts the number at two hundred in his Ten Days That Shook the World (New York, 1935), p. 323, but gives no authority for his statement.

Several additional months of comparative idleness at La Courtine did nothing to revive the patriotism of the Russian troops. About twenty-five hundred accepted Zankevich's request for volunteer workers as a small wage. The rest would have nothing to do with the plan and remained stubborn if peaceable devotees of the revolutionary cause. The November Revolution offered new hope of repatriation, and negotiations to that end were immediately opened by the Bolsheviks. The French government claimed that a renewal of the submarine menace made this impossible for the time being. But submarines did not prevent the removal to North Africa in December of three thousand of the most recalcitrant troops to make room at La Courtine for newly arrived American troops. The others were sent in small groups of twenty or thirty to various parts of France as laborers. Most of the Russian troops in Salonika also refused to continue fighting, and the great majority joined their fellows in North Africa. The rest were sent to the French front with the other patriotic Russians, where further disciplinary problems in some of the units showed that the revolutionary virus could not be stamped out so easily. Most of the offenders were drafted into labor battalions, and the remainder fought with the French army until the end of the war. Many then joined the "White" forces of Baron Peter Wrangel and General Anton Denikin during the civil war. The North African contingent and the Russians in France who wished to return to their homeland were finally sent back in 1919 and early 1920 in exchange for French nationals.[62]

The rigid French censorship prevented any news leaks about the mutiny of the Russian troops during the war. Thus almost the only information available to the outside world was that contained in a brief factual statement released by the Provisional Government on October 30, 1917.[63] It raised more questions than it answered, and the news served only to arouse further discontent among the Russian masses at the brutal treatment accorded their comrades by the "French imperialists."[64] Yet compared to the

[62] Noulens, II, 140-41; Poitevin, pp. 173-88.
[63] Serge Persky, *De Nicolas II à Lénine* (Paris, 1919), pp. 126-31.
[64] Reed, p. 22.

effect of the Kornilov affair, it was but a minor grievance. The ignominious collapse of the counterrevolution, far from strengthening Kerensky and the Provisional Government, as most of the Allied press professed to believe, constituted a tremendous impetus to the Bolshevik movement. "An adventure of a small group," complains Kerensky, "was transformed in the inflamed imagination of the masses to a conspiracy of the whole of the bourgeoisie and of all the upper classes against democracy and the working masses."[65] If the workers and soldiers really were overly hasty in their judgment, Kerensky's conduct was not the least of the reasons. The Bolsheviks had only to reap where Kornilov had sown. They soon obtained a majority in the Soviets of Moscow and Petrograd, as well as many other cities, and throughout the country their rapid gains were startling. Trotsky, who was released from prison on the seventeenth, was elected president of the Petrograd Soviet in early October. The government, pending another cabinet reorganization, was run by a directorate of five. The Soviet ministers, including Chernov and Skobelev, refused to continue in office so long as the Cadets were not excluded and withdrew from the cabinet.

Tereshchenko, reporting the situation to Russia's representatives abroad, expressed great confidence in the future. The whole country, he claimed, was now united in a common unity of purpose, and the government had not only been strengthened by its recent ordeal but was resolved to "follow the path of prosecuting the war at any cost" and to "carry out with renewed energy the task of reconstructing the army."[66] Such statements were designed more for the edification of the Allied Foreign Offices, each of which duly received a copy, than for Russia's diplomats. But the statesmen of Britain and France were no longer moved by promises and manifestoes. They had long ago become disillusioned with Kerensky and a revolution which stubbornly refused to follow the course which had been prescribed for it in London and Paris. The Revolution had been considered a fine thing for Russia until it became

---

[65] Alexander Kerensky, *The Prelude to Bolshevism* (New York, 1919), p. xxii.
[66] *Foreign Relations*, I, 193.

plain that the soldiers were strangely unenthusiastic about fighting the Germans. As a prominent Englishman in Petrograd so succinctly expressed it, "These damn Russians had no right to have a revolution in time of war."[67] The American government, though sobered by the events of the summer, remained faithful to Kerensky, still relatively unsullied by the doubt and cynicism of its allies. While Lansing was personally inclined toward pessimism—or so he later maintained—and complained that Kerensky compromised too much "with the radical element of the Revolution,"[68] the State Department, buoyed up by the glowing report of the Root mission and the optimistic naïveté of Francis's dispatches from Russia, seemed not at all downhearted by the situation. With every appearance of purposeful accomplishment, Lansing transmitted to Russia inspirational messages from the American Federation of Labor and the Chamber of Commerce.[69] "The soul of American labor and democracy beats in unison with the spirit and aspirations of Russia's people," A. F. of L. President Gompers assured them in all seriousness. To be informed further that "the democracies of the world are united in a life and death struggle to crush autocracy, imperialism, and militarism" had little meaning to the average Russian citizen, who, if he had ever heard of Gompers at all, was far more likely to have remembered him as a determined foe of the Stockholm conference than as a friend of the working man. Nor was the assurance of the Chamber of Commerce that Russia had the support of "hundreds of thousands of American business men" in its struggle to defeat the "autocratic militarism of Germany" and spread "democratic ideals throughout the world" particularly comforting.

Scornful of this altruistic approach, but overly enamored of the possibilities of direct pressure, the British government, in accordance with the war cabinet's decision at the time of the Kornilov affair to take a firmer stand toward Russia, instructed Buchanan to consult his colleagues and collectively present the Provisional

---

[67] Quoted by Samuel N. Harper, undated draft of an address (1918?), Harper Papers, University of Chicago Library.
[68] Robert Lansing, *War Memoirs* (Indianapolis and New York, 1935), p. 337.
[69] *Foreign Relations*, I, 194 and 205-6.

Government with a stiff note of protest concerning its remiss be-havior. The ambassador reworded the proposed text and waited for an opportune moment to call upon Kerensky. On October 9, just after the new cabinet had been installed, the British, French, and Italian ambassadors were received at the Winter Palace, the government's new headquarters. Francis did not join them because he had not received an answer from Washington to his repeated queries about the course of action to be taken. Buchanan, after a few preliminary remarks, began to read the note in French. In an apparent effort to conceal his embarrassment at the disagreeable task to be performed, his tone was unduly harsh and seemed to Noulens to give the "rather harmless complaints" of the Allies the "character of peremptory injunctions."[70] Considering the normal allusiveness of diplomatic phraseology, these "harmless complaints" were worded very strongly indeed for an ally-in-arms. "It behooves the Russian government," the note read, "to show by acts its re-solve to employ all proper means to revive discipline and true military spirit among the fighting troops, at the same time that it will insure the operation of the public services and the reestablish-ment of order at the front as at the rear." Furthermore, Russia was warned, "the Allied Governments might soon find themselves confronted by a trend of opinion which would put on trial the responsibility concerning the utility of the considerable sacrifices in arms, munitions, material of every kind accorded without count-ing to Russia, while they would be reproached with not having reserved them for the western front, where the wish to conquer appears without faltering."[71]

Kerensky took the verbal message almost as a personal insult and replied in Russian—Tereshchenko translating—to the effect that Russia would remain in the war to the end despite the crip-pling heritage of the tsarist regime and the hesitation of the Allies in sending war matériel. In conclusion, he testily reminded his listeners that Russia was still a great power. Tereshchenko had hardly finished translating the last sentence before Kerensky brusquely rose to leave, waving his hand as a sign that the inter-

<hr>

[70] Noulens, I, 89.　　　　[71] *Foreign Relations*, I, 207-8.

view was at an end. His behavior offended the ambassadors, and Buchanan later complained to Tereshchenko that Kerensky had no business treating the representatives of the Allied Powers in such a cavalier manner.[72] Kerensky immediately called at the American embassy to thank the ambassador for not participating in the protest. Francis had just left for an appointment with the Foreign Minister and returned as soon as he learned of the visit, too late to receive the Prime Minister's misplaced gratitude. Kerensky was particularly bitter about the incident because the Allies, now so concerned about the lack of "order" in Russia, had given every encouragement to the very man he held responsible for the trouble—General Kornilov. He might have been even more bitter had he known that the man whose report and recommendations to the British war cabinet was instrumental in actuating the protest was General Knox, perhaps Kornilov's most influential non-Russian supporter. The Provisional Government sent formal protests through its representatives in London, Paris, and Rome with the polite demand that the whole matter be kept secret to avoid a "dangerous irritation" of Russian public opinion. Lansing was informed through Bakhmetev that the abstention of the United States from the Allied note was greatly appreciated.[73] The British and Italian ambassadors received instructions to apologize; Noulens, claiming his government stood by the statement, refused to do so.

Kerensky's new cabinet, which had been announced only the day before the unfortunate events of the ninth, was a makeshift affair, even weaker than its three predecessors had been. Its advent had been delayed in order to obtain the approval of the Democratic Conference, an assembly of the nonpropertied elements in Russian society which had opened in Petrograd shortly before. But the delegates failed to arrive at any clear agreement on the composition of the new government, and Kerensky proceeded to select his ministers as he saw fit. The presence of several Cadets in the new coalition was decidedly unpopular. The Petrograd Soviet lost no

---

[72] Noulens, I, 91-92; G. Buchanan, II, 192-93; Kerensky, *Crucifixion of Liberty*, pp. 357-59.
[73] Manchester *Guardian*, Dec. 26, 1917.

time in denouncing it as a "government of civil war."[74] Kerensky issued an appeal for support in the hope that "all citizens will unite . . . for common work in the name of the fundamental and prime questions of our time—the defense of the country from the external enemy, the restoration of law and order, and the safe conduct of the country until the convocation of the Constituent Assembly." While asserting that the government would continue its "firm resistance to all attempts to force a foreign will on Russia," he promised that the Russian representative at the forthcoming Allied conference would endeavor, "in addition to coming to an agreement with our Allies regarding our common war aims, to effect an agreement with them on the basis of the principles announced by the Russian revolution."[75]

The Democratic Conference was followed by the convocation on October 20 of a more conservative but no less futile body, the so-called "Pre-Parliament," or Provisional Council of the Russian Republic, which was to function in an advisory capacity until the oft-postponed Constituent Assembly should meet. Against Lenin's advice a Bolshevik delegation took part in the proceedings but withdrew during the first session following Trotsky's thundering denunciation of a government, which, as he put it, "under the dictation of Cadet counterrevolutionists and Allied imperialists, without sense, without force and without plan, drags out the murderous war, condemning to useless destruction hundreds of thousands of soldiers and sailors and preparing the surrender of Petrograd and the throttling of the Revolution."[76] Francis referred contemptuously to "sixty [Bolsheviks who] bolted amid jeers of the Council" in his report to Washington,[77] but the walkout was an act of strength, not weakness. Having rid themselves of the troublesome left wing, the delegates devoted the succeeding days to ways and means of restoring the army's fighting capacity. As usual, the discussions were doomed to sterility, not only by the lack of agreement in the assembly itself, but even more so by the

[74] Milyukov, *Istoria*, Vol. I, Pt. III, p. 75.
[75] *Foreign Relations*, I, 212-14.
[76] Chamberlin, I, 283.
[77] Oct. 21, 1917, *Foreign Relations*, I, 210.

absence of any sentiment among the mass of ordinary soldiers in favor of continuing the war.

In contrast to the phenomenal success of Bolshevik antiwar propaganda—a success which must, of course, be ascribed to war weariness rather than to any inherent superiority of dogma—patriotic counterpropaganda, by no means negligible, made little headway. The bourgeois press remained unread by those for whom its patriotic homilies were intended, while the circulation of such Bolshevik organs as *Okopnaya Pravda* [*Trench Truth*] attained enormous proportions at the front. What little influence the Allied representatives had been able to exert declined to almost nothing by the autumn months.

Very nearly alone in their belief that revised tactics would yield the hoped for resurgence of martial spirit were Lieutenant Colonel William Boyce Thompson and Major Raymond Robins, two members of the nominally nonpolitical American Red Cross mission in Russia. The mission in question, consisting of some twenty persons, had arrived during the summer, with Dr. Franklin Billings, a prominent Chicago physician, at its head. Lacking executive experience and a grasp of Russian conditions, he left many practical matters to Thompson, a wealthy financier and copper magnate, whose money had much to do with the mission's presence in Russia. Early in September Billings returned to the United States, partly because of ill health, leaving Thompson in charge. Robins, his chief assistant, a social worker and formerly one of the leading backers of Theodore Roosevelt and the Progressive party, was as liberal in his social outlook and political sympathies as Thompson was conservative in his. Each had had misgivings about the other at the start of the journey. Robins wondered what "that Wall Street reactionary" was doing on such a mission and Thompson exclamed in amazement at the presence of an "uplifter, trouble-maker, and Roosevelt-shouter."[78] During the long and monotonous trip to Petrograd, the two men had ample time to thaw out and

[78] Statement of Raymond Robins, Jan. 31, 1931, William Boyce Thompson Papers, Library of Congress. The Thompson Papers consist of the material gathered by Hagedorn for his biography of Thompson. See Hermann Hagedorn, *The Magnate: William Boyce Thompson and His Time* (New York, 1935).

gradually came to admire each other, for both shared an eagerness to probe beneath the surface of events in Russia for the unadorned reality. In Petrograd they observed the growing power of the Soviet and realized that the war weariness of the people was not to be explained by German and Bolshevik propaganda; and their contempt grew for the "seven per cent mind," as Robins characterized the mental outlook of that small section of the population—an estimated seven per cent—which had always controlled Russia and expected to continue doing so.[79] It was this group which preferred the Germans to a deepening of the Revolution, and to the two patriotic Americans this sounded very much like treason. In his efforts to transport grain from the Ukraine to Petrograd, Robins obtained firsthand evidence of the power of the Soviet and the weakness of the Provisional Government. His government credentials were so much waste paper, but when he saw the chairman of the local Soviet, his transportation difficulties were solved.[80]

Convinced of the importance of the Soviet in determining Russia's future policy, Robins spoke occasionally and then daily by mid-September before groups of peasants and workers in and around Petrograd. His argument did not differ radically from that employed by the Allied emissaries who had preceded him but his choice of audiences was a far more realistic one. He sought to persuade them that Germany was the real menace to the Revolution and that the old landlord regime would return behind German bayonets if she were not defeated. While Robins was a brilliant speaker, his success was not spectacular. There was little that one individual could do; only propaganda on a large scale could make an impression. The cost, he told Thompson, would be at least a million dollars to start and three million monthly for six months.[81] Thompson had already consulted Kerensky about the possibility of such a campaign. He expressed interest and referred Thompson to Catherine Breshkovskaya, "the grandmother of the Revolution," famous for her revolutionary activity during the

[79] *Bolshevik Propaganda,* pp. 768, 772-73, and 783.
[80] *Ibid.,* p. 765.
[81] *Ibid.,* pp. 771-72; Hagedorn, p. 204.

tsarist regime. She thought the plan feasible, and with this encouragement, Thompson decided to advance one million dollars
of his personal fortune to begin the project, confident that Washington would support so worthy a purpose with practically un-
limited funds. At a meeting which Kerensky, Robins, and Thompson attended, Breshkovskaya founded a "Committee on Civic Education in Free Russia," with the aid of her old revolutionary colleague, Nicholas Chaikovsky, David Soskice, Kerensky's private
secretary, and General Constantine Neslukovsky of the Russian
general staff.[82]

Thompson's money was placed at the disposal of the committee. Scores of newspapers were established, a printing plant purchased, and several news bureaus supported. Soldiers' clubs were
organized and supplied with books and papers. More than eight
hundred speakers, both men and women, were sent into the
trenches, barracks, and villages of the country. At such a rate,
even a million dollars could not last long. In late August Thompson had cabled Henry P. Davison, the director of the American
Red Cross, and asked him to lay his plan before the proper Washington officials. After a ten-day interval Lansing replied in the
same equivocal terms with which he had answered the dispatches
of the Root mission.[83] In September Breshkovskaya herself appealed to Wilson for funds in the guise of a greeting from one free
people to another. Lest it be misunderstood, Thompson asked
Davison to explain to Wilson what she was really hinting at. The
President made no reply for three weeks, and when he did so, the
message ignored the matter of financial aid and was couched in
terms of those universal moral principles of which he was so fond:
"Intellectual development and moral fitness are the most powerful
elements of national advancement"; a nation "should embody the
highest individual ideals of civil perfection" and maintain its honorable position in the world-family, "strong in the might of right and
fearless in the cause of truth and justice."[84]

By this time an emissary from Thompson, H. Grosvenor Hut-

[82] *Bolshevik Propaganda*, pp. 776-77; Hagedorn, p. 205.
[83] *Bolshevik Propaganda*, pp. 777-78; Hagedorn, pp. 206-7.
[84] Oct. 10, 1917, Wilson Papers; Baker and Dodd, V, 107.

chins, vice-president of the New York Bank of Commerce, had arrived in the United States from Petrograd. Thompson's grandiose plan had so inspired him that he felt the fate of the world lay in his hands. He hurried to Washington and spread his story widely in influential capital circles but could not gain an audience at the White House. Despite the various stratagems that were employed, including an attempt to enlist the aid of Colonel Edward M. House, the President's unofficial adviser, Wilson remained inaccessible as cable after cable from Thompson and his friends pleaded for immediate action. In late September Davison was able to see the President and showed him one of Thompson's cables requesting a million dollars in ten days and three million monthly beginning in October. Wilson was not favorably impressed. "Three million a month!" he exclaimed. "What's the matter with your friend? Has he gone crazy?"[85]

Hutchins managed to stir the interest of George Creel, who, as director of the Committee on Public Information, was mobilizing American public opinion for an all-out war effort. Finally, on October 23, five weeks after his arrival, the President consented to see Hutchins, accompanied by Creel and one of his assistants, Edgar Sisson.[86] Wilson had already decided to send Sisson to Russia as a representative of Creel's committee but with the vaguest of instructions as to what his mission was to accomplish. Hutchins told his story, and, though the President listened with his usual unfailing courtesy, it was apparent that he had already made up his mind that the proper approach to Russia was the idealistic one of reassuring her of "our friendliness, our unselfishness . . . and our desire of helpfulness," with the expectation that unpleasant subjects like Bolshevism and a separate peace would somehow take care of themselves.[87] He spoke brilliantly of the Russian psychology, but "amid an aura of ethnological generalities," Hutchins found that the interview was at an end.[88]

[85] Hagedorn, p. 219. A slightly different version is contained in a letter to Hagedorn by William Wallace, Aug. 21, 1931, Thompson Papers.
[86] Baker, VII, 320.
[87] Edgar Sisson, *One Hundred Red Days* (New Haven, Conn., 1931), pp. 8-9.
[88] Hagedorn, p. 230; statement of Grosvenor Hutchins, May 11, 1932, Thompson Papers.

Sisson sailed for Russia four days later, carrying with him credit for only a fraction of the amount Thompson considered essential. He also bore a letter to Thompson from the President praising him for "the great thing" he had done on behalf of "Russia's fight for freedom" but with the implied suggestion that he do no more of it.[89] The letter was actually written by Creel, who had meanwhile soured on Thompson. It did not seem to him that "a rockbound conservative" at home and a "roaring radical" in Petrograd "was quite the man we wanted to preach American gospel."[90] By the time Sisson arrived, the Bolsheviks had been in power nearly three weeks. It was the belief of Wilson, Creel, and himself, Sisson afterwards related, that he was "going as a friend to a friendly country"; there was no reason "to believe that Bolshevism was even a cloud on the Russian horizon." Having spent thousands of dollars cabling the actual situation to Washington and requesting money to combat Bolshevism, Thompson might well have been justified, as his biographer acidly comments, in quoting the well-known observation regarding "the infinite capacity of the human mind to withstand the introduction of knowledge."[91]

Thompson was hardly mollified by Wilson's left-handed gesture of support. Without monetary aid to back it up, his ambitious program was necessarily curtailed. Robins continued his speaking tours, but, since he was realistic about the situation, his optimism had somewhat flagged. "The war is dead in the heart of the Russian soldier," he admitted on October 22 in the privacy of his diary.[92] Nevertheless, he fully co-operated with Thompson's last desperate effort to stave off the imminent seizure of power by the Bolsheviks. They both knew that the Soviet held the key to political power. If the Provisional Government could be persuaded to accept Soviet control and distribute the land to the peasants, they reasoned, something might yet be salvaged. When Kerensky was approached on the matter, he indicated a

[89] Oct. 24, 1917, Wilson Papers; Thompson Papers; Hagedorn, p. 231; Baker, VII, 323.

[90] George Creel, *Rebel at Large* (New York, 1947), p. 176.

[91] Hagedorn, p. 231.

[92] William Hard, *Raymond Robins' Own Story* (New York, 1920), p. 46.

willingness to co-operate were it not for the Allies. It was their money which was supporting his floundering government. "Why won't the allies really understand Russia?" he burst out irritably. "They force me to talk western European liberalism two-thirds of the time for their benefit, while I have to talk Russian Slavic social-ism one-third of the time for the sake of living 24 hours."[93]   It was plainly left up to Thompson to secure the consent of the Allies.

On November 3 there was a meeting in Thompson's hotel room of the British, French, and American military attachés, Thompson, Robins, General Neslukovsky, and Soskice, the latter representing Kerensky. The ambassadors had not been invited as too hope-lessly conservative to bother with. Thompson opened the discus-sion by briefly outlining his plan. Then Robins spoke of the need for land distribution. General Knox was appalled at the sug-gestion. Who would compensate the landowners, and on what terms, if such a wild scheme were actually carried out? Thomp-son thought the time inappropriate for haggling over details. "Dis-tribute the damned land and settle the compensation afterward," he exclaimed. Knox remained unsatisfied; his political instincts revolted at the very thought of such an idea. "Distribute the land in Russia to-day," he warned, "and in two years we will be dis-tributing it in England." The general was not interested in the Soviet or land reform. In order to unburden his resentment about the Russian situation on someone, and particularly for the benefit of the two Russians present, he launched into a lengthy tirade on the incompetence, futility, and general worthlessness of the Pro-visional Government. What little he left unsaid was supplied by General Henri Niessel, the French representative, who concluded his remarks on Russia's poor military showing with something to the effect that her soldiers were cowardly yellow dogs. At this open insult, Soskice and Neslukovsky, flushed red with anger, stalked from the room. Then Knox joined the fray again. Thomp-son was just wasting his money on Kerensky; it should have been back of Kornilov. Military dictatorship, he declared, was the solu-

[93] Robins in *Bolshevik Propaganda*, p. 779.

tion: the people simply needed a whip over them. Robins pointed out that he might get a dictatorship of a very different character. "This Trotsky-Lenin-Bolshevik stuff—this soap-box stuff?" snorted the general. "Military men know what to do with that kind of stuff. We stand them up and shoot them." Although Robins expressed doubt as to the efficacy of this method—there were probably several million Bolsheviks and their sympathizers—well over two hours of this kind of argument only made it clearer than ever that no agreement was possible.[94]

General William V. Judson, the American military attaché in Russia, has estimated that the activities of Thompson and Robins set back the advent of Bolshevism by from four to six weeks.[95] There is little tangible evidence to support such a contention, but whatever their influence in this respect, the Allies, by sabotaging the prospective discussion of war aims, probably did as much during this critical period to undo the work of prowar propagandists in Russia as a whole army of Bolshevik agitators. The one hope which sustained the moderate Russian socialists in their devotion to the Allied cause was the government's assurance that an Allied conference for the revision of war aims would meet in the near future. All through the summer Kerensky and Tereshchenko had tried to convince Britain and France that such a conference should be held without further delay. After the disastrous ending of the Stockholm conference, a substitute of some kind, no matter how inadequate, was more than ever imperative from the Russian point of view. But the only effective weapon at her disposal, a threat to make a separate peace unless the Allies complied with this demand, was never invoked or even considered. Even after a grudging consent had been obtained—and then with no assurance that war aims would be discussed—the conference suffered repeated postponements. Finally the meeting was definitely set for Paris at the end of November. Tereshchenko, as Foreign Minister, almost automatically became Russia's official representative, with

---

[94] *Ibid.*, pp. 779-81; Hard, pp. 49-52; Hagedorn, pp. 234-37.
[95] Judson to Secretary of War, June 18, 1919, William V. Judson Papers, Newberry Library, Chicago.

General Alexeyev proposed as the military delegate. On the unwarranted assumption that a Soviet delegate would be admitted to the proceedings, Skobelev, the former Minister of Labor, was chosen by the Soviet executive committee to go to Paris and spread the gospel of "peace without annexations or indemnities." An elaborate set of instructions was drawn up very similar in nature to Wilson's later and much more famous "fourteen points."[96] But on many matters of detail the Soviet proposals went beyond Wilson's. Such recommendations as the neutralization of the Panama and Suez canals, the return of Germany's colonies, the restoration of Greece and Persia, autonomy for Turkish Armenia, and a sweeping ban on reparations, were not likely to receive a favorable hearing at Paris—or even a hearing of any kind. A Cadet newspaper inquired sarcastically: "What will Skobelev do if the Allies unceremoniously reject his conditions? Will he threaten them with another appeal to the people of the whole world?"[97] The gibe was only too apt. Had Skobelev and his fellow socialists been able to provide a satisfactory answer, their plight would never have become as hopeless as it did shortly thereafter when socialists of a more active persuasion wrested the power from the feeble grasp of the Provisional Government.

An adverse response from the West to Soviet presumptions was not long delayed. Nabokov was informed in no uncertain terms that Skobelev was not welcome. "We do not understand in what capacity the Soviet representative intends to come to Paris," said the British Foreign Office. "One thing is certain. He will not be admitted to the Allied Conference."[98] Francis became unnecessarily alarmed about the meeting and told Lansing that it should be at least postponed so as not to increase the peace sentiment in Russia. The latter replied that the discussions were to center on a "vigorous and successful prosecution of the war" and that the ambassador was authorized to say so publicly if need be. The Romanian and Serbian governments had to be pacified and assured

[96] See Ross, pp. 260-63, for this comparison.
[97] Quoted in Trotsky, *History of the Russian Revolution*, III, 69.
[98] Nabokoff, p. 166.

that their interests would not be sacrificed at the behest of Russian radicals. The Romanian Prime Minister had gone so far as to call a special meeting of all the Allied representatives in Bucharest to request that they protest to their governments against the presence of a Soviet delegate.[99] Buchanan thought it unwise to veto the discussion of peace terms or to raise difficulties about Skobelev's attendance because it would not commit the Allies in any way and would "humor" the socialists. Furthermore, he told his government, Tereshchenko could be relied upon to keep Skobelev in his place. The ambassador's advice was disregarded, and on October 29 and again on the thirty-first, Andrew Bonar Law, Chancellor of the Exchequer, curtly stated in the House of Commons that the conference would consider the prosecution of the war and not war aims.[100] A spokesman for the French ministry of foreign affairs also declared flatly on the thirty-first that only "members of governments" would be allowed to attend because the subject of war aims would not be considered.[101]

Tereshchenko spoke at great length on the government's foreign policy before the Pre-Parliament on the twenty-ninth. It was a patriotic address and strongly appealed to the Allied ambassadors, all of whom were in attendance. He condemned the Soviet claim to separate representation at the conference and attacked the instructions given to Skobelev. Two days later, when the moderate socialists had an opportunity to reply, Tereshchenko was bitterly criticized for his attitude. Considerably sobered by the weak support for his policy in the Pre-Parliament and the belligerent tone of the left-wing press, he complained to Buchanan of Bonar Law's unfortunate statement in the House of Commons. It had added greatly to his difficulties, he told the ambassador, and though the conduct of the war was naturally the main object of the meeting, it was certainly impolitic to inform the Russian democracy that all discussion of war aims would be barred.[102]

[99] Foreign Relations (1917, suppl. 2), I, 284-86.
[100] Parliamentary Debates, XCVIII, 1187 and 1447.
[101] New York Times, Nov. 1, 1917.
[102] G. Buchanan, II, 202.

Buchanan had made preparations to leave with the Foreign Minister on November 4 in order to attend the conference and to report on the Russian situation. Tereshchenko was warned that his train would be halted should he try to leave, and the date of departure was put off four days to allow matters to calm down.[103] By the eighth the Bolsheviks were in power; instead of on the way to Paris, Tereshchenko found himself in a prison cell.

Russian prestige during the last weeks of the Provisional Government's existence was at its lowest point. An appeal to the British late in October for naval aid to help repulse a German expedition in the Baltic Sea met a negative response. It was presumably refused for sound strategic reasons, yet Buchanan significantly remarked to Tereshchenko that Russia could hardly expect an ally to risk its fleet when the Russian army, numerically stronger than the forces opposed to it, did little or no fighting. Disturbed by the resentment which this news aroused in Russia, Kerensky did not conceal his disappointment. He could understand the British position, he told Buchanan, but it was difficult to explain to the growing number of persons who complained that the Allies were giving Russia the cold shoulder. The ambassador was not in an apologetic mood and steered the conversation around to Russian sins. It was no longer a time for half-measures; iron discipline must be introduced at all costs, he told the Prime Minister. Bolshevism was at the root of all the evils from which Russia suffered, and if he would only eradicate it, he would go down in history not only as the leading figure of the Revolution but as the savior of his country. Though the prospect must have been an inviting one, Kerensky protested that he would have to wait until the Bolsheviks made the first move, a move which he expected in the course of the next few weeks. Buchanan did not fail to express the hope that the government would not let the opportunity to eradicate Bolshevism (i.e., Bolsheviks) slip by as it had the previous July.[104] The embassy circles still lived in a dream world in which the possibility of an armed rising meant only the oppor-

[103] M. Buchanan, *Dissolution of an Empire*, pp. 244-47; also her *City of Trouble* (New York, 1918), p. 173.
[104] G. Buchanan, II, 194-96.

tunity to scotch the Bolshevik monster and thus, by some mysterious alchemy, restore the fighting vigor of the army. That the Bolsheviks might win and establish their own government was not considered a serious possibility.

Kerensky faced something of a mutiny within his own cabinet in the last week of its existence when the War Minister, General Verkhovsky, no longer able to persuade himself that the army could be rehabilitated, appeared before a secret committee of the Pre-Parliament and came dangerously near advocating peace as the only means of saving the country. The news leaked out, and Verkhovsky was denounced furiously in the patriotic press. He has "jumped on the footboard of Comrade Trotsky's chariot," cried one such organ.[105] Vladimir Burtsev, an old Socialist Revolutionary whose own paper was heavily subsidized by French funds, falsely charged that the War Minister had advocated a separate peace and hinted at the presence of German gold as a reason for his sudden change of heart. The errant minister was given an enforced vacation under the guise of a "leave of absence," and an official statement was issued denying that he had proposed a separate peace.[106]

As his sacrifice of Verkhovsky illustrated, Kerensky clung grimly to the notion that the resurgence of Russia would come in time if the Allies would only be patient. In an interview with a correspondent for the Associated Press on November 1, he flatly denied reports that Russia was virtually out of the war. But reflecting his irritation at Allied pressure, he admitted that Russia was worn out by the strain of fighting and has "the right to claim that the Allies now take the heaviest part of the burden on their shoulders." The question now agitating Russian public opinion, he added, was the whereabouts of the British fleet now that the German fleet was out in the Baltic.[107] The first accounts of this interview to appear in the United States were badly garbled and

---

[105] Quoted in Trotsky, *History of the Russian Revolution,* III, 73.

[106] Chernov, pp. 390-91; Yakhontoff, p. 181; for the details of the secret meeting see James Bunyan and H. H. Fisher, *The Bolshevik Revolution: Documents and Materials* (Stanford University, Calif., 1934), pp. 45-48.

[107] Cumming and Pettit, pp. 39-41.

conveyed the impression that Russia was nearly out of the war. Headline writers went even further and flatly asserted in some instances that Russia had already given up the struggle. Both the State Department and the Russian embassy were quick with denials. All reports which have been received from Petrograd, Lansing declared, "show that Premier Kerensky and his government, far from yielding to discouragement, are still animated by a strong determination to organize all Russia's resources in a whole-hearted resistance and carry the war through to a victorious conclusion." Yet in his dispatch to Francis on the same day, Lansing exhibited less official optimism and asked for a copy of the original interview because the "general impression, after careful reading, remains unfavorable."[108] In view of the adverse press comment on the interview, particularly in England, Kerensky authorized an explanatory statement in which he emphasized that Russia would "continue to do her duty."

While Kerensky and Tereshchenko—none too friendly in their personal relations—were busily engaged up to the very eve of their overthrow in furnishing proof of the government's fidelity to the Allied cause, the Bolsheviks were actively preparing the seizure of power. Their intention was no secret, and the conservative press, nervous but absurdly overconfident, asserted that any attempt against the government would be crushed. Kerensky also was outwardly confident and repeatedly told Buchanan that he wished the uprising would occur so that it could be put down.[109] Lenin, who had been in hiding in Finland since late July, had returned to Petrograd in disguise on October 20. Three days later at a secret meeting of the Bolshevik central committee, he insisted that the political situation was ripe for insurrection and that to delay longer might be fatal. The ensuing discussion was a stormy one, and it was only after many hours of argument that Lenin won a majority to his side. The decision once made, only Zinoviev and Kamenev continued to oppose it as a dangerous and premature step. Lenin excoriated the "strikebreaking" tactics of his

[108] Foreign Relations, I, 218.
[109] G. Buchanan, II, 201.

two old comrades and called for their expulsion from the party. Though his analysis later proved to be the correct one, at the time other party leaders shared the doubts and hesitations which Zinoviev and Kamenev ventured to express openly. Nevertheless, Lenin's will prevailed, and under Trotsky's leadership the Petrograd Soviet organized a "Military Revolutionary Committee" to take care of the practical end of the insurrection. Of the original members of this committee, forty-eight were Bolsheviks, fourteen were Left Socialist Revolutionaries, and four were Anarchists. Representatives were sent to all units of the Petrograd garrison to gain their support—or failing that, their neutrality. It was in this type of work, rather than in planning the actual details of military strategy, that the committee proved its value. The core of the striking force at the disposal of the Bolsheviks was the Red Guard, composed of approximately twenty thousand armed factory workers. They had been training since the Kornilov rebellion, and while they would have probably fared poorly against a trained body of troops, it was a measure of the Provisional Government's strength and prestige that no such body of troops was available to it.

In the face of these aggressive preparations, which could not, of course, be satisfactorily concealed, the government took countermeasures. Military units believed to be reliable were called up from the surrounding area; a squad of junkers (military cadets) raided the printing plant of the Bolshevik newspapers on the morning of November 6; other junker detachments were stationed about the city to guard strategic buildings, bridges, and installations; the cruiser *Aurora,* stationed on the Neva River uncomfortably close to the Winter Palace, was ordered out to sea. The Military Revolutionary Committee replied swiftly and efficiently. Within a few hours the Bolshevik press resumed operations, and the crew of the *Aurora,* receiving the committee's counterorders, refused to obey the government edict.

Kerensky appeared before the Pre-Parliament in the afternoon to rally support for his regime. He delivered a tirade against the Bolsheviks, with particular attention to "that wanted but fugitive state criminal, Ulyanov-Lenin,"[110] and demanded a vote of unconditional confidence. After a long intermission for discussion, the delegates reassembled and gave the Prime Minister his meaningless vote of confidence by a small majority. But they severely qualified their support of Kerensky's leadership by calling for "an immediate decree transferring the land to the administration of the land committees and a decisive move in foreign policy, with a proposal to the Allies to proclaim conditions of peace and begin peace negotiations."[111] Thus two of the most important planks in the Bolshevik platform were taken over in the same resolution which condemned the approaching insurrection in unmeasured language. Kerensky was quite incensed by this uncalled for advice and threatened to resign. What had once been an effective political weapon was now but an empty gesture. Grudgingly supported by the Mensheviks and Socialist Revolutionaries and openly scorned by the Cadets and other right-wing opinion, the Provisional Government, like the tsarist government which it had replaced, was a hollow façade unprepared to withstand a determined assault against its authority.

On the same afternoon Ambassador Francis paid his customary daily call at the Foreign Office. After discussing routine business, Francis went over to the window and noticed a thousand or more government troops drilling in the square. "I expect a Bolshevik outbreak to-night," said Tereshchenko nervously.

"If you can suppress it, I hope it will occur," Francis replied.

"I think we can suppress it," said the Foreign Minister with apparent calm. But then he added abruptly: "I hope it will take place whether we can or not—I am tired of this uncertainty and suspense."

"I realized to the full," Francis afterwards related, "the terrible strain under which this young man was living.... Having lost faith in his chief, Kerensky (a fact which I did not know at this time), he undoubtedly felt that the chief responsibility for saving his country from the terrible fate that threatened her rested upon his

---

[110] Gorky *et al.* (eds.), *The History of the Civil War in the U.S.S.R.*, Vol. II: *The Great Proletarian Revolution* (Moscow, 1946), p. 218.

[111] Chamberlin, I, 310.

shoulders." He took his leave in a hopeful mood and directed his driver to go past the soldiers. They were called to attention and smartly returned the ambassador's salute. "I wanted to impress these men," says Francis, "with the fact that America and her Ambassador were back of the threatened Provisional Government."[112]

To judge from the following day's events, they were not sufficiently impressed to do battle on its behalf. Indeed, the whole Petrograd garrison showed a strange reluctance to fight, and only a pitiful remnant of junkers, Cossacks, and women soldiers remained to defend the Winter Palace, the last bastion of the Kerensky regime.

[112] Francis, pp. 178-79.

CHAPTER VII

The Allies and Bolshevism

LATE in the evening of November 6 and in the early morning hours of the seventh the Bolshevik offensive began in earnest. Detachments of the Red Guard seized the railroad stations, the bridges, the telephone and telegraph agencies, the post office, and the state bank. These strategic points were occupied without bloodshed, since little more than token resistance was offered—when it was offered at all. By daylight the capital was practically in the hands of the Bolsheviks. Only the Winter Palace, where Kerensky had spent an anxious and sleepless night, remained to be taken; and it too could have been captured with ease had not the government's strength been grossly overestimated. Kerensky expected reinforcements momentarily, for the promises had been many, but none ever materialized. The Cossack troops, as distinct from their officers, chose to remain neutral; yet they were invariably in the act of "saddling their horses" whenever an inquiry was directed as to their whereabouts.[1]

About ten o'clock, when it became apparent that the Cossacks would continue to saddle their horses and that no help was forthcoming, Kerensky decided to go to the front in search of loyal troops. This was by now a risky enterprise because Red Guard patrols controlled the streets and the government automobiles had been put out of commission during the night. One of Kerensky's adjutants asked for the use of a car belonging to Sheldon White-

[1] Kerensky, *The Catastrophe*, pp. 332-34.

house, the secretary of the American embassy, which, in addition to furnishing the necessary means of locomotion, carried a near guarantee of unmolested passage in the form of an American flag. Whitehouse drove to military headquarters, across the street from the Winter Palace, to verify the adjutant's story. Kerensky confirmed his need for the vehicle, and after some hesitation, Whitehouse decided that since it had been "commandeered" anyway, there was no point in objecting too strenuously. He did ask that the flag be removed but soothed his conscience by registering a "protest" when his proposal was declined. Kerensky asked him to request Francis not to recognize the Soviet government and said he expected to return within five days with enough troops to put down the insurrection. Whitehouse left for the embassy to report the affair, while Kerensky and a few officers made good their escape. The ambassador approved of his secretary's action, but fearing that news of the incident might leak out, gave orders to his staff not to mention Kerensky's unorthodox method of departure to anyone.[2]

In the afternoon the Pre-Parliament was dissolved, and Lenin made his first public appearance before a meeting of the Petrograd Soviet. One of the immediate tasks of the Workers' and Peasants' Revolution, he said, was to put an end to the war, which could best be accomplished by the overthrow of capitalism. "A just and immediate offer of peace by us to the international democracy will find everywhere a warm response among the international proletariat masses," Lenin predicted.[3] The Russian Revolution was to him chiefly significant as the opening stage of the world revolution, but he was to discover that the proletariat of the West was not as class-conscious as Marxist theory had assumed.

The blockade of the Winter Palace was tightened as the revolutionaries waited for the arrival of the Kronstadt sailors before attempting to seize it by force. The morale of the defenders was very low; a part of the garrison deserted early in the evening, and

[2] Francis to Lansing, Nov. 20, 1917, Lansing Papers, Library of Congress; Francis, pp. 179-80; Kerensky's version of his escape in *The Catastrophe*, pp. 336-38, is apparently not reliable. The only new evidence (Gorky *et al.*, II, 258) supports Francis's account. See also Trotsky, *History of the Russian Revolution*, III, 245-46.

[3] Golder, pp. 618-19.

few of the remaining soldiers were concerned enough with the government's fate to wish to die for it. At nine o'clock a blank shot from the cruiser *Aurora* inaugurated a wild fusillade of rifle and machine-gun fire which lasted about an hour. Later, shells from the Fortress of Peter and Paul were fired intermittently, and though only two hit the palace, their effect upon the morale of the beseiged troops more than compensated for the insignificance of the material damage. By midnight a large number of sailors and Red Guards had succeeded in infiltrating the huge building. At first they were successfully disarmed, but as more and more poured through the numerous entrances, the defenders were gradually overwhelmed. Neither side appeared anxious for bloodshed, and by 2 A.M. the capture of the palace had been completed at a cost of six fatalities on the Bolshevik side and evidently none at all in government ranks. The ministers were marched across the bridge through hostile crowds and imprisoned in the Fortress of Peter and Paul. Their period of confinement was a short one; within a few days most of them were released, for the Revolution was as yet tolerant of its enemies.

Ill-founded rumors of killing, looting, and rape gained wide credence in the Allied embassies and other conservative circles. To save the captured women's battalion from a supposed "fate worse than death," General Knox was prevailed upon by the agitated Lady Buchanan to beard the Bolsheviks in their lair. He took the ambassador's car and went to Smolny Institute, once a fashionable ladies' finishing school, where the party maintained its headquarters, and demanded of the secretary of the Military Revolutionary Committee the immediate release of the women soldiers. After some initial procrastination, an order to that effect was issued and promptly carried out.[4] This was the first contact between an Allied official and the new Soviet power, and it was to be the last for some time to come.

Shortly before the fall of the Winter Palace, the second All-Russian Congress of Soviets had convened at Smolny. The first session had been notable mainly for the walkout of the Mensheviks

---

[4] Knox, II, 712-13.

and Socialist Revolutionaries, who withdrew to the city Duma and organized an abortive protest march to the beseiged Winter Palace. At the second session, on November 8, Lenin rose, and after a prolonged ovation, read two historic decrees, one on peace and one on the distribution of the land. The first proposed "to all warring peoples and their governments [that they] begin immediately negotiations for a just and democratic peace," with an armistice to begin at once and to last for a period of at least three months. In its emphasis on a just peace the language was reminiscent of that used in previous government pronouncements under moderate socialist auspices. But in the promise to begin publication of all the secret treaties to which Russia had been a party and the declaration that they were now annulled, a striking change in foreign policy was noticeable. New too was the distinction implied between the people and their governments: "While addressing this proposal of peace to all the governments and peoples of all the warring countries, the Provisional Workers' and Peasants' Government of Russia appeals also in particular to the classconscious workers of the three most forward nations of the world and the largest States participating in the present war—England, France, and Germany."[5] Despite the hostility to capitalism and capitalist governments apparent in the proclamation, the over-all tone was moderate and even conciliatory, probably in the hope that some or all of the belligerents would reply in a friendly spirit. If such was the reason, the Bolsheviks were doomed to disappointment, for neither the Allies nor the Central Powers deigned to reply.

The peace resolution was given overwhelming approval, as was the following decree, which abolished all private ownership of land and transferred the estates of the landlords and the Church to local land committees for distribution to the peasants. Likewise approved was the new governing body, the Soviet of People's Commissars, of which Lenin was President and Trotsky the Commissar of Foreign Affairs. The ease with which the new regime was established in Petrograd manifestly did not mean that Bolshevik authority was automatically established in the rest of the

[5] Cumming and Pettit, pp. 41-44.

country. In Moscow the transition was made only after a week of sanguinary fighting; in more remote areas the period required was even longer, though in few cases did the anti-Bolshevik forces put up as strong a resistance as they did in Moscow. Kerensky, who had gone to Pskov in his quest for loyal troops, succeeded in enlisting the support of a small group of about seven hundred Cossacks under General Peter Krasnov. This tiny force marched on Petrograd with the expectation of securing additional aid along the way. But no reinforcements appeared, and on the twelfth the Cossacks were forced to retreat before a much larger contingent of Red troops massed outside the city limits of the capital. As on previous occasions, the already low morale of the counterrevolutionary soldiers was further undermined by propagandists who slipped in among them and induced a large proportion to desert. An armistice was arranged on the fourteenth, Krasnov was arrested, and Kerensky fled in the disguise of a sailor. He later managed to escape to England with the help of Bruce Lockhart, the special emissary of Lloyd George in Russia.[6] Kerensky's naval aide managed to slip back into Petrograd on the sixteenth and saw the American ambassador at Kerensky's instructions. He gave an account of Kerensky's defeat and maintained that both Krasnov and Kerensky were of the belief that the Bolshevik army was commanded by German officers, apparently because of the "German tactics" it used. Francis was unable to help the aide in his request to escape to the United States, and he was arrested shortly afterward.[7]

With the collapse of Kerensky's futile enterprise, the Soviet regime faced no serious internal threat for several months, and by giving peace to the soldiers, land to the peasants, and the factories to the workers, the Bolsheviks placed their authority on a firm foundation of mass support. In the Allied countries the momentous events of November 7, which for the first time in history brought into being a government avowedly based on the principles of Marxian socialism, were greeted with horror and dismay but with little comprehension of the magnitude of the upheaval. The

[6] Lockhart, pp. 275-76.
[7] Francis to Lansing, Nov. 20, 1917, Lansing Papers.

initial shock was tempered by the widespread opinion that the Bolshevik victory was but a freakish happenstance which would be remedied when "reason" and "sanity" reasserted their rightful heritage in the affairs of man. With a predictable unanimity, the new revolution was denounced by the press as furiously as the preceding revolution had been enthusiastically praised. The conservative organs cited the fall of the Provisional Government as an object lesson in the failure of temporizing methods. The London *Times* characteristically blamed Kerensky and claimed that the latest developments in Russia were no surprise: "When constitutional authority is palpably incapable of backing words by deeds, when anarchy is allowed to increase daily, when arms are recklessly given to the mob, then the end cannot be far off." Inaccurately, and with anti-Semitic overtones, the Bolsheviks were described as "fanatics and anarchists," whose leader, Lenin, and "several of his confederates are adventurers of German-Jewish blood and in German pay, whose sole object is to exploit the ignorant masses in the interests of their own employers in Berlin."[8] The influential *Saturday Review*, to which Kerensky and Lenin were equally abhorrent, traced the Revolution to "international Socialism" and the "cabals of Geneva and Stockholm" and warned its readers that England must "never be led away by the demagogue-doctors who are poisoning Europe."[9] To the London *Daily Telegraph* Lenin and his cohorts were "architects of ruin," a party of "hare-brained visionaries" who have "set up by violence a thing [called] . . . a government, which nobody dreams of obeying save at the rifle's mouth." But a consequence of these proceedings may be "the long delayed drawing together of the sane and patriotic elements of the nation and the army for the purpose of putting an end to the chaos in which such things are possible."[10] A few journals, of which the London *Nation* was one of the best representatives, managed to give a more coherent interpretation of the Revolution. "The real cause of the Leninite rising," it maintained, "was the Western veto on the Stockholm conference and the postponement of the Allied conference on war aims which Russia proposed last May." "The

---

[8] Nov. 9 and 23, 1917.   [9] CXXIV (Nov. 17, 1917), 385-86.
[10] Nov. 9 and 19, 1917.

practical elimination of Russia from the alliance will be the penalty for our lack of sympathy and statesmanship," concluded the *Nation*.[11]

The French press was, of course, rabidly anti-Bolshevik, and the opinion of the *Journal des débats* that "all the people who form the scum of the Russian Revolution have triumphed" was the consensus of the Parisian dailies.[12] *Excelsior* called for the use of "iron and fire" against the usurpers but confidently asserted at the same time that the affair was already in the process of liquidation and was only a "passing incident."[13] *Victoire* warned that "these unfortunate creatures may sign an armistice with Germany and dishonor their country by abandoning the Allies in the midst of the struggle,"[14] and the editor of the *Revue* somberly declared that this new outburst of "Russian anarchy" had "profoundly surprised all the stubborn warning of common sense and the logic of History."[15] The new Russian ambassador to France, Basil Maklakov, a replacement for the old tsarist diplomat, Alexander Izvolsky, began his career rather inauspiciously by arriving in Paris on the very morning of the Bolshevik Revolution. Like almost every other person of middle-class environment, he expressed the view that the success of the Bolsheviks would be momentary only, isolated as they were in Petrograd. "The abscess has burst," he declared, and suggested a "radical surgical operation" as the proper cure for Russia.[16]

American public opinion, in so far as it was reflected in the press, showed no departure from the uniform hostility of the Allies toward the new revolution. The New York *Times*, like its London namesake, placed a major part of the blame on Kerensky's shoulders for compromising with "anarchy." "It seems probable," said the *Times*, that Russia "is aroused at last; and not until she is aroused can the forces of sanity be listened to."[17] "God knows the Bolsheviki are as dangerous to organized government as are the Hohen-

[11] XXII (Nov. 17, 1917), 230.   [12] Nov. 10, 1917.
[13] Nov. 13, 1917.
[14] Quoted in the New York *Times*, Nov. 10, 1917.
[15] CXXII (1918), 1.
[16] New York *Times*, Nov. 10, 1917; *Journal des débats*, Nov. 10, 1917.
[17] Nov. 9 and 13, 1917.

zollerns and Hapsburgs, and probably more so," exclaimed the Houston *Chronicle,* with pious horror. "We must not only undermine the idea of the divine right of kings, but we must also repress the mob."[18] "In all probability," said the weekly *Independent,* "German intrigue was a large factor in promoting the pacifist coup d'état which has thrown Russia into confusion."[19] The enraged New York *Russkoe Slovo* [*Russian Word*] anathematized the Bolsheviks for their "high treason," declaring that a "handful of madmen and fanatics" could not seize a whole country. It predicted that the Russian people would refuse to follow "mad Petrograd," where the bloody scenes of the Paris Commune of 1871 would be re-enacted. "But this Commune of our days," the *Russkoe Slovo* warned in anticipation, "will be shattered to splinters by cannon and machine guns."[20]

The Revolution found Ambassador Bakhmetev on a speaking tour, attempting to bolster the Provisional Government's prestige in the eyes of the American people. Only the day before he had told a Memphis audience that his countrymen were "heart and soul with the Kerensky government" and would "fight to the end" with the Allies. But the ambassador's optimism was not to be ruffled by contradictory evidence, and he confidently asserted that the "intent and spirit of Russia as a whole can in no way be judged by the news from Petrograd."[21] Numerous unofficial "authorities," such as professors, bankers, and visiting Russians, were as one in maintaining that Bolshevik supremacy was only temporary and that Russia would remain in the war. Perhaps a more accurate barometer of the real significance of the news to the Allied cause was the New York Stock Exchange, where leading stocks dropped from four to eleven points in a wild hour of trading and Russian bonds and exchange rates suffered a similar decline.[22] President Wilson departed briefly from his customary policy of silence on the internal troubles of his allies to take an indirect slap at the Bolsheviks in a speech before the American Federation of Labor

[18] Quoted in the *Literary Digest,* LV (Dec. 8, 1917), 16.
[19] XCII (Nov. 17, 1917), 313.
[20] Quoted in the *Literary Digest,* LV (Nov. 17, 1917), 9.
[21] New York *Tribune,* Nov. 9, 1917.
[22] New York *Times,* Nov. 9, 1917.

convention in Buffalo on the twelfth, in which he equated the misguided persons who remained apathetic toward the German menace with the "fatuous . . . dreamers of Russia."[23]   On the same day a correspondent in Washington reported that government and diplomatic circles were predicting the complete overthrow of the Bolsheviks and were debating whether the new leader would be Kerensky, Kornilov, or some more obscure figure.[24]

A majority of the newspapers in all the Allied countries featured rumor and second- or third-hand reports from Stockholm and Copenhagen, no matter how fantastic, in preference to more accurate but suspect accounts from Petrograd. Kerensky himself was variously reported to be defeated, victorious, a suicide victim, and concluding a compromise truce, all within the space of a few days, while many other prominent Russian politicians and generals received their brief hour of glory in the headlines.[25]   Official statements were few, though the American State Department and the Russian embassy remained outwardly confident at all times. Only on the seventeenth were doubts expressed in Washington that Kerensky might not be successful, but the ultimate downfall of Lenin's government was held to be only a matter of time.[26]

This continued optimism was due in part to the unreliable dispatches of Ambassador Francis and the American minister to Sweden, Ira N. Morris, whose information was largely a compound of rumor and wishful thinking. Francis, though not the most conservative of the ambassadors, seems to have looked upon Bolshevism with particular abhorrence. Writing to inform the American consul at Moscow of events in the capital, he mentioned a report that a cabinet had been formed with Lenin and Trotsky at its head. "Disgusting!" he commented. "But I hope such effort will be made, as the more ridiculous the situation the sooner the remedy."[27]   The ambassador gave his staff strict orders to refrain from

[23] *Ibid.*, Nov. 13, 1917.   [24] *Ibid.*

[25] This curious treatment of Russian news was not, of course, confined to the period of the Bolshevik Revolution. For an analysis of the New York *Times* and its treatment of the news from Russia (March, 1917, to March, 1920), see Walter Lippmann and Charles Merz, "A Test of the News," *New Republic*, XXIII (Aug. 4, 1920), 1-42 (special supplement).

[26] New York *Times*, Nov. 18, 1917.   [27] Francis, pp. 186-87.

any act which might be construed as recognition of the new government and expressed his displeasure when told that the Allied military attachés had requested protection for the embassies from the commander of the Petrograd military district.[28] Both orally and in writing Francis warned General Judson against any contact with the "Bolshevik officials who are attempting to administer affairs from Smolny Institute."[29] There was no possibility of Allied recognition of the Soviet regime, though Trotsky, as the new Foreign Minister, was anxious to be friendly and asked the Provisional Government's protocol expert whether he ought to call on the ambassadors first or whether they should call on him. When told that a new minister should inform them of his assumption of office by letter, he replied that while such a procedure may have been all right under the old regime, it was not suited to present conditions.[30] One newspaper reported that Trotsky had called on Buchanan and was turned away at the door, but he made no overtures until later in the month—and then only by letter. Trotsky's conception of diplomacy was not at first clearly distinguished in his mind from revolutionary agitation. When asked by a comrade what kind of work he would do, he replied, "I will issue a few revolutionary proclamations to the peoples of the world and then shut up shop."[31] The retort was purposely exaggerated but indicative of the mood of the Soviet leaders, impatient of custom and routine in the face of what they believed to be the opening stage of world revolution.

The difficulties Trotsky encountered in taking over the foreign ministry were similar to those of his colleagues. The old bureaucracy was uniformly hostile to its new masters. Only among the lower ranks of state employees did the Bolsheviks find sympathizers or at least persons who were unwilling to join the strike of officials and white-collar employees. Offices and desks were found locked and the keys withheld. Money for current expenses had to be obtained from the state bank practically at the point of

[28] Ibid., p. 183.
[29] Francis to Judson, Nov. 20, 1917, Lansing Papers.
[30] G. Buchanan, II, 210.
[31] Trotsky, My Life, p. 341.

the bayonet. When Trotsky entered the Foreign Office and ordered the peace decree translated into foreign languages, six hundred employes walked out. His assistant, Michael Uritsky, was literally thrown out of the archives when he tried to obtain the secret treaties. When they had finally been secured, Trotsky promised immediate publication. The documents are "more cynical in their provisions than we had supposed," he announced.[32] The first installment was printed on November 23 in *Izvestia,* which had become the official government organ. In an introductory statement Trotsky declared secret diplomacy to be a "necessary weapon in the hands of the propertied minority . . . compelled to deceive the majority in order to make the latter serve its interests," and its abolition the "first essential of an honorable, popular, and really democratic foreign policy."[33] "In revealing to the whole world the work of the governing classes as it is expressed in the secret documents of diplomacy," the statement concluded, "we offer to the workers the slogan which will always form the basis of our foreign policy: 'Proletarians of all countries, unite!' "[34] Publication continued in *Izvestia* and *Pravda* over a period of several months, but except for short summaries and excerpts in some of the big city dailies, only the Manchester *Guardian* and the New York *Evening Post* of the Allied press printed these significant documents in full. Many papers ignored them altogether, some hinted at forgery, and others minimized the importance of the disclosures; a few, however, such as the New York *Times,* went so far as to accuse the Bolsheviks of "an act of dishonor" in making them public, although the Allies had been caught red-handed, so to speak.[35]

Meanwhile the Bolshevik peace decree had not been allowed to lapse by default. On the twenty-first the Soviet government authorized fraternization with the enemy on all fronts and ordered the commander-in-chief, General Nicholas Dukhonin, to contact the "military authorities of the enemy armies with the proposal

---

[32] Judah L. Magnes, *Russia and Germany at Brest-Litovsk* (New York, 1919), p. 12.

[33] Bunyan and Fisher, pp. 243-44.   [34] *Ibid.*

[35] Nov. 25, 1917.

of an immediate cessation of hostilities for the purpose of starting peace negotiations."[36] On the same day Trotsky officially informed the Allied ambassadors of the existence of the new government and called their attention to the peace decree, which was to be considered as a "formal offer for an armistice on all fronts and an immediate opening of peace negotiations." He politely assured each ambassador of the "profound respect" in which the people of his country were regarded by the Soviet government but added a good deal less politely that they were "as eager for peace as are all the other peoples exhausted and bled by this unparalleled slaughter."[37] The neutral representatives were circularized the next day and urged to bring the armistice proposal to the attention of the enemy governments. "The laboring masses of neutral countries," said Trotsky, "are suffering the greatest misfortunes as the result of that criminal butchery which, if it should not be ended, threatens to draw into its whirlpool the few peoples still outside of the war."[38]

The Allied ambassadors met to consider the note and decided unanimously to take no notice of it. Each ambassador agreed to request his government to make no reply because the "pretended government" had been "established by force" and was "not recognized by the Russian people."[39] Lord Cecil, as spokesman for the British government, declared that the action "taken by the extremists in Petrograd . . . if approved and adopted by the Russian nation would put them practically outside the pale of the ordinary councils of Europe" but that he did not believe "the Russian people will confirm this action or approve a proclamation . . . to open all along the line peace negotiations with the enemy across the trenches."[40]

At Russian military headquarters in Mogilev General Dukhonin gave no indication that he had received instructions to make overtures to the enemy for an armistice. When reached by direct wire on the twenty-second, he replied evasively to all questions

[36] Bunyan and Fisher, p. 233.   [37] Ibid., pp. 243-44.
[38] Cumming and Pettit, pp. 45-46.
[39] Francis to Lansing, Nov. 22, 1917, Foreign Relations, I, 245.
[40] Magnes, p. 14.

but finally admitted his unwillingness to obey orders. Only a government "supported by the army and the country can have sufficient weight to impress the enemy," he protested. The general was promptly informed of his dismissal for "refusing to carry out the orders of the government and for pursuing a course that will bring incredible misery to the toilers of all countries." He was told to remain at his post until relieved by the new commander-in-chief, Ensign Nicholas Krylenko, a veteran Bolshevik propagandist.[41] Lenin and Krylenko immediately issued a proclamation to the soldiers explaining the circumstances of the change and authorizing the regiments at the front to elect representatives for the purpose of obtaining an armistice. As if foreseeing trouble for Dukhonin, the troops were cautioned by indirection against excesses: "You will not permit counter-revolutionary generals to frustrate the great cause of peace. You will surround them with guards, so as to avoid lynchings unworthy of revolutionary armies and to prevent these generals from escaping the judgment that is in store for them."[42]

Krylenko started for headquarters on the twenty-third, proceeding at a leisurely pace in order to remove untrustworthy generals and to consolidate the Bolshevik regime in the area of the front. Dukhonin replied with vigorous counterproclamations, but aside from the open support of the Allied military and diplomatic representatives, his position was isolated and precarious. The chiefs of the numerous Allied military missions accredited to headquarters (excluding the United States) sent him a formal note on the twenty-third protesting the proposed armistice and calling attention to the treaty of September 5, 1914, by which the Allied Powers had agreed never to make a separate peace. The message warned in conclusion that any violation of that treaty would "entail the gravest consequences."[43] By this precipitate step the Allies not only made a direct appeal over the heads of the *de facto* rulers but also made a clear and unmistakable threat, which was generally interpreted to mean that Japan would be called upon to attack Russia from the rear. Buchanan, whose anti-Bolshevism

[41] Bunyan and Fisher, pp. 233-35.   [42] *Ibid.*, pp. 336-37.
[43] *Ibid.*, p. 245.

was secondary to his diplomatic sense, considered the step harmful and ill-advised. Washington, with no prior knowledge of the protest, was reported to have received the news with a "large grain of salt" because it was believed to be "part of the German game of propaganda being played for the purpose of throwing dust in the eyes of the outside world and stirring up trouble in Russia against the Allies."[44] Dukhonin had the note printed in leaflet form and widely distributed among the troops.

Trotsky swiftly countered this feeble effort at patriotic propaganda by issuing a fiery manifesto to all army units and local Soviets denouncing the Allied protest as a "flagrant interference in the domestic affairs of our country with the object of bringing about civil war." The soldiers were exhorted to continue their fight for an immediate armistice. "The peoples of Europe will not allow their imperialist governments to harm the Russian people who are guilty of no crime but the desire to have peace and to assert the brotherhood of man. Let us all know that the soldiers, workers, and peasants of Russia did not overthrow the governments of the Tsar and Kerensky just to become cannon fodder for the Allied imperialists."[45]

Trotsky's blast, though it helped to arouse the soldiers to burning resentment against those who would continue the war, had no appreciable effect upon the Allies or Dukhonin. On the twenty-fourth the chiefs of the Allied missions again addressed the supreme commander, asking him to "do everything possible to make clear by an appeal to all political parties, as well as the army, that honor and patriotism require them to make every effort to preserve and consolidate order and discipline on the front." Georges Clemenceau, who had become the new premier of France only the week before, wired the French military representative to inform Dukhonin that France refused to recognize the Soviet government and that the supreme command was expected to "categorically repudiate all criminal negotiations" and "hold the Russian army at the front facing the common enemy."[46] In a note to the Bolshevik military authorities General Judson, the American military attaché

[44] New York *Times*, Nov. 28, 1917.   [45] Bunyan and Fisher, pp. 245-46.
[46] *Ibid.*, pp. 247-48.

172 THE ALLIES AND THE RUSSIAN REVOLUTION

in Petrograd, quoted a report published in the United States that no more aid for Russia would be forthcoming until the "formation of a stable government" and warned that while no formal verification had been received, the report was undoubtedly accurate.[47] Although Colonel Thompson tried to soften the blow with the assurance that Red Cross supplies would continue as heretofore, *Izvestia,* reflecting the heightened tension of Russia's relations with the West, remarked in an ill-tempered editorial that the "North American plutocrats" seemed "ready to trade locomotives for the heads of Russian soldiers." "The Russian people are interested in having economic and political relations with the Allies, but they are not willing to pay for them with blood to the satisfaction of Clemenceau and the New York kings of war industry."[48] Judson hastened to reassure the Bolsheviks that his letter should not be construed to mean that the American government had expressed preference for the success of "any one political party or element over another." While the evidence indicates that "no important fraction of the Russian people desires an immediate separate peace or armistice," said Judson, Russia has a perfect right to "bring up the question of a general peace."[49]

Whatever propitiatory effects Judson's second communication may have had were quickly dissipated by two more notes addressed to Dukhonin, one by Judson's subordinate, Lieutenant Colonel Monroe Kerth, and the other by General Lavergne, the head of the French military mission at headquarters. Lavergne's message did little more than repeat Clemenceau's remarks; Kerth, acting under Francis's instructions, for the first time made the United States a party to the general Allied protest against the proposed armistice.[50] The objection had to be based on moral rather than legal grounds, however, for the United States had not been a participant in the 1914 treaty. In his answer to these additional protests, Trotsky declared that such a state of affairs could no longer be tolerated. "The Soviet government," he asserted, "cannot allow

[47] *Ibid.,* pp. 249-50.   [48] *Ibid.,* pp. 250-51.
[49] Cumming and Pettit, pp. 48-49.
[50] For the Kerth note, see *ibid.,* pp. 53-54; for Lavergne's, see Serge Oldenbourg (ed.), *Le Coup d'état bolcheviste* (Paris, 1929), p. 459.

Allied diplomatic and military agents for any purpose to interfere in the internal life of our country and attempt to fan civil wars. Further steps in the same direction will immediately provoke the most serious complications, the responsibility for which the Soviet of People's Commissars refuses beforehand to accept."[51]

These mutual recriminations in no way deterred the conclusion of an armistice which, without benefit of formal agreement, had already existed for some time. Contact with the Germans at the front was established on the twenty-sixth, and two days later the cease-fire order was announced officially. In separate notes to the ambassadors and the military attachés Trotsky again invited the Allies to take part in the preliminary deliberations scheduled to begin on December 2. Aside from these invitations sent in his capacity as Foreign Minister, Trotsky aimed a manifesto at the peoples of the belligerent countries in his capacity as revolutionary agitator. The armistice negotiations had been postponed for five days, he declared, in order to give the Allies another opportunity to join the discussions. So far their only reply had been a refusal to recognize the Soviet government. "The government of the victorious revolution stands in no need of recognition from the technicians of capitalist diplomacy, but we do ask the people: Does reactionary diplomacy express their thoughts and aspirations? Will they allow such diplomacy to pass by the great opportunity for peace offered by the Russian Revolution? . . . We want a general peace, but if the bourgeoisie of the Allied countries force us to conclude a separate peace, the responsibility will be theirs."[52]

The Allied governments could afford to remain silent, for the peoples of Europe, even if they had been as ripe for revolution as the Bolsheviks seemed to believe, knew little or nothing of these exhortatory proclamations. Only the British made any kind of reply to these repeated invitations. The embassy issued a statement in Petrograd claiming that the Allies had been "confronted by an accomplished fact" in the Bolshevik armistice negotiations and that the "ambassador of Great Britain cannot possibly reply to notes addressed to him by a government not recognized by his own gov-

[51] *Izvestia*, No. 229, Dec. 1, 1917.   [52] Bunyan and Fisher, pp. 258-59.

ernment." Furthermore, stated the embassy, "governments like that of Great Britain whose authority comes directly from the people, have no right to decide problems of such importance until they are definitely informed whether their intended decision will meet with the complete approval and support of their electors."[53] This answer was obviously an evasion of the real issue of whether or not the Allies would agree to join the peace discussions, and relations were only worsened by the exchange.

General Judson, largely upon his own initiative, tried to patch up the badly deteriorating diplomatic situation by visiting Trotsky at Smolny on December 1. Though there was perhaps an element of mutual distrust, the meeting was a friendly one. The general emphasized the unofficial character of the visit and stated that the "time for protests and threats against the Soviet power has passed, if there ever was such a time." The main subject of conversation centered on the armistice, and Trotsky agreed to co-operate in every way he could to prolong the negotiations and to keep the interests of the Allies in mind on such matters as the shifting of troops and the exchange of prisoners and supplies.[54] The interview, as the first of its kind between a Soviet leader and an Allied official, aroused wide attention in the press, both in Russia and abroad. Most of the comment in the latter was hostile because it seemed to imply partial recognition of the Bolsheviks, and the State Department was not slow to reprimand Judson, in a message to Francis, for breaking the prohibition against direct contact with the Soviet regime. Francis, though he had fully sanctioned Judson's visit in advance, quickly joined the other diplomatic and military representatives in voicing his condemnation and informed Washington that the step had been taken without his knowledge or approval.[55] The unfortunate Judson, one of the few Allied officials on the scene who did not allow the prevailing anti-Bolshevik animus to distort his judgment, was recalled within a few weeks.

[53] Cumming and Pettit, pp. 51-52.
[54] Judson's diary, especially for Nov. 30 and Dec. 1, 1917, Judson Papers; Judson to War Department, Dec. 1, 1917, Foreign Relations, I, 279; Trotsky, My Life, p. 345; Sisson, pp. 80-83.
[55] Francis to Lansing, Dec. 9, 1917, Foreign Relations, I, 294-95.

The improvement in relations which the Judson-Trotsky interview might have portended did not materialize. Even at the time Britain was involved in a dispute with Russia concerning two Bolsheviks, Peter Petrov and George Chicherin, who had been interned in London because of their propaganda work. Trotsky wished to make use of their talents in the Soviet Foreign Office, especially those of Chicherin, who had once been an official in the tsarist Foreign Office. Buchanan ignored a Soviet note requesting their release, and in retaliation it was announced that henceforth no British subject would be allowed to leave the country until the two prisoners had been allowed to return to Russia. Trotsky moreover threatened to arrest the ambassador for his alleged counterrevolutionary activity on behalf of certain "White" generals then organizing their forces in south Russia. Buchanan advised his government to relent in its stand. "There is, after all," he admitted, "something in Trotzky's argument that, if we claim the right to arrest Russians for making a pacifist propaganda in a country bent on continuing the war, he has an equal right to arrest British subjects who are conducting a war propaganda in a country bent on peace." London agreed to a compromise, and within a short time the Soviet decree was rescinded and the two Russians repatriated to their homeland.[56]

Powerless to stop the armistice with Germany and yet gravely worried by the prospective loss of a second front against the common enemy, the Allies floundered aimlessly amid a welter of conflicting testimony as to the best course to pursue in dealing with this perplexing semi-ally, whose rulers were regarded by many men of influence, both in and out of government, as far more dangerous to the traditional values of Western civilization than the German autocrats against whom the war was supposedly being waged. The one thing that all agreed upon was that Bolshevism was an evil thing and that an attitude of disapproval and nonrecognition of an evil government, even though a nominal ally, was morally correct and probably politically correct. But so long

[56] Captain Jacques Sadoul, *Notes sur la révolution bolchevique* (Paris, 1919), p. 124; G. Buchanan, II, 226-28 and 230-31; Trotsky, *My Life*, p. 348; Francis to Lansing, Nov. 30, 1917 (861.00/743½), National Archives.

as the separate peace did not become a reality, there continued to be doubt, disagreement, and confusion as to the political wisdom of this policy.

For a time the Allies appeared to believe that General Dukhonin was a force to be relied upon in resisting the Bolshevik peace plans. His usefulness in this capacity came to an abrupt end when he was deposed as supreme commander, and though he continued to appeal to the troops and the population in general with an array of forceful manifestoes, he was helpless to do anything more. Prominent Socialist Revolutionaries had gathered at Mogilev, sensing a possible center of resistance to Bolshevism, but soon returned to Petrograd in a state of disillusion. The Allied military missions joined the exodus, leaving for Kiev on December 1. Two days later Krylenko finally arrived and found that the local garrison had already mutinied. Feeling ran high against Dukhonin, particularly as the news of the escape of Kornilov and other generals had just been received. A frenzied mob of soldiers gathered in front of Krylenko's private railway coach, where the deposed commander had been confined. Against Krylenko's somewhat half-hearted attempt to save his prisoner, the mob pushed into the car and dragged the general out. He was beaten into unconsciousness and then dispatched beyond a doubt when a sailor fired two shots into his body.[57]

The conspicuous failure of the Allied military missions to prevent the Bolsheviks from concluding an armistice had caused Buchanan to recommend a drastic shift in tactics. He advised London on November 27 that it was no use trying to force an exhausted nation to fight against its will. "For us to hold to our pound of flesh and to insist on Russia fulfilling her obligations, under the 1914 Agreement, is to play Germany's game," he warned. "Every day that we keep Russia in the war against her will does but embitter her people against us."[58] The wisdom of this contention can now hardly be disputed. But at the time the "pound of flesh" approach had staunch adherents, firmly convinced that

[57] Bunyan and Fisher, pp. 267-68; Tyrkóva-Williams, pp. 310-12; Captain George A. Hill, Go Spy the Land (London, 1932), pp. 109-10.
[58] G. Buchanan, II, 225-26.

a resolute stand against Bolshevism and against a separate peace would rally the Russian people to the cause of patriotism and righteousness. To be against Bolshevism was equivalent to being against sin, and the right-thinking statesman would no more have raised his voice in dissent than he would have thought of praising opium dens or houses of ill-fame.

Buchanan's proposal arrived at a propitious time, for the long-awaited Allied conference, at which Kerensky had hoped to secure a revision of war aims, was scheduled to begin in Paris on the twenty-ninth. The next day Foreign Secretary Balfour read the ambassador's dispatch to the assembled representatives, but, aside from Balfour, only Colonel House of the United States seemed sympathetic. Clemenceau raised objections and Baron Sidney Sonnino, the Italian Foreign Minister, was even more outspokenly hostile. Maklakov, who still maintained his anachronistic status as the Russian ambassador to France—and continued to do so even after Trotsky had formally notified him of his dismissal for his part in the Paris deliberations—was called in for his opinion and sided with Clemenceau and Sonnino. He proposed a resolution to be sent to Russia declaring that the Allies would "proceed to a revision of war aims together with Russia, so soon as there shall be a Government aware of its duties to the country and defending the interests of the country and not of the enemy."[59] House, who considered Sonnino an "ultra-reactionary," was strongly in favor of a reconsideration of war aims but opposed tying it in with a statement which amounted to a deliberate insult to the Soviet government.

Not only had the events in Russia made a statement on war aims imperative, but a growing peace sentiment in Western Europe had to be placated. This had been brought into sharp focus on the opening day of the conference by the publication in the London *Daily Telegraph* of a letter from Lord Henry Landsdowne, an elder statesman of impeccably Conservative views, which suggested the possibility of a negotiated peace. House offered the

[59] Charles Seymour, *The Intimate Papers of Colonel House* (Boston and New York, 1928), III, 290.

conference a simple resolution to the effect that the Allies were not waging war for the purpose of aggression or indemnity. It met with little support, and Lloyd George managed to accomplish the difficult feat of combining the House and Maklakov resolutions into a single statement. Again the American delegate raised objections, and Sonnino then tried his hand at the task of drafting a suitable message. All the delegates approved it except House, who flatly stated that the United States would never sign a document so divergent from the progressive aims which Wilson had so often expressed in his public speeches. This effectively quashed the resolution, and it was finally agreed that each country should send a note at its own discretion, the substance of which should read that the Allies were willing to reconsider their war aims in conjunction with Russia as soon as she had a stable government with which they could act.[60]

The outcome of the conference, in so far as it concerned Russia, reflected that continued estrangement from the Western World which had begun so noticeably with the Bolshevik Revolution. House left for the United States more than ever convinced that a definite and liberal basis of peace would have to be formulated, and that if the Allies refused to take the initiative, America—technically still an "associated" power—would have to supply it. Wilson's famous "fourteen points" address later filled this gaping void in the moral armament of the democracies. But even then the President indicated that the problem was in his mind and that the "Russian question" was intimately bound up with it. "I cannot help thinking," he said in his message to Congress of December 4 calling for a declaration of war against Austria, "that if they [liberal war aims] had been made plain at the very outset the sympathy and enthusiasm of the Russian people might have been once for all enlisted on the side of the Allies, suspicion and distrust swept away and a real and lasting union of purpose effected.

[60] House to Wilson, Dec. 2, 1917, *ibid.*, pp. 284-85. For additional material on Russia and the conference, see Lloyd George, V, 108-9; *Foreign Relations (suppl. 2, 1917)*, I, 352-53; Poincaré, IX, 394-96; and the diary of Edward M. House, XII, 390 and 393-94 (Nov. 30 and Dec. 1, 1917), House Papers, Yale University Library.

Had they believed these things at the very moment of their revolution and had they been confirmed in that belief since, the sad reverses which have recently marked the progress of their affairs toward an ordered and stable government of free men might have been avoided."[61]

Representatives of that disordered and unstable government, which by Wilson's implication now controlled the destinies of the Russian people, were at the time he spoke engaged in making their government more stable, if not more orderly, by negotiating an armistice with the Central Powers in the town of Brest-Litovsk in Polish Russia, where the Germans had set up military headquarters for the Eastern Front after the retreating Russians had abandoned it in July, 1916. The period of negotiations at Brest, which did not bring peace to Russia until March, was a time of anxiety, frustration, and uncertainty for the horde of official and unofficial representatives of the Allied Powers in Petrograd. The former lived in a world apart in self-imposed isolation, disdainful of the Soviet government and forbidden by orders from home even the slight contact which routine diplomatic business required. This awkward situation was partially remedied by the use of unofficial agents who served as a link between Smolny and the embassies and who could be repudiated whenever the exigencies of diplomacy demanded a sacrificial offering.

The chief emissaries in this *sub rosa* contact were Raymond Robins for the United States, Bruce Lockhart for Britain, and Captain Jacques Sadoul for France. These men possessed initiative and open-mindedness, qualities which the ambassadors so obviously lacked, and if not uncritical of the Soviet regime, they were willing to accept the Revolution as an accomplished fact and to judge its progress with as much objectivity as could reasonably be mustered. Through frequent meetings with Lenin and Trotsky, they came to admire the idealism and tenacity of purpose of the two leaders, however harsh it became in practice, and unanimously rejected the facile doctrine that the Bolsheviks were in the pay of Germany or subservient to German policy. Trotsky was

[61] Baker and Dodd, V, 128-39.

"a fourkind son of a bitch, but the greatest Jew since Christ," said Robins. "If the German General Staff bought Trotsky, they bought a lemon."[62]

Sadoul had arrived in October with the French military mission headed by General Henri Niessel. A socialist and a good friend of Albert Thomas, he had known Trotsky during his residence in Paris and found a place with the mission upon Thomas's recommendation.[63] The Robins-Thompson partnership had broken up late in November when Thompson left Russia, increasingly disturbed by the blindness of Allied policy and with the feeling that while there was nothing that could be done about it in Petrograd, something might yet be accomplished in the Western capitals. He arrived in London too late to see Colonel House, but through the help of his friend, Thomas W. Lamont, a well-known New York financier, he met and talked to a number of high British officials, including the Prime Minister. Thompson argued that instead of treating Russia as a pariah nation, a sympathetic policy might induce her to co-operate with the Allies to the extent that she was still able. Opposition to the regime in power would only throw her into Germany's arms. "At present they are nobody's Bolsheviks," he told Lloyd George. "Don't let us let Germany make them her Bolsheviks. Let's make them our Bolsheviks." Lloyd George was greatly impressed by Thompson's advice and resolved to institute a change, the initial step of which involved sending a representative to Russia for the express purpose of establishing unofficial relations with the new government.[64]

Thompson left for the United States with the Prime Minister's request to tell Wilson of their talk and to try to get from him a concrete suggestion on the improvement of Allied-Russian relations. Thompson now had the comforting feeling that his advice was at last beginning to carry weight in Allied diplomatic circles and that a conference with the President would similarly affect American

[62] Lockhart, p. 222.

[63] General Niessel, Le Triomphe des bolcheviks et la paix de Brest-Litovsk (Paris, 1940), p. v.

[64] Statement of T. W. Lamont, June 4, 1932, Thompson Papers; Lamont to Wilson, Jan. 29, 1918, Wilson Papers; Hagedorn, p. 255.

policy.[65] His disillusion was rapid when he tried to obtain an interview at the White House. Wilson informed him indirectly that he did not care to speak to the kind of man who would spend a million dollars for political purposes. Though his efforts to influence Wilson did not cease, Thompson gradually came to be looked upon by conservatives as a Bolshevik apologist, so anxious was he to gain support and possible recognition of the Soviet government as the best means of forestalling a separate peace. The legend grew that Thompson's million had been spent on Bolshevik propaganda, and no amount of denials ever quite caught up with the original story.[66] In Russia, on the other hand, the Bolsheviks used the Thompson million as effective propaganda to discredit Breshkovskaya and her faction of Socialist Revolutionaries for taking money from an American capitalist. "And these political prostitutes who have been selling the Russian people . . . to the Allied purse," growled *Pravda,* "have dared to accuse the Bolsheviks of getting German money. Forsooth, one could not have sunk any lower. On the bottom of the stenching pit the traitors of Socialism are wrestling."[67]

Thompson's old headquarters in Petrograd were taken over by Edgar Sisson, whose arrival corresponded with Thompson's departure. At his disposal were two hundred and fifty thousand dollars for "educational" purposes, and he immediately set to work organizing a news service with branches in Petrograd and Moscow. Wilson's speech of December 4 was printed in a Russian translation, fifty thousand copies of which were posted on Petrograd billboards and three hundred thousand copies distributed as handbills.[68] In his work Sisson was thrown with Robins a great deal until their sharp disagreement on Russia and Bolshevism caused a rupture in their friendly relations.

[65] An eight-page "Memorandum of the Present Situation in Russia" accompanied Thompson's letter to Wilson, Jan. 3, 1918, Wilson Papers; copies are also in the Thompson and Polk Papers.

[66] Hagedorn, pp. 258-67.

[67] Quoted in Sisson, p. 47.

[68] Sisson, pp. 109-10 and 141-42; George Creel, *How We Advertised America* (New York, 1920), pp. 375-77.

Sisson was consistently hostile in his attitude toward the Soviet regime, while Robins, like Thompson, became convinced that the Allies could never hope to restore the Eastern Front by opposing those who for good or ill were ruling Russia. He realized that the Bolsheviks were securely in power for the present and that glib predictions of their early overthrow were "bunk."[69] Furthermore, the Red Cross had supplies which might be confiscated as counterrevolutionary property unless the sympathy of the new regime could be obtained. In a conciliatory spirit Robins called on Trotsky soon after the November Revolution about the future status of the Red Cross. Kerensky supporters were distinctly unwelcome in Trotsky's office, but Robins managed to placate him by speaking of the Provisional Government as a corpse—and the thing to do with a corpse, he said, was "to bury it, not to sit up with it."

Trotsky showed his willingness to co-operate by personally authorizing the transmission of thirty-two freight cars of supplies from Petrograd to the Red Cross in Romania. Later, upon Robins's request, he saw to it that four hundred thousand cans of condensed milk were moved from Murmansk to Petrograd for relief work and confiscated fifty-four cars of contraband raw materials bound for Finland, where they would have reached Germany by way of Sweden.[70] This was proof enough for Robins that the Soviet leaders were not German henchmen. He remained on friendly terms with both Lenin and Trotsky and proved to be such a valuable source of information to Francis that the ambassador, despite his pronounced antipathy toward Bolshevism, successfully requested the State Department to withdraw its order against Robins's visits to Smolny.[71]

Lockhart, the third member of the unofficial Allied triumvirate, arrived on the scene much later than Sadoul and Robins. He had served at the British consulate in Moscow since 1912 and had been recalled to England in the fall of 1917, ostensibly for reasons of health but actually to avoid scandal over an indiscreet

[69] *Bolshevik Propaganda,* p. 783; Hagedorn, p. 242.
[70] Hard, pp. 55-62.
[71] Francis to Lansing, Dec. 27, 1917, Cumming and Pettit, p. 60.

extramarital affair. Perhaps the only man in England with diplomatic experience and a first-hand knowledge of recent Russian events, Lockhart was the logical choice to fill the position of special agent to Russia which Lloyd George, after his talk with Thompson, had decided to create. He met many persons of social and political importance and did his best to combat the firmly rooted conviction that the Soviet leaders were in German pay. His success on that score was indifferent, and though he got a more favorable response to his argument that it was madness not to establish some contact with the men who, whatever their political views, were now controlling Russia, the prevailing sentiment was one of hatred toward Bolshevism and fear of its effect upon England.[72] Young and self-confident, perhaps even brash at times, Lockhart favorably impressed Lloyd George with his ability at their first meeting and was informed of his selection on the spot. His instructions—other than to establish unofficial relations with the Bolsheviks—were of the vaguest. If the Soviet leaders were prepared to receive Lockhart on this basis, the British government promised to grant a similar concession to Maxim Litvinov, only recently appointed Russian ambassador to England. Through an intermediary Lockhart arranged a meeting with Litvinov, who, unable to obtain a passport to Russia after the March Revolution, had remained in England. Litvinov wrote a letter of introduction to Trotsky in which Lockhart was pronounced a "thoroughly honest man who understands our position and sympathises with us" and whose sojourn in Russia should be "useful from the point of view of our interests."[73]

Lockhart and his small entourage did not arrive in Petrograd until late in January. During the long and difficult journey he had an opportunity to talk briefly to Buchanan, Knox, and other embassy officials who crossed his path on their way back to England. Because of the ambassador's ill health and the arrival of the new mission, with a consequent overlapping of authority, the British government had recalled most of its Petrograd staff and left the embassy in the hands of a chargé d'affaires.

[72] Lockhart, p. 195.   [73] Ibid., pp. 197-202.

The intervening weeks between the beginning of peace negotiations and the departure of Buchanan were marred by several incidents illustrative of the poor state of relations between Russia and the West. One of the most prominent—though undeservedly so—was the Kalpashnikov affair, in which a Russian officer by that name in the service of the American Red Cross was imprisoned for alleged dealings with General Alexis Kaledin and his White army in south Russia. By a strange quirk of fate Kalpashnikov had been in the United States earlier in the year on a mission for the Russian Red Cross to obtain some ambulances and on his return home had been asked to act as interpreter in questioning Trotsky, then a British prisoner in Halifax.[74] Kalpashnikov had complied, and so he was well remembered, probably none too kindly, by the Red leader for his part in the unpleasant episode. The ambulances had reached Petrograd too late to be of use on the front and were to be shipped, together with some trucks and other supplies to Jassy, Romania, for use there. Early in December an order had reached the American embassy from Colonel Henry Anderson, the head of the Red Cross mission in Romania, to send the vehicles instead to Rostov, the capital of the Don Cossack territory. Francis co-operated with Kalpashnikov in carrying out the directive, but Robins suspected that the shipment's destination might be Kaledin's headquarters, also in Rostov. Anderson's motive was apparently to keep the material from falling into German hands, for Romania, which had fared no better than Russia in the war, was also considering a separate peace. However suspicious the circumstances may have appeared to the Bolsheviks, the Rostov order was countermanded a short time later and the shipment again directed to Jassy. Thus on this evidence alone, Anderson seems to have been innocent of any connection with Kaledin. Kalpashnikov, whose motives were more open to suspicion, was arrested before his preparations had been completed and incarcerated in the Peter and Paul Fortress.

[74] See above, pp. 40-41 for Trotsky's Halifax experience. The Kalpashnikov affair is discussed in Sisson, pp. 144-66; Hard, pp. 111-20; correspondence in *Foreign Relations*, I, 321-22 and 326-30; and Andrew Kalpashnikov, *A Prisoner of Trotsky's* (Garden City, N. Y., 1920) (with a foreword by Francis).

Robins went to Smolny to try to explain matters and found that he himself was suspected of being a party to the plot along with Anderson and Francis. But as American citizens of considerable importance, it would have been inadvisable to arrest them, particularly on the flimsy evidence at hand. Fortunately for Robins and his unsullied reputation at Smolny, one of the documents found on Kalpashnikov was a letter to Anderson complaining of Robins's unco-operative attitude, and this soon restored him to favor. Trotsky made the most of the affair—much more, in fact, than it was worth—by attacking Francis for his complicity in the supposed plot. "This Sir Francis will have to break his golden silence which has remained unbroken since the Revolution," he stormed in a speech to Bolshevik partisans at the Alexandrovsky Theater. The Allied ambassadors would have to understand "that from the moment that they interfere in our internal strife they cease to be diplomatic representatives—they are private counterrevolutionist adventurers and the heavy hand of the Revolution will fall upon their heads!" Francis issued a detailed refutation of the charges, and although it did not appear to convince the Soviet government, the matter was allowed to rest. Kalpashnikov, as a Russian citizen, bore the brunt of official anger and remained in prison. In May he was released, probably because of lack of evidence, and the following September managed to leave the country with false papers.

The Bolsheviks judged correctly the Allied interest in Kaledin, an interest which was to develop more fully later into open support of numerous White armies, some of them then in the process of formation on Russian territory, but unfortunately the Kalpashnikov affair was a poor choice for purposes of exploitation. The attitude of the United States, less hostile, on the whole, toward the Soviet regime than that of Britain or France, was officially one of non-recognition but "hands off." American representatives in Russia, it was "authoritatively stated" in Washington on December 26, would "carefully avoid any interference with the internal politics of the country" and "permit the Russian people themselves to work out their own salvation, free from any American interference."[75] Yet two weeks earlier Lansing had cabled the American ambassador in London to consult "the proper British and French authorities" about a loan to Kaledin and cautioned him with the "necessity of acting expeditiously and impressing those with whom you talk of the importance of avoiding it being known that the United States is considering showing sympathy for the Kaledine movement, much less of providing financial assistance."[76] Wilson, in a glaring example of the dichotomy of his thought regarding the Russian problem, gave his "entire approval" to this message on behalf of Kaledin.[77] But the general's career came to an abrupt end in February when the hopelessness of his military position caused him to commit suicide. Though the reliance placed upon him by Lansing and other Allied leaders proved to be illusory, other White leaders were ready and eager to step into the breach of the anti-Bolshevik movement, particularly if they could rely upon moral and material assistance from abroad.

Another *cause célèbre* in Allied-Russian relations occurred only a few weeks after the Kalpashnikov incident and was in fact part of an undeclared small-scale war between Russia and Romania. This was the Diamandi affair, involving the arrest of the Romanian minister, Constantine Diamandi, in reprisal for the hostile treatment and in some cases, arrest, of Russian troops by Romania.[78] A large force of Russians on the southwestern front had attempted to retreat through Romanian territory after the armistice with Germany. Hemmed in between the unfriendly Romanians and the Austrians, and faced with the growing threat of the Ukrainian separatist movement organized around the Central Rada (assembly) at Kiev, the Russians, forced to live off the country or starve, were continually involved in provocative incidents with their former comrades-in-arms. The imprisonment of Diamandi on January

[75] New York *Times,* Dec. 27, 1917.
[76] Lansing to Page, Dec. 13, 1917, *Lansing Papers,* II, 346.
[77] *Lansing Papers,* II, 345 n.
[78] For this affair, see the Judson Papers, esp. Judson's diary, Jan. 13-16, 1918; Sisson, pp. 221-32; Francis, pp. 216-21; Noulens, I, 182-93; Anet, III, 226-34; correspondence in *Foreign Relations,* I, 477-82 and II, 707-22; William J. Oudendyk, *Ways and By-Ways in Diplomacy* (London, 1939), pp. 254-56; and Jules Destrée, *Les Fondeurs de neige* (Brussels and Paris, 1920), pp. 240-49.

13 was a retaliatory measure which aroused the whole diplomatic corps in Petrograd to immediate protest. Francis, the dean of the corps following the departure of Buchanan, led his colleagues of the Allied and neutral embassies—nineteen strong—to Smolny the next day for a prearranged meeting with Lenin. He received them courteously, listened quietly to the collective protest which the American ambassador read, and then proposed that the matter be discussed. Francis curtly replied that there could be no discussion when the principle of diplomatic immunity was involved. Notwithstanding the finality of his remark, the meeting continued for another hour as some of the other ambassadors proceeded to lecture Lenin on the iniquity of the deed and threatened to leave Russia unless Diamandi were released. Lenin pointed out that the niceties of international law did not concern him nearly so much as the fate of the Russian soldiers but promised to give his decision later that evening after a meeting of the Soviet of People's Commissars. The minister was given his freedom the next day, presumably after the question had been discussed at the meeting. *Pravda* incorrectly stated the same day, possibly as a face-saving gesture, that Francis had agreed to protest to Diamandi after his release about Romania's treatment of the Russian troops. This allegation naturally aroused the latter's resentment until Francis had a chance to deny the story. On the twenty-eighth Diamandi was given ten hours to leave the country, and the Romanian gold reserve, which had been shipped to Moscow for safe-keeping earlier in the war, was ordered to be "preserved as the property of the Rumanian people and kept inaccessible to the Rumanian oligarchy." The sum was probably confiscated as part payment for the loss of Bessarabia when it was officially annexed by Romania several months later.

In the long run, of course, these diplomatic incidents, unpleasant though they were, had no permanent ill-effects upon Allied-Russian relations; they were, rather, symptoms of a more serious malady which still plagues the relations of East and West. This root cause of conflict is regarded by many as Bolshevism (or Communism); to others, of contrary viewpoint, the cause is capitalism.

But the problem had lain dormant until the November Revolution suddenly institutionalized capitalism's hitherto unsuccessful rival as the official doctrine of a great national state. But even this fundamental difference did not inevitably mean friction. So long as the war lasted, the German menace officially superseded the Bolshevik menace, even though it did not do so in the minds of all the Allied leaders. And Bolshevik Russia, no matter how subversive to the established order, no doubt would have remained a somewhat suspect partner in the common struggle had its leaders chosen to remain at war. But under the circumstances peace was the logical and necessary choice. The Allies faced the problem of accepting it with good grace or of resisting it and thereby alienating the Russian people.

Despite divided counsels and often contradictory policies, the second course prevailed. The disastrous period of intervention followed and continued for more than two years, begun for the avowed purpose of opposing Germany but ending with no other excuse than that of eliminating Bolshevism. But that intervention was a calculated conspiracy of the capitalist world designed to crush economic heresy in its infancy is—certainly in its early stages—an oversimplification of Allied policy, based as it was upon day-to-day improvisation with no integrated and rational goal in view. The United States, certainly as powerful a capitalist country as either Britain or France, continuously lagged behind its more aggressively anti-Bolshevik partners, frequently an unwilling and obstreperous accomplice.

Russia's new rulers, world revolutionists first and Russian revolutionists second, attempted by every means in their power and with a fine sense of impartiality to undermine the capitalist order wherever it existed, and though their sanguine hopes were not to be realized, the virility of Bolshevik propaganda was quite enough justification to the interventionists—if they actually thought at all in terms of "justifying" what was assumed to be so righteous a cause—for an armed assault on the motherland whence this aggressive and subversive doctrine first sprang. Such, for example, was the unconscious reasoning of the New York *Times,* long before the intervention question had arisen, when it asserted that Russia had been ruined by "German socialism" and that both countries were breeding places of "foul contagions" like "socialism, anarchism, nihilism, and communism," which have spread to "free and well-governed nations where they have become a pest and a menace."[79]

Besides the Bolshevik ideological offensive, a Soviet decree of January 14 (ratified on February 3) repudiating the debts of the preceding regimes[80] brought home to men of substance, whether they suffered personal loss or not, the reality lurking behind what might otherwise have been regarded as "mere doctrine." The Allied and neutral ambassadors immediately issued a collective protest in which they reserved "the right to claim from the Russian Government at an opportune time damages for all loss which these decrees may cause their nationals."[81] The finance section of the Inter-Allied Council then meeting in London adopted a resolution declaring that Russia's obligations could not be repudiated "without shaking the very foundations of the law of nations."[82] *Pravda* confidently asserted that the decree would be a blow to the Allies no less severe than the German victories on the Western Front and that as soon as the French people discovered how they had been deceived into buying tsarist bonds the hour of punishment for the Clemenceaus and Poincarés would sound. "The petty bourgeois Frenchmen may pardon the millions of victims upon the battlefield, but he will not forgive his material ruin."[83] Other Bolshevik decrees, most of them concerning the nationalization of various kinds of property, were protested by the diplomatic corps, with the sole exception of Francis, who maintained that such decrees pertained to domestic affairs and should not be protested "in the form proposed."[84]

The question of intervention had arisen only a few weeks following the November Revolution. At the Allied conference in Paris Clemenceau had approached House on the feasibility of such

---

[79] Nov. 25, 1917.
[80] Bunyan and Fisher, pp. 602-3.
[81] *Foreign Relations,* III, 33.
[82] *Ibid.,* p. 34.
[83] Feb. 17, 1918, quoted in Noulens, I, 152.
[84] Francis, p. 297.

action, but nothing like a consistent policy emerged until the secret Anglo-French convention of December 23, 1917, in which Russia was divided into "spheres of influence."[85] Negotiated chiefly by Lord Milner and Clemenceau and signed at Paris, the agreement saw very little practical fulfilment until the end of the war but indicated the economic and political interests of the two countries even at this early date. Britain was allotted the Cossack territories, the Caucasus, Armenia, Georgia, and Kurdistan, while the French zone encompassed Bessarabia, the Ukraine, and the Crimea. Allied activity during the ensuing intervention conformed to this pattern laid down late in 1917 and confirms the authenticity of the agreement, which, so far as official publication is concerned, still remains a secret.

The Allied diplomats, even when they had become convinced of the usefulness of intervention, were baffled by the difficulties of exerting direct pressure on the Soviet regime. Japan, whose presence in the Allied coalition was not an unmixed blessing, had easier access to Russian territory than Britain and France and thus became the logical mandatory power. And her leaders were not backward in evincing undue interest in the problem of "upholding order" in Siberia. Britain, with some reluctance, and France, more enthusiastically, proposed that Japan be given permission to intervene in Siberia, ostensibly as part of the grand strategy designed to hasten the enemy's capitulation. How Japanese troops in Siberia, fully five thousand railroad miles from the nearest enemy troops, were to contribute in any substantial measure to ultimate victory was never adequately explained. The most rational presentation of the scheme, indicating mixed motives, some of them quite at variance with publicized objectives, may be found in a note to Lansing by the French ambassador to Washington early in January urging American assent to the "desirability of some joint action" in Siberia. The purpose, said the ambassador, would be to "protect"

---

[85] Text of the agreement in Louis Fischer, *The Soviets in World Affairs* (London, 1930), II, 836 (appendix). See also Winston Churchill, *The Aftermath* (New York, 1929), pp. 167-68; Poincaré, IX, 428; Leonid I. Strakhovsky, "The Franco-British Plot to Dismember Russia," *Current History*, XXXIII (March, 1931), 839-42; and Madden Summers (American Consul in Moscow) to Lansing, Feb. 21, 1918 (861.00/1177), National Archives.

Siberia from Bolshevik "contagion," to secure the use of the Trans-Siberian and other railroads for "the advantage of the Allies," and to safeguard the vast amount of war matériel stored at Vladivostok.[86] Wilson remained cool to direct intervention, and Lansing informed the ambassador that the plan "would be likely to offend those Russians who are now in sympathy with the aims and desires which the United States and its cobelligerents have at heart in making war and might result in uniting all factions in Siberia against them."[87]

Later in the month the British tried their hand at overcoming American objections by pointing out the propitious changes in the Russian situation. Whereas "the whole country presented a spectacle of unredeemed chaos" only a few weeks ago, now "local organisations appear to have sprung up in south and southeast Russia which, with encouragement and assistance, might do something to prevent Russia from falling immediately and completely under the control of Germany." Turning to the argument which Lansing had used in opposing intervention in Siberia, the note flatly stated that all the information obtainable "appears to indicate that the Russians would welcome some form of foreign intervention in their affairs"; moreover, that the Russians would find Japan, on a mandate from the other Allied powers, "with no thought of annexation or future control," greatly preferable to the Germans, "who would make Russia orderly only by making it German."[88] Still the American attitude remained unchanged, and for the same reasons, the British being informed that "any foreign intervention in Russian affairs would, at the present time, be most inopportune."[89]

Though Wilson's stand precluded an armed intervention for the time being, Japan's interest in Siberia had become too strong to be denied indefinitely for purely idealistic reasons, particularly as she had received the backing of France and Britain. Since early December reports and rumors had been prevalent of Japanese

---

[86] Jusserand to Lansing, Jan. 8, 1918, *Foreign Relations*, II, 21.
[87] Lansing to Jusserand, Jan. 16, 1918, *ibid.*, p. 29.
[88] Memo., British embassy to the Department of State, Jan. 28, 1918, *ibid.*, pp. 35-36.
[89] Memo., Department of State to the British embassy, Feb. 8, 1918, *ibid.*, p. 42.

troops and warships at Vladivostok, which her Foreign Office spokesman branded "absurd and nonsensical." These persistent reports were very probably semiofficial "feelers," a standard diplomatic technique designed to gauge the reaction of world opinion before embarking upon perilous undertakings. The hostility of the United States being evident, the Japanese ambassador in Washington assured Lansing late in December that his government had no intention of sending troops to Vladivostok, even though London and Paris had been the first to suggest it.[90]

A few days after this interview took place a Japanese cruiser entered the harbor at Vladivostok for the usual reasons assigned in such cases—that of protecting Japanese citizens and property. The early arrival of two more Japanese vessels and a British warship concentrated a formidable amount of naval strength in the harbor. The American ambassador in Tokyo was instructed to protest this action because, as Lansing diplomatically phrased it, "the presence of more than one Japanese war vessel at Vladivostok at present is likely to be misconstrued and create a feeling of mistrust as to the purposes of the Allied Governments which Japan does not desire any more than the United States."[91] A Japanese landing would probably have followed soon afterward had Wilson given his consent. His closest advisers agreed that Japanese intervention would be a mistake and, as House informed Balfour early in March, might cause "a serious lowering, if not actual loss, of our moral position in the eyes of our peoples and of the whole world, and a dulling of the high enthusiasm of the American people for a righteous cause."[92] Increasing pressure from Britain and France, as well as the strongly favorable recommendations of the various American representatives around the globe, anti-Bolshevik and pro-interventionist almost to a man, did much to weaken Wilson's determined opposition. Several companies of Japanese troops landed in April, followed by a small contingent of British sailors, on the excuse of Russian atrocities against Japanese citizens. This was the entering wedge, soon to be widened when the Czech troops on Russian soil,

[90] Lansing memo., Dec. 27, 1917, *ibid.*, p. 13.
[91] Lansing to Morris, Jan. 20, 1918, *ibid.*, p. 31.
[92] House to Balfour, March 4, 1918, Wilson Papers.

returning by way of Vladivostok to fight with the Allies on the Western Front, clashed with the Soviet authorities and ignited the smoldering civil war which was to last until 1920. This incident, in addition to exaggerated reports that the Bolsheviks were arming German and Austrian war prisoners for all kinds of nefarious purposes, finally wrung a reluctant consent from the American government in the summer of 1918 for "limited intervention."[93]

Concurrently with military intervention and the efforts at friendly collaboration which Robins, Lockhart, and Sadoul were making in Petrograd, there existed a third aspect of Allied policy— the subsidization of anti-Bolshevik military adventurers who had been able to attract some support in the remoter areas of Russia. Actually this was but a nonmilitary phase of intervention. While the avowed purpose was to build up an organized force in Russia capable of resisting Germany, the practical effect of this form of "anti-Germanism," as the Allied representatives on the scene were well aware, was rather to create centers of resistance to Bolshevik rule. In the Far East the best known of these anti-Bolshevik leaders was the Cossack chieftain, Gregory Semyenov, who operated near the Manchurian border and soon came to be regarded as little more than a bloodthirsty bandit under Japanese sponsorship. Britain and France, though not without a small financial stake in his activities even at this early date,[94] were more interested in the possibilities of south Russia as a focal point for Russian "patriotism," and as far as possible their agents operated within the spheres assigned them under the Anglo-French convention of December 23. The United States played a subordinate role in this activity, and when aid was forthcoming, as in the case of Kaledin,[95] it was given indirectly in the form of loans to the other Allied Powers. Generals Kaledin, Alexeyev, and Kornilov, together with such former political leaders as Milyukov and Rodzyanko, were prominent in this early period prior to the signing of the Brest-Litovsk

[93] The story of intervention has been told many times, and it is not here proposed to retell it. For some of the relevant documents and a bibliography, see James Bunyan, *Intervention, Civil War, and Communism in Russia* (Baltimore, 1936).

[94] Paul S. Reinsch (American minister in Peking) to Lansing, Feb. 15, 1918 (861.00/1093), National Archives.

[95] See above, p. 186.

peace. It was on behalf of such "democrats" as these that the American consul in Moscow urged moral and material support. Undoubtedly a beginning has been made, he informed Washington, "for bringing into a close working union the regenerative elements in Russia which can be expected to act effectively against the Bolsheviki and the Germans."[96] By late December substantial monetary aid had been promised by Britain and France for the purpose of "restoring order in Russia and continuing the war against the Central powers," though actual payment was delayed because of the inaccessibility of the region.[97]

The Soviet government was highly suspicious of Allied activities but had little concrete evidence for specific charges. The press, unable to cite names, dates, and places, except in the case of the Kalpashnikov affair, usually spoke in rather general terms when attacking the Allied representatives for alleged counterrevolutionary acts. Thus *Izvestia* warned the ambassadors that they "must once and for all renounce their criminal attempts to influence the internal life of Russia with the help of corruption, intrigue, plots, lies, and slander."[98] The French military mission was regarded with particular disfavor because of its aggressively anti-Bolshevik attitude. General Niessel had received several hundred thousand dollars for propaganda work, and French officers were continually in contact with Kaledin and the Ukrainian Rada. On December 18 Trotsky called on the French ambassador about the activities of these officers. Noulens maintained that they had received instructions not to interfere in internal affairs, and in any case were attached to the Romanian and not to the Russian mission. The meeting was a friendly one, and for a time the Bolshevik press adopted a moderate tone. But two weeks later Trotsky sent a stiff note to Niessel accusing the French mission of inciting civil war and demanding specific information about its activities in Russia. The Red leader was not satisfied with the explanation

[96] Summers to Lansing, Dec. 29, 1917, *Foreign Relations*, II, 602.

[97] Page to Lansing, Dec. 21, 1917, *ibid.*, p. 595; report of Consul De Witt Poole, Jan. 26, 1918, *ibid.*, p. 609; Poole to Lansing, Jan. 13, 1918 (861.00/271½) and Page to Lansing, Feb. 14 (861.00/1101), National Archives; General Loukomsky, *Memoirs of the Russian Revolution* (London, 1922), p. 143.

[98] No. 27, Feb. 17, 1918.

offered and ordered the recall of the officers in south Russia and the closing of the propaganda bureau and the radio receiving station. Niessel promised to comply with these terms and banished one of his subordinates as a scapegoat. A brief and uneasy truce ensued, which remained unbroken until the period of open military intervention by the Allies.[99]

Despite the open hostility between Russia and her nominal allies, a situation which showed no signs of improvement as the Soviet regime continued to defy all predictions from abroad of its imminent collapse, unofficial relations were usually friendly, if not cordial. In so far as Robins, Lockhart, and Sadoul could persuade their governments that Bolshevism was not irrevocably bound to the German chariot and that Russia could yet be salvaged for the Allied cause, they were able to exert some influence in favor of collaboration as the more realistic—if not ideologically comfortable—alternative to continued hostility. But it was the tense and prolonged drama unfolding at Brest-Litovsk that meant success or failure of their attempts to mold Allied policy.

[99] Judson Papers, esp. diary entries for Jan. 3-5, 1918; Trotsky, *My Life,* pp. 346-47; Noulens, I, 171-74; Niessel, pp. 157 and 161-63.

CHAPTER VIII

A Separate Peace

"History willed it," writes Trotsky, "that the delegates of the most revolutionary regime the world has ever known had to sit at the same diplomatic table with the representatives of the most reactionary caste among all the ruling classes."[1] The Bolshevik delegation which left Petrograd late in November for the purpose of negotiating an armistice with the Central Powers was probably the most unusual ever to appear at a peace conference in modern times. It was headed by Adolf Joffe, an ascetic-looking intellectual who later became the first Soviet ambassador to Berlin. Closer to the orthodox concept of the typical revolutionary were Kamenev, now restored to favor after his heresy at the time of the November Revolution, Gregory Sokolnikov, and Leo Karakhan, the latter as secretary of the delegation. The Left Socialist Revolutionaries, in temporary alliance with the Bolsheviks, were allotted two places. One of them was filled by Anastasia Bitsenko, famous for her assassination of a tsarist official twelve years before. In addition to representing her party she served the added purpose of illustrating Marxist ideas on sex equality. But by far the most curious delegates were the four representatives of the masses: a sailor, a soldier, a worker, and a peasant. They were added purely for decorative purposes to provide the proper revolutionary atmosphere and appeared to enjoy themselves even if they were not always sure of

[1] L. Trotsky, *The History of the Russian Revolution to Brest-Litovsk* (London, 1919), p. 5.

what was going on. The peasant had been fortuitously acquired on the way to the railroad station when it was suddenly realized that a man of the soil was lacking to round out the party. Attached as technical advisers were nine military and naval officers, as well as the usual complement of clerks, orderlies, and translators.

The armistice proposals which the Germans were prepared to offer contained no punitive or otherwise humiliating terms, and it was hoped that the matter could be disposed of within a few hours, the formal peace conference to follow shortly. The German High Command was above all interested in an immediate cessation of hostilities which would facilitate the transfer to the Western Front of the bulk of its forces facing Russia. A spring offensive was planned, a final gigantic thrust in which the Allies could be smashed before the immense resources of the United States in men and matériel could be brought into effective use. Already American troops were arriving in a steady stream to belie the German boast that her policy of unrestricted submarine warfare would prevent the arrival of a single soldier from across the Atlantic. Victory for the Central Powers would have to come soon—or never. Austria, Bulgaria, and Turkey were close to the point of exhaustion and could no longer be relied upon for effective military support; everything depended on the German army, still a formidable fighting machine and for the first time since 1914 potentially able to concentrate an equal or superior force in the West. The morale of the civilian population, however, subjected to increasing privation by the Allied blockade, left much to be desired. Though organized peace sentiment was negligible, the workers showed signs of restlessness which erupted into serious industrial strikes in January. The naval mutiny at Kiel during the summer had not only alarmed the government, but also, because of the political repercussions, unfavorably affected the national spirit.

Allied morale, while it was to display a dogged fortitude during the coming year, was not markedly superior. Italy had been very near to complete collapse after the disastrous rout at Caporetto in October, and though she rallied to make a remarkable military recovery, the popularity of the war—never high among the mass of the people—was at its lowest ebb. France, bled nearly white, with England hardly better off, had no manpower reserves to fall back upon. War weariness was pervasive, but politically the situation was somewhat improved. Clemenceau had brought new life into the French war effort after his assumption of leadership in November, and Lloyd George continued in office with little opposition. But even the addition of the United States to the coalition could not as yet offset the loss of Russia. The winter of 1917-18 was a critical one for the Allies; for the first time in more than three years of fighting the initiative lay with Germany.

Such was the situation of the leading belligerents as the first session of the Russo-German armistice conference began on December 3. A Soviet proposal for complete freedom of publicity regarding the meetings was accepted at the outset, a tactical success for the Russians which, to the later regret of the Germans, opened the way to long orations with an unduly large propaganda content. Joffe then spoke, giving in broad outline the Soviet viewpoint on peace based on the familiar formula of no annexations or indemnities and the right of all nationalities to self-determination. He proposed that it be a general and not a separate peace, but when pressed by Major General Max Hoffmann, the head of the German delegation, as to whether Russia was empowered to speak for her allies, Joffe was forced to admit that the invitations already extended to the Allied Powers to participate in the negotiations had not been answered. The Russian armistice proposals called for a six months' truce, the immediate cessation of all German troop movements on the Eastern Front, and the evacuation of German forces from the islands in the Gulf of Riga. Germany preferred a much shorter armistice and refused to consider the evacuation as out of the question, coming as it did from a defeated power. Only the second point was accepted without objection, since all the troops which were to be shifted to the Western Front were already in transit or had received orders to go.[2]

[2] Major General Max Hoffmann, *War Diaries and Other Papers* (London, 1929), II, 191-94; U. S. Department of State, *Proceedings of the Brest-Litovsk Peace Conference* (Washington, 1918), pp. 13-35; John W. Wheeler-Bennett, *The Forgotten Peace* (New York, 1939), pp. 88-90.

The conference was suspended on the fifth at the end of the third session with an agreement to postpone the proceedings for a week to enable the Russian delegates to consult their government and to allow the other Allied belligerents another opportunity to join the negotiations. Karakhan was left for liaison purposes, while his colleagues departed for Petrograd. The next day Trotsky informed the Allied ambassadors in some detail of the progress of the deliberations and called upon their governments to define their attitude toward the peace conference—"that is, to express their readiness or their refusal to participate in the negotiations for an armistice and peace, and in the case of a refusal to openly state before the world, clearly, definitely, and correctly, in the name of what purpose must the people of Europe bleed during the fourth year of war."[3]

This communication, like the others which preceded it, was ignored, though Buchanan authorized a long statement in the non-Bolshevik press two days later which discussed the armistice in part without directly replying to the numerous appeals for Allied participation.[4] Attention was again called to the 1914 agreement against a separate peace which the Soviet government had broken. Nevertheless, the ambassador maintained, "We do not desire to induce an unwilling ally to continue to contribute her share to the common effort by an appeal to our treaty rights." The Allies could not send representatives to Brest-Litovsk, but they were "ready, so soon as a stable Government has been constituted that is recognized by the Russian people as a whole, to examine with that Government the aims of the war and the possible conditions of a just and durable peace." The remainder of Buchanan's statement was devoted to defending his country's good name from the frequent attacks in the Bolshevik press. He appeared to be particularly disturbed by the revolutionary proclamation issued only the day before to the Moslems of Russia and the East,[5] presumably because of the unsettling effect it might have in India. The British Foreign

[3] Cumming and Pettit, pp. 56-57.
[4] G. Buchanan, II, 233-37.
[5] The Soviet Union and Peace, with an Introduction by Henri Barbusse (New York, n.d.), pp. 28-30.

Office was even more alarmed as to the dangers of this sort of propaganda and showed unusual diligence in seeing that the proclamation was suppressed in all the Allied countries.[6] The ambassador's presentation of the Allied viewpoint was naturally received with sharp criticism in the Bolshevik newspapers. Trotsky alluded to it in a speech in which he said the ambassador had expressed his affection for Russia in five columns of the press and that while the warmth of his sentiments had been gladdening, deeds were preferable to words.[7]

The siren song of Bolshevism was not feared by the Allies alone. Germany too was to experience this stealthy invasion, where it was to wreak far greater havoc than it did in the more remote Western democracies and to play a significant if largely unpublicized role in her subsequent collapse. Shortly after Trotsky's assumption of office as Foreign Minister he had created a special press bureau headed by Karl Radek, a Bolshevik of Austrian nationality. A section of this bureau was devoted to international revolutionary propaganda, and Boris Reinstein, who had gone on to Russia after his appearance as one of the three unofficial American delegates to the Stockholm conference,[8] was placed in charge. He supervised the publication of *Die Fackel* [*The Torch*], a propaganda organ especially designed for German consumption, its successors, and several other newspapers in Hungarian, Bohemian, Romanian, and Croatian. He was aided by Albert Rhys Williams and John Reed, two American writers sympathetic to the Bolshevik cause. Reed, who became one of the founders and leaders of the American Communist movement and whose body now lies in a Kremlin vault in Moscow after his death there from typhus in 1920, was named Soviet consul to New York in January, 1918, an entirely hypothetical post in the absence of American recognition of the Soviet government.[9]

It was in the week of grace before the resumption of the armistice talks that the Soviet propaganda offensive against the Central

[6] Sir Cecil Spring Rice to Frank L. Polk, Dec. 8, 1917 (861.00/782½), National Archives.

[7] G. Buchanan, II, 238-39.   [8] See above, pp. 75-76.

[9] *Bolshevik Propaganda*, pp. 564-66 and 591; John Reed, "How Soviet Russia Conquered Imperial Germany," *Liberator*, II (Jan., 1919), 16-25.

Powers began in earnest. Hoffmann had flatly refused a Russian request at the conference to allow the admission into Germany of "Bolshevik propaganda and literature" but generously offered his assistance in the "export of this to France and England."[10] He was also obliged to resist Soviet demands for fraternization between the troops. But hardly had the delegates returned from Brest-Litovsk before the first issue of *Die Fackel* was on its way to the front in editions which later reached as high as half a million copies a day. It was sent by special train to various key cities and turned over to army committees. From there it was distributed to a number of places along the front and conveyed to the German lines in small quantities, usually in a surreptitious fashion, since strenuous efforts were made to keep the contaminating material from the troops.

The prisoners of war within Russia were subjected to a more systematic "educational" program. So saturated with revolutionary ideology were these troops that before being allowed to re-enter Germany they were confined for thirty-day periods in "political quarantine camps" to be "deloused" and reinculcated with patriotic values.[11] The Allies, of course, heartily approved of Bolshevik ideas when they were directed against the Central Powers. Edgar Sisson, in his work in Russia on behalf of the Committee on Public Information, shared the printing presses used by Radek's bureau and, in spite of his hostility to the Bolsheviks, gave Robins a sizeable sum of money for the use of the Soviet government in its propaganda activity.[12] German protests and threats were ineffective in stemming the deluge. As early as December 6 Hoffmann complained to Karakhan of the "unwarranted interference in the internal affairs of Germany, placing in jeopardy the successful continuation of the negotiations and evincing a lack of knowledge of the real state of affairs in Germany."[13]

Regardless of this incontrovertible evidence that the Germans and the Bolsheviks were not working together—evidence which was to grow more impressive as the peace negotiations progressed and sharp disagreements arose—Allied opinion persisted in the

[10] Hoffmann, II, 194.   [11] Reed, *loc. cit.*, p. 21.
[12] *Bolshevik Propaganda,* p. 1017; Hard, pp. 85-86; Sisson, pp. 101-2.
[13] Sisson, pp. 107-8.

legend of a German-Bolshevik conspiracy. The New York *Times* quoted an unidentified report from Paris which claimed that the French government had "absolute proof" that Lenin had been sent to Russia by the German spy system and "is a creature of the Prussian propaganda service."[14]   The London *Morning Post* referred to Krylenko as a "German-Jewish spy" and to Lenin as a Judas Iscariot named Zederbaum. "Considering that Lenin is exposed beyond doubt as having been in German-Austrian pay," said the *Post*, "we are not surprised at the report that he will take refuge in Germany after the armistice."[15]   The *Figaro* of Paris, citing as its informant an important financier who had just returned from Petrograd with "stupefying details" on the stream of German gold which was still flowing into Russia, asserted that millions of rubles are daily . . . directed into the hands and pockets of the partisans of Lenin." "That a majority of the Bolshevik leaders are in the pay of Germany," concluded *Figaro*, "is a matter as clear as day."[16]

Nor was it solely the press which had formed this conclusion regarding the Bolsheviks. The Allied governments, too, apparently labored under this delusion. A confidential memorandum of the American State Department dated December 1, though admitting the difficulties in the way of getting "any connected information as to the career of Lenin," seemed confident of the existence of "ample evidence that the considerable amounts which he has spent since [his arrival in Petrograd] are of German origin" and that "there seems little if any doubt as to his being a German agent" as well as a "convinced and rabid social agitator."[17]

In an atmosphere of this kind, which was even stronger among the personnel of the embassies in Petrograd, it is not surprising that an ample supply of forged documents rose to meet the demand for more concrete evidence of collusion. A sample had been published after the "July Days" but quickly forgotten when its purpose had been served.[18]   With the Bolsheviks in power, spurious docu-

---

[14] Nov. 23, 1917.   [15] Dec. 5, 1917.
[16] Dec. 22, 1917.
[17] U. S. Department of State, "Periodical Report Relating to Russia," Dec. 1, 1917, Hoover Library, Stanford University.
[18] See above, p. 144.

ments were hawked about to all the Allied representatives in Petrograd in the hope that a gullible buyer would snap them up for suitable monetary compensation. They were not to be disappointed in the case of Edgar Sisson, who was suitably impressed with their value and conveyed them to the United States to be published later by the government.[19] They purported to show that the Bolsheviks were taking orders from the German general staff, and while a few of them may have been genuine communications between the Russian and German governments, they were hardly proof of a "conspiracy." The bulk of the "Sisson documents"— and the most startling—were rather unskilful forgeries, almost all of them composed on the same typewriter. They had first been offered to two British secret service men in Russia, George Hill and Sidney Reilly, who rejected them after an expert had pronounced them fraudulent.[20] Sisson acquired them from Eugene P. Semyenov, an anti-Bolshevik journalist, presumably in contact with certain unnamed persons in the Soviet Foreign Office.[21]

Sisson left Russia early in March, and the documents were released to the newspapers the following September. Since the propaganda was ideally suited to the war hysteria of the times, the authenticity of the source was seldom questioned. Some adverse comment, however, made it advisable to obtain expert corroborative opinion before formal publication was attempted. Accordingly the documents were examined by historians Samuel Harper and J. Franklin Jameson and all but a few pronounced genuine in a statement which was appended to the published text. The two scholars unfortunately left the added but quite incorrect impression that they also agreed with all of Sisson's extreme conclusions regarding the depravity of the Bolsheviks with which he regaled his readers in an introduction.[22] The British Foreign Office con-

---

[19] *The German-Bolshevik Conspiracy* (Washington, 1918); also reprinted in the appendixes of Sisson's book.

[20] Hill, pp. 200-1; Lockhart, pp. 219 and 228-29.

[21] Semyenov's story has been told in a series of articles in *Poslyedny Novosty* [*Latest News*] (Paris), April 3-8, 1921. Typewritten English translation entitled "German Money to Lenin" in the Hoover Library, Stanford University.

[22] For further information on the documents, see the Harper Papers; Sisson, pp. 357-86; Creel, *Rebel at Large*, pp. 183-85; Granville Hicks, *John Reed* (New York, 1936), pp. 321-22; Arthur Bullard, "Memorandum: German Gold," Bullard

tinued to view the documents skeptically on the advice of its experts, and the American State Department was apparently none too anxious to sponsor the publication. But it was forced to bow to Wilson's decision after the President had become convinced by Creel that the documents were authentic.[23] The incident remains, in the words of one impeccably anti-Bolshevik commentator, a monument to "that paralysis of the critical faculties which seems inseparable from a state of war."[24]

If Sisson's documents are to be believed, the conclusion is inescapable that the peace conference at Brest-Litovsk was a farce from beginning to end, stage-managed from Berlin and conducted only for the sake of appearances.[25] But the armistice negotiations which were resumed on December 13 bore no resemblance to this Arabian Nights version of history. The Russian delegates came prepared to accept the terms of the truce—and later the treaty—because there was no reasonable alternative in view of Germany's overwhelming military supremacy, not because the Bolshevik leaders were corrupted with German gold or otherwise subservient to orders from Berlin. The armistice agreement was formally signed on the fifteenth with little change from the previous German proposals.[26] It was to last until January 14 and to be automatically prolonged unless a week's notice of termination was given by either party. Only in the "fraternization clause" did the Germans blunder. At several places within each section of a Russian division "organized intercourse between the troops" was permitted of not more than "twenty-five unarmed persons belonging to either side." The exchange of news and newspapers was also allowed, though everything of an incendiary nature was confiscated by the German officers. Fraternization was likewise conducted on a clandestine

to House, March 7, 1918 (861.00/1283½), National Archives; and James R. Mock and Cedric Larson, *Words That Won the War* (Princeton, N. J., 1939), pp. 314-20, which gives additional references.

[23] Sir Eric Drummond to Sir William Wiseman, Oct. 3, 1918, and Wiseman to Drummond, Oct. 5, 1918, William Wiseman Papers, Yale University Library.

[24] Wilcox, p. 248.

[25] So Sisson seriously maintained in a cable to Creel, April 3, 1918 (861.00/1421), National Archives.

[26] U. S. Department of State, *Texts of the Russian "Peace"* (Washington, 1918), pp. 1-10.

basis, generally at night, with secret meetings in remote areas where Bolshevik literature was handed out.

The successful conclusion of an armistice was announced in a manifesto to the "toiling, oppressed, and exhausted peoples of Europe."[27] "After nearly three and a half years of uninterrupted slaughter, with no issue in sight," declaimed Trotsky, "the workers' and peasants' revolution in Russia has opened the way to peace." But the capitalist governments are not capable of peace: "They are endeavouring to postpone the hour of their ultimate bankruptcy. Are the peoples willing to go on patiently enduring the criminal work of Stock Exchange cliques in France, Great Britain, Italy, and the United States?" Evidently they were, for no responsive chord was as yet discernible among the masses in any of the countries named. The myth of the international class-conscious proletariat, straining at the chains of capitalism for its freedom, was to die hard in Russia. But the call to world revolution continued with unabated fervor as the first session of the peace conference drew near.

The Allies, if they remained aloof to the Bolshevik appeals for a general peace, could not remain indifferent to the consequences of a separate one. Lloyd George emphasized the gravity of Russia's retirement from the war in a public address on the fourteenth. "[It] strengthens the Hohenzollerns and weakens the forces of democracy," he complained. "Her action will not lead, as she imagines, to universal peace. It will simply prolong the world's agony and inevitably put her in bondage to the military dominance of Prussia."[28] Reviewing the course of the war in the House of Commons a few days later, he admitted that "it would be idle to pretend that the hope we had formed at the beginning of the year has been realized, and our disappointment has been attributable entirely, in my judgment, to the Russian collapse."[29] Winston Churchill, Britain's Minister of Munitions, proclaimed in stately prose the Allied will to win, notwithstanding Russia's defection, in a speech before a cheering audience at Bedford. "Russia has

[27] *The Soviet Union and Peace,* pp. 30-33.
[28] Magnes, p. 26.
[29] *Parliamentary Debates,* C (Dec. 20, 1917), 2209.

been thoroughly beaten by the Germans," he frankly stated. "Her great heart has been broken, not only by German might but by German intrigue; not only by German steel but by German gold." "It is this melancholy event," he continued after expounding this fashionable interpretation of the rise of Bolshevism, "which has prolonged the war, that has robbed the French and British and Italian armies of the prize that was, perhaps, almost within their reach this summer; it is this event, and this event alone, that has exposed us to perils and sorrows and sufferings which we have not deserved, which we cannot avoid, but under which we shall not bend." To Churchill the war was a struggle to the finish on behalf of "the British Empire and of democracy and of civilization," and he would have nothing to do with "specious peace terms that would leave Germany stronger than before."[30] His blunt if graceful language confirmed the Bolshevik view of the Allied cause and could not have been happily received by patriotic idealists in any of the Allied countries, but it undoubtedly expressed what the bulk of the population still believed about the war.

On the afternoon of December 22 Prince Leopold of Bavaria opened the formal peace negotiations at Brest-Litovsk with a speech of welcome. Large delegations representing Austria-Hungary, Turkey, and Bulgaria were present in addition to Germany's. The Russian delegation remained approximately the same except for the addition of Michael Pokrovsky, whose writings were to epitomize for many years the Soviet conception of historical studies. The Russian proposals, as set forth in principle by Joffe, closely adhered to the idealism of the Bolshevik peace decree of November 8 and were still based upon the notion of a general rather than a separate peace: no forceful expropriation of territories taken during the war, no war indemnities, and political freedom for all nationalities. Baron Richard von Kühlmann, the German Foreign Minister, and Count Ottokar Czernin, the Austrian Foreign Minister, thought it good strategy to accept these conditions providing "the Entente Powers would also agree to negotiate a Peace on similar terms."[31] Hoffmann opposed such a reply "because at

[30] *Times* (London), Dec. 11, 1917.   [31] Hoffmann, II, 199.

bottom it was a lie." Russia had never been empowered to speak for her allies, and until she could he saw no point in pretending that a general peace was in the realm of possibilities. Hoffmann's objections were overcome without great difficulty, but Bulgaria, which had entered the war on a frankly annexationist basis, presented an additional problem. Her head representative stubbornly refused to agree even when assured that an acceptance of the Russian proposition was just a matter of form, and it was not until a telegraphic order had been obtained from Tsar Ferdinand in Sofia that Bulgaria fell into line.

The Russians joyfully received the declaration read by Czernin on Christmas Day that the Central Powers agreed in principle to their formula. They naïvely seemed to believe that Germany would actually return the conquered territories of Poland, Lithuania, and Courland. On the following day Hoffmann proceeded to disabuse their minds of any such intention when he told Joffe at luncheon that the Central Powers did not consider it a forcible annexation if portions of the former Russian empire broke off and decided "of their own free will" to unite with some other state. Joffe, looking "as if he had received a blow on the head,"[32] immediately arranged for an informal meeting to discuss this astonishing interpretation of Germany's "no annexation" policy. The Russians, bitterly disappointed and angry, could not budge the German position and finally threatened to disrupt the negotiations and depart for Petrograd. Czernin desperately sought a compromise formula, for the Dual Monarchy needed peace and needed it badly. Joffe had previously confided to him his hope that "we may yet be able to raise the revolution in your country too," and Czernin had commented in his diary: "We shall hardly need any assistance from the good Joffe, I fancy, in bringing about a revolution among ourselves; the people will manage that, if the Entente persist in refusing to come to terms."[33] When the frantic Czernin received no support from Kühlmann, he threatened to make a separate peace with the Russians and dispatched his military adviser to

[32] *Ibid.*, p. 203.
[33] Count Ottokar Czernin, *In the World War* (New York and London, 1920), p. 246.

make a similar pronouncement to Hoffmann. The German general, cynically appraising Russia's military position, could see no reason for Czernin's agitation and coolly replied that he thought the idea a brilliant one, since it would release for duty elsewhere twenty-five German divisions that were currently supporting the Austrian army on the Eastern Front.

The Austrian bluff was thus called with scant ceremony, and Czernin withdrew into baffled silence. The negotiations were interrupted on the twenty-eighth to enable the Russians to proceed with the hopeless ritual of inviting their "allies" to participate in the conference. Except for a number of technical experts who remained at Brest-Litovsk, the delegates returned to their respective capitals to await the resumption of the next plenary session on January 9. Sadder but wiser men, Joffe and his colleagues arrived in Petrograd as Trotsky's expected proclamation to the "peoples and governments of the Allied countries"—part invitation and part revolutionary manifesto—was released to the press. Though admitting the program of the Central Powers was "highly inconsistent" and a plan of "unprincipled compromise between the aims of imperialism and the resistance of the labour democracy," the very fact that it was proposed at all was pronounced "a great step forward" and in sharp contrast to the Allied policy of mouthing "general phrases about the necessity of carrying on the war to a finish." "If the Allied Governments," warned Trotsky, "in the blind stubbornness which characterizes decadent and perishing classes, once more refuse to participate in the negotiations, then the working classes will be confronted by the iron necessity of taking power out of the hands of those who cannot or will not give the people peace." We promise full support, the statement concluded, "to the working class of each country which will rise against its national imperialists, against chauvinists, against militarists, under the banner of peace, brotherhood of peoples, and socialist reconstruction of society."[34]

While Lloyd George, Clemenceau, and Wilson were in too stable a position to take seriously Trotsky's warning of the wrath

[34] *The Soviet Union and Peace,* pp. 35-39.

to come if they persisted in their contemptuous silence, the Allies could no longer, with any assurance of success, pose before world opinion as the champion of freedom and democracy and still maintain a stubborn taciturnity in regard to their war aims. To be sure, there had been no lack of public declarations, pervaded with a tone of moral superiority, in which the just and pacific nature of the Allied aims were acclaimed. Yet nothing really definite was forthcoming, and the course of the Russian Revolution—the vain pleas of the Petrograd Soviet, the abortive Stockholm conference, the triumph of the Bolsheviks, the publication of the secret treaties, and the Brest-Litovsk conference—demonstrated to the ever-increasing embarrassment of liberals, socialists, and idealists the vast distance between promise and performance.

France's new Foreign Minister, Stephen Pichon, expressed the usual stereotypes on the subject when he told the Chamber of Deputies on the twenty-seventh, in reply to a heavy socialist barrage against the government's policy, that France could not accept a peace based on the status quo after the suffering she had endured on behalf of the "cause of right, justice, and liberty."[35] He scorned the Bolshevik peace invitation and repeated the formula which House had so decisively rejected at the Allied conference in Paris: when Russia has a government recognized by the whole population France will be ready to join it in "an examination of war aims and the conditions of a just and durable peace." Meanwhile, said Pichon, "we have the duty of remaining in contact with all the healthy elements in Russia, with all ethnic groupings where the sentiments of independence and loyalty, the instinct of legitimate defense, and the need of order and liberty still resides."[36]

Lloyd George took a more enlightened view in an address before the Trades Union Congress on January 5 in which he stated emphatically that the Allies were "not fighting a war of aggression against the German people," nor for the "disintegration of their State or country." He rightly criticized the reticence and vagueness of the enemy powers in stating their aims but was not entirely clear or candid in his own formulation of Allied aims. For example,

[35] *Débats parlementaires* (1917), II, 3631.
[36] *Ibid.*, p. 3627.

with regard to the secret treaties—though he carefully avoided calling them that—he was content to say only that "new circumstances, like the Russian collapse, and the separate Russian negotiations, have changed the conditions under which those arrangements were made" and that Britain was and always has been "perfectly ready to discuss them with our allies." Russia was elsewhere referred to without recrimination or slander as simply a victim of German designs: "Whatever phrases she may use to delude Russia, she does not mean to surrender one of the fair provinces, or cities, of Russia, now occupied by her forces. Under one name or another—and the name hardly matters—these Russian provinces will henceforth be in reality a part of the dominions of Prussia."[37]

The Prime Minister's effort was intended as an answer to the increasing restiveness of British labor, whose leaders had prepared their own statement of war aims a short time before. Easily the most detailed and least cliché-ridden of the many utterances on this subject which belligerent leaders had made during the war, and quite satisfactory for home consumption, the Lloyd George declaration was nevertheless clearly inadequate to put the Central Powers on the defensive in the war of ideology raging parallel to the more obvious military struggle. This task could have been fulfilled only by Woodrow Wilson, unfettered as he was by secret commitments and with the sincerity of a rigorous moral idealist, convinced that the cause of the democracies was the cause of world civilization. It was admirably performed by the American President in his historic "fourteen points" address of January 8 before a joint session of Congress, which one of his biographers, extravagantly but not inaptly, has described as "the most effective piece of propaganda ever designed by any human brain in the history of mankind."[38] It was a momentous and startling document, a powerful if silent weapon in the assault which led to the German collapse some ten months later. Wilson's message, though brought forth by the impending resumption of the Brest-Litovsk deliberations,

[37] James Brown Scott (ed.), *Official Statements of War Aims and Peace Proposals* (Washington, 1921), pp. 225-33.

[38] George Sylvester Viereck, *The Strangest Friendship in History: Woodrow Wilson and Colonel House* (New York, 1932), p. 210.

had a period of gestation stemming directly from House's recommendations upon his return from Paris.[39] Most of the research upon which the specific proposals were based was conducted by the "Inquiry," a group of scholars previously assembled by House to gather data for the future peace conference. The outline was completed on January 5 in a meeting between Wilson and House, but when news of Lloyd George's speech was received the next day, the President was at first inclined to abandon his own as unnecessary. House was able to dissuade him, however, and the address was delivered substantially without change.[40]

Unaware of Wilson's intention, which was kept a secret until he actually appeared before Congress, Sisson had approached Creel in an attempt to enlist the President's aid in exploiting the dissension between Russia and Germany for the benefit of the Allies. Sisson cabled from Petrograd on the third: "If President will re-state anti-imperialistic war aims and democratic peace requisites of America thousand words or less, short almost placard paragraphs, short sentences, I can get it fed into Germany in great quantities in German translation and can utilize Russian version potently in army and everywhere."[41] Sisson put the message on the open wire without the usual coding precaution, positive that the contents would expedite its passage through both Russian and British censorship. It reached Washington in record time, and Creel took it to the White House at once. While the appeal probably strengthened Wilson's belief that the time was propitious for his address, it would be absurd to say (as has been said) that the famous declaration resulted from Sisson's cable. "If I were to state," says Sisson, "that I suggested the formula for it, knew what that formula would be, or what the effect of it was to be upon the nations, I would appear as ridiculous as the would-be historian . . . who began his narrative by putting into the mouth of a General the words: 'Men, do your duty! The eyes of the world are upon you who are about to fight the first battle of the Hundred Years' War!' "[42]

[39] See above, p. 178.
[40] House diary, XIII, pp. 7-8 (Jan. 9, 1918), House Papers; Seymour, III, 319-41.
[41] Cumming and Pettit, p. 67.
[42] Sisson, p. 216.

Sisson was not alone in his appeal to the President. Bakhmetev had suggested to House weeks before the advisability of a friendly statement on Russia, and Francis had cabled Lansing on December 29 and again on January 3 strongly urging Wilson to make a generous expression to the Russian people on Allied aims. On January 5 Balfour likewise recommended an idealistic pronouncement, though his advice was implied rather than stated. "The Prime Minister is confident," he wrote, "that such a statement would also be in general accordance with the lines of the President's previous speeches, which in England, as well as in other countries, have been so warmly received by public opinion."[43]

In his address Wilson spoke with sympathy of the sincerity and earnestness of the Russian delegates and their resistance to the German proposals of "conquest and domination," though he mistakenly declared that the negotiations had been broken off. And he went on to speak, in a notable passage, of the Russian people, who were "prostrate and all but helpless . . . before the grim power of Germany," but whose "soul is not subservient" and who "will not yield either in principle or in action." "Their conception of what is right, or what is humane and honorable for them to accept," said Wilson, "has been stated with a frankness, a largeness of view, a generosity of spirit, and a universal human sympathy which must challenge the admiration of every friend of mankind. . . . They call to us to say what it is that we desire, in what, if in anything, our purpose and our spirit differ from theirs; and I believe that the people of the United States would wish me to respond, with utter simplicity and frankness." Then, after a few additional remarks, the fourteen principles of the Wilsonian peace program were laid down. The sixth, relating to Russia, called for the evacuation of all her territory, assistance of every kind "that she may need and may herself desire," the settlement of all questions affecting her in a manner to obtain "an unhampered and unembarrassed opportunity for the independent determination of her own political development and national policy," and the assurance of a "sincere

[43] Balfour to Wilson, Jan. 5, 1918, Wilson Papers; Seymour, III, 330-31 and 340-41; Foreign Relations, I, 405 and 422-24.

welcome into the society of free nations under institutions of her own choosing."

The speech was received with acclaim in the United States, with hardly a dissenting note in evidence. In England, France, and Italy, the chorus of praise did not entirely conceal a certain uneasiness in more conservative quarters that Wilson's utterances might be an embarrassing obstacle to the just and lucrative deserts of a hard-earned victory. In Russia the Bolshevik leaders were not so hostile toward the Allies that they could not recognize its friendly tone and more especially its value as anti-German propaganda. Lenin seemed genuinely pleased, though it was evident that he regarded Wilson not as a fellow thinker but a fair-minded and tolerant class opponent. Sisson took the text to the press bureau at Smolny to get it in the official organs. *Pravda* published most of it but added some skeptical remarks of its own, while *Izvestia* not only printed it in full with a prominent display but added favorable editorial comment. The anti-government press was careful to omit the sections friendly to Russia because it reflected also to the credit of the Bolsheviks. In the form of posters, handbills, and pamphlets, Sisson and his staff printed nearly two and a half million copies of the speech in Russian and approximately a million in German. This total takes no account of huge quantities circulated by other means, nor of the copies distributed by the Bolshevik propaganda service to prisoner-of-war camps and to German troops at the front.[44]

At the annual conference of the British Labor party, held at Nottingham later in the month, a resolution was passed unanimously welcoming the "statements as to War Aims made by the British Prime Minister and President Wilson, in so far as they are in harmony with the War Aims of the British labour movement and make for an honorable and democratic peace." The Allied governments were in addition urged to "formulate and publish at the earliest possible moment a joint statement of their War Aims

[44] Sisson to Creel, Jan. 13, 1918, Wilson Papers; Sisson, pp. 208-11; George Creel, *How We Advertised America* (New York and London, 1920), pp. 377 and 379. An itemized account of the distribution is given in *The Complete Report of the Committee on Public Information* (Washington, 1920), pp. 217-19.

in harmony with the above."[45]   This rather lukewarm attitude toward the idealistic pronouncements of Wilson and Lloyd George was indicative of a decided change from the patriotic atmosphere of the previous year's meeting. Now the delegates who supported the continuance of the war were in a minority, the majority opinion hardly distinguishable from that of the Independent Labor party.[46] Russia's plight was noted in a special "Address to the Russian People" which, more accurately, was a plea to the peoples of Central Europe, for it called upon them to embrace the aims originally advanced by the Petrograd Soviet of no indemnities or annexations and the self-determination of nationalities. The resolution warned: "Do not let your governments drive the British people, as they are driving the Russian people, into the terrible choice between continuing the war and abandoning the only principles that can save the world."[47]

Litvinov, Russia's unrecognized ambassador, had been invited to the conference and was generously given an opportunity to explain the Bolshevik position. He combined a revolutionary harangue with a skilful defense of Russian policy. Regarding Brest-Litovsk he said, "Even if peace does not result from the negotiations, a revolution in Germany—and let me hope somewhere else—becomes one of the immediate possibilities." "The Russian people are fighting an unequal fight, against the imperialists of all nations," Litvinov concluded. "They have begun a work for general peace, which alone they cannot finish. They will fail if they have not the response of the workers of all countries—those of the Central Powers as well as the Allies. I can only say to British labor: speed up your pace. I hope and trust that you will not allow thousands and millions more men to be sacrificed."[48] These bold remarks were greeted with enthusiastic applause by many of the delegates. But it was still a long way from an antiwar position to a prorevolutionary position—and further yet from conviction to action. The conservative press was alarmed. The

[45] *Report of the Seventeenth Conference of the Labour Party*, p. 105.
[46] Snowden, pp. 480-82.
[47] *International Conciliation*, No. 123 (Feb., 1918), pp. 64-66.
[48] Paul U. Kellogg and Arthur Gleason, *British Labor and the War* (New York, 1919), pp. 88-90.

Daily Express cried out that Litvinov had made "the most menacing speech ever delivered by the ambassador of a friendly country,"[49] neglecting to point out that he was not the ambassador, nor, for that matter, could Russia be regarded as a friendly country. The Foreign Office directed Lockhart to warn the Soviet government that such conduct could not be tolerated.[50]

Another delegate whose speech was warmly received was Camille Huysmans, who attended as the representative of the still hopeful Stockholm committee. The committee had telegraphed a renewed appeal for an international socialist conference, and the convention took note of the plea with a resolution calling for an "international congress in some neutral state, preferably Switzerland, at which organized working class opinion of all the countries may be represented, in order that nothing may be left undone to bring into harmony the desires of the working class of all the belligerents."[51] Soon afterward Huysmans was prevented from going to Paris for consultation with French socialists by the obstreperous Seamens' and Firemens' Union, which had effectively vetoed the MacDonald mission to Russia the previous June.[52]

The shift in mood of the British labor movement was also in evidence at the Inter-Allied Labor and Socialist Conference held in London during the following month. Delegates from all the Allied countries were present except the United States and Russia. The Soviet government frowned upon the enterprise as another bourgeois-tainted socialist gathering and had refused passports to the Mensheviks and Socialist Revolutionaries desirous of attending. No American socialists had been invited in an attempt to lure the American Federation of Labor into participation. But Gompers and his associates, more chauvinist than the government, declined to take part anyway, ostensibly because the invitation had not been received in time.[53] Most of the discussion centered upon the Labor party's war aims memorandum, which was finally adopted in an amended form. A lengthy document, it repeated the statement

[49] Quoted in Arthur Upham Pope, *Maxim Litvinoff* (New York, 1943), p. 133.
[50] Lockhart, p. 238.
[51] Kellogg and Gleason, p. 51; *Labour Leader,* Jan. 17, 1918.
[52] See above, pp. 73-74.
[53] Kellogg and Gleason, pp. 57 and 61-62; Gompers, II, 403-4.

made three years before that the war was a "monstrous product of the antagonisms which tear asunder capitalist society and the aggressive policy of colonialism and imperialism, against which International Socialism has never ceased to fight, and in which every government has its share of responsibility."[54] The memorandum received wide publicity, though perhaps not the credence it deserved. Its ideological debt to the formula first expressed by the Petrograd Soviet was obvious, but the absence of any referrence to the problem of Russia was an unfortunate omission.

The "Russian problem" was daily becoming more acute as the "wolves in sheeps' clothing," as *Pravda* called the Germans,[55] were even more openly asserting their annexationist designs at the peace conference. In spite of the brave words of Joffe about breaking off negotiations, there had never been a serious doubt but what the Russian delegation would reappear at Brest-Litovsk. Bolshevik strategy envisaged delaying tactics in the absence of military strength. A revolution in Germany, it was still believed, remained within the realm of immediate possibilities; and with Allied help, the nucleus of a revolutionary army might be formed in case all else failed. But "in order to delay the proceedings," said Lenin, "there must be someone to do the delaying."[56] Joffe, while a competent man, was already beyond his depth. Only Trotsky, unrivaled as a dialectician, measured up to the demanding task, and upon Lenin's urging, he accepted the leadership of the peace delegation. He assumed his new duties with mixed feelings. A vain man, his confident air concealed an inward shyness. "I confess," he says, "I felt as if I were being led to the torture chamber. Being with strange and alien people always had aroused my fears."[57]

Before leaving for Brest-Litovsk, Trotsky tried to secure from Robins and Sadoul some assurance of Allied assistance in the event of a rupture with Germany. Sadoul had been active for some time, not only with Noulens, but with many other Allied officials, in campaigning for a statement promising military support to the

[54] Kellogg and Gleason, pp. 352-66 (appendix II).
[55] Quoted in Magnes, p. 43.
[56] Leon Trotsky, *Lenin* (New York, 1925), p. 103.
[57] Trotsky, *My Life,* p. 363.

Russians. The response he received was typical: the Bolsheviks were German agents, and in any case, their days were numbered. It was quite adequate to ward off any common-sense agreement.[58] Robins had been temporarily successful with the vacillating American ambassador and obtained his signature to two documents which were to be used only in the event of a Russo-German break. The first, headed "Suggested Communication to the Commissar for Foreign Affairs," promised American aid and possible diplomatic recognition "if upon the termination of the present armistice Russia fails to conclude a democratic peace through the fault of the Central Powers and is compelled to continue the war." The second, a suggested dispatch to the State Department, proposed substantially the same thing and advocated continued informal relations with Smolny.[59]

A Russian attempt to transfer the negotiations to neutral soil, preferably Stockholm, was flatly rejected by the Germans, and the conference resumed on January 9. This time the four ornaments of proletarian democracy stayed in Petrograd. Besides Trotsky, another newcomer to the delegation was Radek, who signaled his arrival by throwing propaganda leaflets from his train window to the German troops at the station. Trotsky would stand for no more nonsense about fraternization between the delegations and proceeded to "quarantine" his colleagues from all but formal contact with the representatives of the Central Powers.

Kühlmann opened the first plenary session with a blunt declaration that since Russia had failed to obtain the participation of her allies, the previous formula agreed to by the Central Powers was now "null and void." Czernin, in giving a formal answer to the Bolshevik request to shift the deliberations to a neutral country, emphasized the intrigues which would immediately be launched by England and France. Trotsky scornfully counter-attacked: "The idea of the German Command [in holding the conference at Brest-Litovsk] was to isolate the Russian Delegation from the popular masses. The ideals of the Russian Revolution and of its pacific programme were forced to find expression in a space hermet-

---

[58] Sadoul, pp. 162-65.   [59] *Bolshevik Propaganda,* pp. 1009-10.

ically sealed. Generals and diplomats impervious to those ideas are to form a safety curtain shutting off the fire of the Russian Revolution from the German workers and all Europe." And he concluded, "You are the stronger from the military point of view, but you are forced to hide the motives of your policy from the masses. We are the weaker, but our strength increases in proportion as we unmask your policy, and that is why we are staying."[60]

In Trotsky Kühlmann had found a worthy opponent. For days the two men faced each other across the conference table, the one delivering semirevolutionary harangues brimming over with vituperation and biting sarcasm, the other, never forgetful for a moment that Germany was the master and Russia the slave, shrewdly manipulating his superior position to political advantage. To Kühlmann Trotsky's malevolent expression indicated a desire to bring the negotiations "to a sudden and thorough end by throwing a few hand grenades over the green table."[61] Hoffmann, aroused by the inflammatory Bolshevik appeals to the German troops and impatient to "give the Russians another touch of the whip," finally obtained the consent of his colleagues "to bring the negotiations back to a basis of facts" away from the "theoretical discussions" into which they had degenerated.[62] Taking advantage of a speech by Kamenev on the twelfth—to Hoffmann "a piece of amazing insolence"—he proceeded to remind the Bolsheviks of a few simple truths. "The Russian Delegation," he said, "talks to us as if it stood victorious in our countries and could dictate conditions to us. I would like to point out that the facts are just the reverse; that the victorious German Army stands in your territory." Moreover, "the Russian Delegation demands for the occupied territories the application of a right of self-determination of peoples in a manner and to an extent which its Government does not apply to its own country. Its Government is founded purely on power and, indeed, on power which ruthlessly suppressed by force all who think otherwise."[63]

[60] *Proceedings of the Peace Conference,* p. 55.
[61] Richard von Kühlmann, *Erinnerungen* (Heidelberg, 1948), p. 530.
[62] Hoffmann, II, 211; Czernin, p. 262.
[63] *Proceedings of the Peace Conference,* p. 82.

Though the outburst came as no surprise to Kühlmann, Czernin, accustomed to a little more finesse in such matters, was alarmed by the crudity of Hoffmann's mailed-fist approach. Germany's designs upon Russia were already under heavy attack in the liberal and socialist press at home, and the general's intemperate outburst only provided fresh ammunition for these critics. But this was as nothing compared to its propaganda value to the Allied Powers, where public opinion, fed throughout the war on the horrors of German militarism and aggression, received a practical example of the Prussian military mind in action. To make the story even more lurid, Hoffmann was depicted as pounding the table repeatedly to emphasize his points. In his rebuttal Trotsky gave the delegates a beginners' course in Marxist principles, pointing toward the moral that in a class society every government was based on force. The German government applied repression to protect big property owners, whereas the Soviet government used the same methods to defend the working class. "The thing that surprises and repels the governments of other countries," he said, "is that we do not arrest strikers but capitalists who subject workers to lockouts; that we do not shoot peasants who demand land but arrest the landowners and officers who try to shoot the peasants."[64]

Kühlmann did not force the pace of the discussions after Hoffmann's tirade, and the ensuing sessions fell back into the routine pattern of theory and polemics. Trotsky was again able to seize the initiative and pillory the Central Powers before world opinion as unholy practitioners of power politics. Kühlmann, with no adequate conception of the Allied fear of Bolshevism, missed a splendid opportunity to counterattack and portray his country as the champion of civilization—the remaining barrier between the engulfing Red menace and the West. The Germans at length tried a new tack by sounding out the representatives of the Ukrainian Rada, who had come to Brest with annexationist ideas of their own. By threatening to conclude a separate peace with the bourgeois Ukrainian republic, the Germans hoped to induce Trotsky to come to terms. The Bolshevik leader was uneasily aware of his

[63] *Proceedings of the Peace Conference*, p. 82.

exposed position in that respect. On the eighteenth he asked for a respite of a few days to consult with other party leaders in Petrograd. Already he had conceived of a daring plan to end the war while spurning a formal peace treaty and had written Lenin about it. "We declare we end the war but do not sign a peace," he explained in his letter. "They will be unable to make an offensive against us. If they attack us, our position will be no worse than now, when they have the opportunity to proclaim and declare us agents of England and of Wilson after his speech, and to commence an attack."[65] Lenin wired that the plan seemed "disputable" to him and inquired: "It is not possible to postpone taking the final decision until after a special session of the central executive committee here?"[66] The Germans assented to Trotsky's request, though not without presenting their demands in unmistakable terms, and he left for Petrograd on the evening of the eighteenth, carrying the map upon which Hoffmann had drawn a blue line showing the future boundary of a badly truncated Russia.

While Trotsky was on his way to the capital, what vestige of legal opposition to the Soviet regime remained—the Constituent Assembly—was disbanded under circumstances more anticlimactic than heroic. The elections to this body had been repeatedly postponed during the life of the Provisional Government. The Bolsheviks had capitalized on the delay, charging Kerensky with deliberately thwarting the will of the people, yet were themselves faced with the embarrassing problem of what to do about the Assembly after the November Revolution. Lenin, always contemptuous of bourgeois democracy, advocated postponing the elections but was overruled by the party's executive committee.[67] As a result of the balloting, which took place on November 25 and the following few days, the Socialist Revolutionaries, because of their strength in the rural areas, received a decided majority, while the Bolsheviks, whose influence lay in the big cities, particularly Petrograd and Moscow, came off second best. The Cadet and Menshevik vote was surprisingly small. The Bolsheviks complained

[65] Wheeler-Bennett, pp. 185-86.
[66] Leon Trotsky, Stalin (New York and London, 1946), p. 248.
[67] Trotsky, Lenin, pp. 119-20.

with some justice that because the split in the ranks of the Socialist Revolutionaries occurred after the electoral lists had been drawn up, the voters who wished to support the pro-Bolshevik left wing had no opportunity to do so.

The delegates met in the Tauride Palace on the afternoon of the eighteenth, the heavily armed sailors and Red Guards in evidence indicating an uncertain future for the Assembly. Ambassador Francis failed to persuade his colleagues to attend in a body, and since no one would accompany him, he decided not to go by himself. "If we had gone," says Francis, "the presence of the Diplomatic Corps, representing Russia's allies, might have had a pacifying effect on the assemblage."[68] As always, the ambassador was inclined to exaggerate the moral prestige of his office. Even the comparatively conservative Assembly was not favorably disposed toward the Allied cause. Indeed, a resolution was passed "in the name of the peoples of the Russian Republic" expressing the "firm will of the people immediately to discontinue the war and conclude a just and general peace." The Allies were called upon to "define jointly the exact terms of a democratic peace acceptable to all the belligerent nations."[69]

The meeting continued hour after hour, with much turgid oratory from all factions, the speakers frequently being interrupted by catcalls and remarks from the gallery, where soldiers, sailors, and workers of Bolshevik persuasion held forth. About one o'clock in the morning a Bolshevik deputy got up and read a statement presenting the party's view and announcing the withdrawal of their delegation, at which point the Assembly seemed on the verge of a free-for-all fight. The Left Socialist Revolutionaries also quit the hall a short time later, leaving the remaining delegates to pass their resolutions with greater ease. Toward five o'clock the head of the military guard approached the rostrum, laid his hand on the chairman's shoulder, and asked him to disband the meeting because the guard was tired. The chairman tried to ignore him and went on speaking; but the lights began to go out, and it was decided to adjourn until noon. Before the second session could be

---

[68] Francis, p. 203. [69] Bunyan and Fisher, pp. 378-79.

held, a Soviet decree was passed dissolving the Assembly as an aid only to "the bourgeois counterrevolution in its efforts to crush the power of the Soviets."[70] The forceful breakup of the Constituent Assembly was received with apathy by the masses, and the would-be legislators dispersed quietly to their homes.

This mild threat to their domestic rule disposed of, the Soviet leaders turned their attention to the much more serious threat emanating from Berlin. The dissolution of the Assembly, Trotsky admits, adversely affected Russia's position because it signified to the Germans a willingness to "end the war at any price." "Kühlmann's tone," he says, "became more brutal at once."[71] The indignation of the Allied press at the event served only to increase Trotsky's conviction that a "pedagogical demonstration" was more than ever necessary to prove to the European proletariat the deadly enmity actually existing between Hohenzollern and Bolshevik. Lenin remained skeptical. "One could want nothing better," he told Trotsky, "if it turns out that Hoffmann is not strong enough to send troops against us. But there is little hope of that. He will find specially selected regiments of rich Bavarian farmers for it. And then, how many of them does he need? You say yourself that the trenches are empty. What if the Germans resume fighting?"

"Then," said Trotsky, "we will be compelled to sign the peace, but every one will realize that we had no choice. By this act alone, we will deal a decisive blow at the story of our secret connection with the Hohenzollerns."

"Of course, there are certain advantages in that," replied Lenin. "But it is too risky. If it were necessary for us to go under to assure the success of the German revolution, we should have to do it. The German revolution is vastly more important than ours. But when will it come? No one knows. And at the moment, there is nothing so important as our revolution. It must be safeguarded against danger at any price."[72]

Bukharin, joined by a group of "Left Communists," including, among others, Radek, Pokrovsky, and Kollontai, went beyond

[70] *Ibid.*, pp. 384-86.   [71] Trotsky, *Lenin,* p. 105.
[72] Trotsky, *My Life,* pp. 381-82.

Trotsky's position to advocate a "holy war" against the German invaders. With but indifferent success Lenin warned against this "intoxication with the revolutionary phrase." Radek, rising to speak at one meeting of party leaders, glared at Lenin and said, "If there were five hundred courageous men in Petrograd, we would put you in prison."

"Some people, indeed, may go to prison," Lenin replied in an icy tone, "but if you will calculate the probabilities you will see that it is much more likely that I will send you than you me."[73]

In his notable "twenty-one theses" Lenin calmly appraised the merits of the Bukharin-Radek plan and decisively rejected it in favor of signing the peace. "A revolutionary war at this time," he argued in his tenth point, "would place us in the position of agents of Anglo-French imperialism in so far as we should be aiding the cause of the latter. The English have offered our Supreme Commander Krylenko, one hundred rubles a month for every one of our soldiers if we continue to fight. Even if we do not accept a penny from them, we should still be helping them by detaining German troops."[74] Lenin's comment on the supposed offer to Krylenko must have been a bit of rhetorical exaggeration, because Lockhart, the only man who might have had the authority to make such an offer on behalf of the British government, did not arrive in Petrograd until the end of the month. Nor did the other Allied governments seem disposed to commit themselves. Robins had nothing new to report. Sadoul had a look at the Hoffmann map in Trotsky's office and was asked to show it to Noulens and Niessel. "We shall not sign this peace, but what can we do?" asked Trotsky. "The holy war? Yes, we shall declare it, but with what result? The moment has come for the Allies to decide."[75]

The reluctance of the Allies to make a definite promise apparently confirmed Trotsky's suspicion that they were making secret overtures to Germany at Russia's expense. In his speech before the third Congress of Soviets on the twenty-sixth, he declared that England had given "its tacit approval of Kühlmann's

[73] Hard, p. 94. It should be borne in mind that Hard was writing a "popular" account and that the quotations here (as elsewhere) may lack strict accuracy.

[74] Bunyan and Fisher, pp. 500-5.   [75] Sadoul, p. 204.

terms" and was "ready to compromise with Germany at the expense of Russia." "The peace terms which Germany offers us are also the terms of America, France, and England," he charged; "they are the account which the imperialists of the world are making with the Russian Revolution."[76] He went on to speak with contempt of the Ukrainian republic. A British officer, Captain Gerald Fitz-Williams, was then in Kiev along with several French officers trying to win over the Rada to the Allied cause with large-scale bribery, and Trotsky in referring to this "cynical support," pointed out that the Rada "has followed the course of those bourgeois governments of small Balkan states who took bribes at the same time from Russia and from Austria-Hungary." "History will show," he predicted with remarkable accuracy, "that the Rada played a malicious trick on those who have supported them because of their hostility to us."[77]

The Bolshevik central committee, by a vote of nine to seven, finally decided to accept Trotsky's formula of "No war, no peace" if all else failed but meanwhile to delay the negotiations as long as possible. Trotsky promised Lenin that if the Germans advanced he would then be in favor of signing the peace. Some Russian territory would be overrun, but Lenin thought the experiment might not be so dangerous and in any case not nearly so adventurous as the proposed revolutionary war. "For the sake of a good peace with Trotsky," he said with a chuckle, "Latvia and Esthonia are worth losing."[78] Upon his return to Brest-Litovsk Trotsky found the representatives of the Central Powers in a less tolerant mood. They were anxious for a quick decision and an ending to this overly prolonged "spiritual wrestling match."[79] To offset the embarrassing presence of the Ukrainian Rada delegation, Trotsky brought with him two Ukrainian Bolsheviks, for the Red forces were then (January 29) in the process of occupying Kiev and overthrowing the bourgeois government. He sarcastically declared that the Rada delegates had only their lodgings at Brest-Litovsk to

---

[76] Bunyan and Fisher, p. 506; Fisher, I, 50-52, implies that the Bolsheviks may have been correct in their suspicions.

[77] Sisson, pp. 268-69.   [78] Trotsky, *My Life,* p. 383.

[79] Ludendorff, II, 177.

represent, since they could no longer claim to represent any Ukrainian territory. "Judging from the reports from the Ukraine that I had before me," writes Hoffmann, "Trotsky's words seemed unfortunately not to be without foundation."[80] But the disappearance of the Rada failed to dissuade the Central Powers from continuing separate negotiations with the nonexistent Ukrainian government. As Hoffmann puts it: "The difficulties were transitory; at any time we could support the government with arms and establish it again."[81] The peace treaty with the Ukraine, signed on February 9, in exchange for certain territorial concessions obtained for the Central Powers badly needed grain and other produce, as well as vital raw materials. The Anglo-French bribery attempt thus collapsed dismally. As Fitz-Williams said philosophically, "The plan failed, so it has to be called bad. If it had succeeded, it would have been called good."[82]

Bolshevik propaganda had continued unabated through January, and for a time late in the month an epidemic of strikes and workers' demonstrations in Berlin, Vienna, Hamburg, and other cities actually seemed to presage the great awakening of the Central European proletariat. Zinoviev, as president of the Petrograd Soviet, greeted the strikers as "brothers" and hailed their "glorious fight against German and universal Imperialism." "The workers and soldiers of Petrograd," he declared, "have welcomed the news with transports of indescribable enthusiasm. . . . You have shown that the Austro-German working class will not allow the hangmen and spoilers to impose a peace of violation and annexations on the Socialist Republic of the Soviets."[83] Unhappily for this idyll of revolutionary solidarity, the authorities dealt harshly with the strikers and by February 3 the whole movement was in a state of collapse. Bolshevik radio appeals to the German troops became more daring and the soldiers were called upon to murder their officers, the High Command, and the Kaiser himself. Emperor Wilhelm was angered by these incendiary proclamations and at the request of Field-Marshal Paul von Hindenburg wired Kühlmann to present a twenty-four-hour ultimatum to the Russians, requiring as the

---

[80] Hoffmann, II, 216. [81] *Ibid.*, pp. 216-17.
[82] Sisson, p. 269. [83] Magnes, pp. 116-17.

condition of peace the surrender of the Baltic littoral (Estonia and Livonia) in addition to the territory already demanded.[84] The German Foreign Minister, believing himself on the verge of an agreement with Trotsky, courageously stood his ground and threatened to resign unless the order were rescinded.

Kühlmann emerged victorious from this test of will only to find that he had risked his position in vain. On the tenth Trotsky astounded the conference by announcing Russia's withdrawal from the war but her refusal to sign the peace terms. "We can not," he declared, "place the signature of the Russian Revolution under these conditions which bring with them oppression, misery, and hate to millions of human beings. The Governments of Germany and Austro-Hungary are determined to possess lands and peoples by might. Let them do so openly. We can not approve violence. We are going out of [the] war, but we feel ourselves compelled to refuse to sign the peace treaty."[85] Until this concluding statement the delegates had listened with confident satisfaction, assured that Trotsky's denunciation of imperialism was only a rhetorical gesture of defiance before bowing to the inevitable. But when he finished and placed a signed declaration of the Russian position on the conference table, the enemy representatives could only stare in stunned amazement. "We were all dumfounded," says Hoffmann simply.[86]

The Russian delegation departed for home that same evening in a mood of exhilaration, exactly as if they had scored a diplomatic triumph. Kühlmann and Czernin, puzzled as to what to do next in a situation seemingly without parallel in recorded history, were nevertheless relieved that they had not been forced to deliver an ultimatum, for they were fully aware of the moral damage their cause had already suffered at Brest-Litovsk. The answer which Chancellor George von Hertling gave to Wilson's fourteen points sounded painfully hollow in the face of Germany's undisguised annexationist demands. The Allied Supreme War Council had issued a joint declaration only a week before calling

---

[84] Ludendorff, II, 181; Hoffmann, II, 217.
[85] *Proceedings of the Peace Conference*, p. 172.
[86] Hoffmann, II, 218-19.

attention to the "contrast between the professed idealistic aims with which the Central Powers entered upon the present negotiations at Brest-Litovsk, and the now openly disclosed plans of conquest and spoliation."[87] The diplomats were content to accept a *de facto* peace, since German troops already occupied the territory in dispute. Kühlmann was loath to "run after the Bolsheviks with pen in hand" because a forced signature on the peace treaty "would prove of little practical value."[88] At first this policy appeared to have some chance of winning out, but the High Command bestirred itself and secured the approval of the Chancellor and the Kaiser for a denunciation of the armistice and a resumption of hostilities.

In Petrograd most of the Bolshevik luminaries remained incurably optimistic. Even those who conceded the possibility of a German advance allowed themselves the luxury of believing that the morale of her troops had been undermined by propaganda and that the working masses would rise in their rear. In a speech before the party's central committee on the fourteenth, Trotsky defended his actions and closed on a typical note of revolutionary bombast. "If we have to face tacit understandings between the Imperialists of the Central Powers and even perhaps between them and the Allied Powers, if we have to face a plot of World Imperialism against the Russian Revolution," he cried, "we have by our tactics in Brest-Litovsk maintained and reaffirmed the bonds with our natural allies, the workmen of France, England, Germany, Austria, and America. . . . But the World Revolution, the rising of the proletariat of Western Europe and of America will destroy this plot."[89] Resolutions were then passed supporting the work of the Russian delegation at the peace conference and calling for the creation of a "Red Army of peasants and workmen."

The next day Lockhart had his first interview with Trotsky, a two-hour conversation in which every aspect of Anglo-Russian relations was reviewed. Lockhart made no promises—most of his telegrams to London had been unanswered—but Trotsky impressed him as "perfectly honest and sincere in his bitterness against the Germans" and a man "who would willingly die fighting for Rus-

[87] Lloyd George, V, 47.   [88] Kühlmann, p. 547.
[89] Sisson, p. 328.

sia provided there was a big enough audience to see him do it."[90] Lockhart returned from Smolny to find that Robins had become involved in a dispute with Ivan Zalkind, the Assistant Commissar of Foreign Affairs. Robins, in high dudgeon, was determined to exact an apology for Zalkind's rudeness or leave the country. Lenin phoned and promised that the Assistant Commissar would be relieved of his post but that as an old member of the party he would have to be employed in some other capacity. Would Robins mind if Zalkind were sent as a Bolshevik emissary to Berne? Robins smiled and said, "Thank you, Mr. Lenin. As I can't send the son of a bitch to hell, 'burn' is the next best thing you can do with him."[91] Lenin thus managed to soothe Robins's feelings without revealing that Zalkind had already been considered for a diplomatic mission to Switzerland, along with Petrov to England and Kamenev to France. Petrov instead succeeded Zalkind in the Foreign Office, and Chicherin, who had acted in Trotsky's place during his absence at Brest-Litovsk, was shortly afterwards installed as head of the foreign ministry. Trotsky thought his resignation, as he told Lenin, "would imply for the Germans a radical change in our policy and would strengthen their confidence in our willingness actually to sign the peace treaty this time."[92]

Kamenev and Zalkind reached England later in the month. The former carried a message asking for Allied assistance to repel the Germans, provided the help offered did not involve intervention in the Far East by the Japanese.[93] Notwithstanding the informal agreement made between Britain and Russia permitting a certain quasi-legal status for Litvinov in London and Lockhart in Petrograd, the two Bolsheviks were received with hostility upon their arrival at Aberdeen on the twenty-third. They were searched and Kamenev's diplomatic pouch, money, luggage, and other personal belongings seized. This unusual treatment was the subject of an attack by MacDonald on the government authorities responsible in the House of Commons a few days later.[94]

[90] Lockhart, p. 224.   [91] Ibid., pp. 225-26.
[92] Trotsky, My Life, p. 389.
[93] Wheeler-Bennett, p. 284. His information was derived from personal sources.
[94] Parliamentary Debates, CIII (February 27, 1918), 1477-79.

In London, where he was shadowed by detectives throughout his stay, Kamenev talked privately with a number of people, including two officials of the Foreign Office, one of whom received his protests against the violation of his diplomatic immunity and the other his report of the peace negotiations. A member of Parliament bluntly told him that neither the French nor the British government would recognize his diplomatic status and that he would have to return to Russia. He at least seems to have impressed those with whom he talked with his appearance. One described him as a "somewhat sinister teddy-bear," and another said he looked like a "cinquecento Christ." His request for aid was unheeded in London. Unable to proceed to Paris, he left for Petrograd in a most embittered state of mind. But his troubles were just beginning. On the Finnish frontier he was arrested by the authorities and regained his freedom only when an agreement was reached in July between the Soviet government and the German embassy, acting on Finland's behalf, exchanging Kamenev and other Bolshevik prisoners for Finnish citizens held in Petrograd.[95]

Meanwhile, German troops had dispelled all Bolshevik illusions by beginning their advance on the morning of the eighteenth. They met no resistance of any kind; the few Russian troops that had not already gone home either surrendered or fled. In an order to his troops, Prince Leopold, the commander-in-chief on the Eastern Front, maintained that Germany's aim was not annexation but the restoration of order and the suppression of anarchy. "Russia is sick and is trying to contaminate all the countries of the world with a moral infection," he asserted. "We must fight against the disorder inoculated by Trotzky, and defend outraged liberty. Germany is fortunate in being the incarnation of the sentiments of other order-loving peoples."[96] Even the most cynical aggression was thus capable of rationalization in terms of a "holy crusade"

---

[95] George Chicherin, *Two Years of Foreign Policy* (New York, 1920), pp. 19-20; U. S. Department of State, *Texts of the Finland "Peace"* (Washington, 1918), p. 53; Bernard Pares, "Notes on Interview with Mr. Vorovsky" (April 5, 1918), Wiseman Papers.

[96] Magnes, p. 149.

against Bolshevism. To Hoffmann, the menace of Bolshevism was already an *idée fixe,* and the order to resume hostilities was as sweet music to his ears. He was concerned lest the Bolsheviks turn the "whole of Europe into a pigsty," for Russia was "no more than a vast heap of maggots—a squalid, swarming mess." The general was gratified by the unexpected ease of the advance. "It is the most comical war I have ever known—it is almost entirely carried on by rail and motorcar," he recorded in his diary on the twenty-second. "We put a handful of infantrymen with machine guns . . . on a train and push them off to the next station; they take it, make prisoners of the Bolsheviks, pick up a few more troops and go on. This proceeding has, at any rate, the charm of novelty."[97]

Lenin was in conference with two leaders of the Left Socialist Revolutionaries when the notice came from Brest-Litovsk of Germany's intention to break the armistice. Trotsky was also present and Lenin handed him the telegram without a word. As before, Trotsky argued for delay in signing the peace terms to allow the German offensive to actually begin. But Lenin's concern was whether the Germans would agree to the original terms, not whether Russia should still refuse to sign. "We can't afford to lose a single hour now," he exclaimed. "The test has been made. Hoffmann wants to and can fight. Delay is impossible. This beast jumps fast."[98] The central committee overruled Lenin by a one-vote margin and chose to procrastinate. When the Germans demonstrated that they were not bluffing, a radio message was sent offering to accept the old peace terms. But the High Command, not yet glutted with territory that was theirs for the taking, was not disposed to be hasty. German troops continued to advance at will as the "socialist fatherland" was declared in danger. The government made preparations to fight a revolutionary war against the "hordes of bourgeois-imperialistic Germany." The Allies too came in for a sharp attack, being accused of sabotaging Soviet peace efforts by aiding Dukhonin, Kaledin, Alexeyev, the Rada, and Romania. "All of us, including Lenin," says Trotsky, "were of the impression that the Germans had come to an agreement

[97] Hoffmann, I, 205-7.
[98] Trotsky, *My Life,* p. 387.

with the Allies about crushing the Soviets and that a peace on the Western Front was to be built on the bones of the Russian Revolution."[99]

However "tainted" the source, aid was nevertheless eagerly sought from the Allies, because even a defensive war for the most just of all causes could not be fought with enthusiasm alone. Trotsky told Lockhart he would sway the decision of the government toward war if the Allies would promise help, but no reply was forthcoming from London in acknowledgment of Lockhart's messages.[100] Robins continued to dispense vague promises of American support, until Trotsky told him humorously but with a note of irritation: "Colonel Robins, your embassy sends you here with a big bag marked 'American Help.' You arrive every day, and you bring the bag into my room, and you set it down beside your chair, and you keep reaching into it as you talk, and it is a powerful bag. But nothing comes out."[101]

Despite the silence in London, Paris, and Washington, the ambassadors agreed in principle to offer assistance. Noulens telephoned Trotsky at Sadoul's insistence and told him the Soviet government could "count on the military and financial aid of France." The French and British military missions offered to cooperate with the Red Guard in destroying the rails over which the Germans might soon enter Petrograd.[102] On the twenty-second Trotsky informed the central committee of the French offer and expressed himself in favor of accepting it on the condition that the Bolsheviks were left completely free in matters of foreign policy. Bukharin, though still a strong advocate of the revolutionary war, spoke against making such arrangements with imperialist governments. Lenin was not present but scribbled a note reading, "I ask to add my vote in favor of taking potatoes and arms from the bandits of Anglo-French imperialism." The motion carried by a single vote. In the long corridor of Smolny after the

[99] Ibid., p. 388.
[100] Lockhart, p. 227.
[101] Hard, pp. 122-23.
[102] Sadoul, pp. 241-43; Noulens, I, 223; Francis to Lansing, Feb. 22, 1918, Foreign Relations, I, 386.

meeting, Bukharin flung his arms around Trotsky and sobbed, "We are turning the party into a dung-heap."[103]

In the face of the German threat to Petrograd the embassies made preparations for a hasty exit. On the twenty-seventh American, Japanese, and Chinese personnel left for Vologda, a city situated at a railroad junction several hundred miles east of the capital. A day later most of the remaining embassies, including those of England and France (the Italians had been refused passports and were delayed several days), attempted to leave Russia by the Finland route. Only the British succeeded in getting through the battle lines of the Finnish Reds and Whites; the others, after waiting vainly on their special trains for two weeks, joined the Americans at Vologda.[104] This hurried flight turned out to be unnecessary, since the Germans eventually stopped some eighty miles short of Petrograd after overrunning the Baltic provinces, the Ukraine, and the rest of Poland. They had at last replied to the Bolshevik offer with an ultimatum beside which the previous terms seemed almost generous. The message was not received until the twenty-third, and a notice of acceptance was to be forwarded within forty-eight hours.

Lenin had no patience with the patriotic delusions of the Bukharin clique. "It is time to put an end to revolutionary phrases and get down to real work," he told the central committee. "If this is not done I resign from the government. To carry on a revolutionary war, an army, which we do not have, is needed. Under the circumstances there is nothing to do but to accept the terms." When the vote was taken, six sided with Lenin, four refrained from voting (including Trotsky), and four voted for war. The latter group then resigned from the party.[105] Lenin went through an even more exhausting ordeal late in the evening before the Soviet executive committee. But after an all-night session his inexorable logic won a clear majority for submission to the German terms. There were howls of "Traitors . . . Judases . . .

---

[103] Trotsky, *My Life,* p. 389; Chamberlin, I, 404.

[104] Francis, pp. 234-35; Niessel, pp. 290-91; Noulens, II, 1-10 and 18-26; and Destrée, pp. 291-306.

[105] Bunyan and Fisher, p. 519.

German spies!" from the Socialist Revolutionaries of the Left as the Bolsheviks prepared to leave.[106]

The Russian delegation, headed by Sokolnikov, left for the familiar scene at Brest-Litovsk on the twenty-fourth. Delayed by transportation difficulties caused by the demolition activities of the Red Guard in opposing the Germans, the delegates did not arrived until four days later. To dramatize the undeniable fact that it was a dictated peace the Russians assumed an air of martyrdom and refused to discuss the terms. "If the German Emperor had demanded Moscow as his capital and a summer residence in the Ural Mountains, the Russians would have signed without winking an eyelash," commented the *Münchener Post*.[107] There was a brief moment of panic in Petrograd when a telegram from Karakhan requesting a train and an armed escort was taken as evidence that the negotiations had been broken off by the Germans.[108] But the situation was clarified with the receipt of an earlier telegram which had been delayed in transit, and the treaty was signed on March 3 as Sokolnikov declared in a prepared statement that it was a peace "which Russia, grinding its teeth, is compelled to accept." "This is a peace," he continued, "which, whilst pretending to free Russian border provinces, really transforms them into German provinces and deprives them of the right of free self-determination, such as was recognized by the Workmen's and Peasants' Government of Revolutionary Russia, as due to them. . . . This is a peace which gives back the land to the landlords, and again drives the workers into the serfdom of the factory owners." But we do not doubt for a minute, said Sokolnikov, "that this triumph of the imperialist and the militarist over the international proletarian Revolution is only a temporary and passing one."[109]

Russia's wealthiest provinces were torn away, territory containing a third of her population, a third of her cultivated land, and half of her industry. It was a lesson and a warning to the Allies which no amount of synthetic anti-German propaganda manufac-

---

[106] Astrov *et al.*, II, 509.
[107] Quoted in Wheeler-Bennett, p. 266.
[108] *Proceedings of the Peace Conference*, p. 180.
[109] *Ibid.*, pp. 185-87.

tured for home consumption could equal. And to judge from the press reaction it was a lesson well learned. "The policy of the German government in respect to Russia," said the *New Republic*, "has only confirmed the conviction of western democrats as to the necessity of putting an end now to this international marauding, and as long as and in so far as fighting is necessary to teach the Germans the insufferability of what they are doing, the fighting will go on."[110]   To the Philadelphia *Press* Germany's course in Russia proved that it would be "quite mad to take the German word for anything,"[111] and the *Daily Telegraph* of London sharply rebuked the Allied "Bolshevists and pacifists" for still speaking "tenderly of German moderation and her self-styled offers of peace." They were urged to "anxiously ponder all that is involved in this tragic episode of Russia's ruin and draw therefrom conclusions which cannot fail to be illuminating and salutary for themselves."[112] The Paris *Temps,* speaking of the peace as "criminal," noted with satisfaction that the judgment of the Allies regarding it had been "firm and clear-sighted."[113]   Yet the more conservative organs of of opinion, of which the *Temps* was one, could not refrain from blaming the Bolsheviks as well as Germany for Russia's plight. The Boston *Evening Transcript* spoke more bitterly of the Bolshevik leaders than the "aggression and rapine" of Germany. The betrayal at Brest-Litovsk was blamed on "a couple of perverted fanatics who . . . were able to incite the ignorant millions of Russia against Kerensky and Kornilov and to persuade these millions that their German brethren were too high minded to take advantage of an unarmed people! Never, we repeat, has there been such a betrayal in the history of the world."[114]   It appeared to the Parisian *Matin* that the Bolsheviks had "given their country to Germany in the hope of saving the socialist revolution which the continuation of the war was fatally compromising."[115]   The London *Times* implied that the harsh peace was only what the Bolsheviks could expect, for it was they who had "broken up the Russian armies

---

[110] XIV (March 23, 1918), 215.
[111] Quoted in *Current Opinion,* LXIV (April, 1918), 231.
[112] March 8, 1918.   [113] March 20, 1918.
[114] March 4, 1918.   [115] March 6, 1918.

and left their own country defenseless before implacable invaders,"[116] and the weekly *Spectator,* although affirming the Allied will to "continue the war to free the world from German tyranny," stated that it was not being done "to protect the cowardly and treacherous Bolsheviks," but for whose "crimes and follies" the war might be ending.[117]

The treaty had been signed but not yet ratified. The "Left Communist" group, in whose militant "revolutionary" patriotism the most ardent nationalist of the old regime could have found little to criticize, raged against Lenin's "obscene" policy in the *Kommunist,* their newly founded organ, and prepared for a last-ditch stand against what they conceived to be a traitorous surrender to Germany. The triumvirate of Allied diplomatic agents also sought to thwart ratification by promising ample support from their governments. In reality their influence on Allied policy was severely limited. Only Lockhart had direct contact with his government, and it was subject to the vagaries of imperfect telegraphic communication and, what was more serious, a great deal of hostility to his conduct within the Foreign Office. One official complained that he treated Trotsky "as if he were a Bismarck or a Talleyrand," and another urged Balfour to "recall this impudent young man."[118]

Robins and Sadoul lacked even the dubious advantage which the Englishman enjoyed. Neither had the confidence of his respective ambassador, and Sadoul especially had frequent clashes with the conservative Noulens. Lockhart met Lenin for the first time on February 29 and was impressed by the man's "tremendous will-power, his relentless determination, and his lack of emotion," even though he looked at first glance "more like a provincial grocer than a leader of men." Lenin did not expect the peace to be kept and told Lockhart that if the Germans tried to install a bourgeois government the Bolsheviks would fight, even if they had to withdraw to the Urals. "We can afford to compromise temporarily with capital," said Lenin. "It is even necessary, for, if capital were

---

[116] March 8, 1918.

[117] CXX (March 23, 1918), 306.

[118] Blanche E. C. Dugdale, *Arthur James Balfour* (London, 1936), II, 258; Wheeler-Bennett, p. 296 n.

to unite, we should be crushed at this stage of our development. Fortunately for us, it is in the nature of capital that it cannot unite. So long, therefore, as the German danger exists, I am prepared to risk co-operation with the Allies, which should be temporarily advantageous to both of us." But, he predicted, "Your government will never see things in this light. It is a reactionary government. It will co-operate with the Russian reactionaries."[119]

Lockhart was not prepared to accept so cynical an estimate of British policy and continued to strive mightily to sway the Foreign Office toward a more friendly attitude. He was aroused particularly by reports of Japanese intervention. To the Bolsheviks intervention by Japan was no more welcome than intervention by Germany. Lockhart warned Balfour that if the Allies were going to allow Japan to enter Siberia all prospect of co-operation with Russia was hopeless. "I feel sure," he wrote, "that you can have no idea of the feeling which Japanese intervention will arouse. Even the Cadet Press, which cannot be accused of Bolshevik sympathies is loud in its denunciation of this crime against Russia, and is now preaching support of any party that will oppose Germany and save the revolution."[120] The stock reply, that "Japan would come, not like the Germans as hostile conquerors, but as allies and friends," was not reassuring even to Lockhart, much less to the Bolsheviks.

"By sheer logic of events the working classes are the only force in Russia which does not welcome German intervention," Lockhart again telegraphed London on March 10. "Already, as in the Ukraine, there are several bourgeois combinations which are plotting to form a Government under the Germans. If by permitting Japanese intervention at the present moment we destroy the only force in Russia which will oppose Germany, we must take the consequences."[121] Yet Balfour apparently did not believe that encouraging the Japanese in their Far Eastern adventure constituted interference. "I have constantly impressed on Mr. Lockhart that it is *not* our desire to interfere in Russian internal affairs," the Foreign Minister commented petulantly. "He appears to be very

---

[119] Lockhart, pp. 235-37.
[120] Cumming and Pettit, pp. 82-84.
[121] Dugdale, II, 258.

unsuccessful in conveying this view to the Bolshevik government."[122]

The Allied embassies at Vologda fed voraciously on wild anti-Bolshevik rumors, and hardly a day passed without orders to the personnel remaining in Petrograd to investigate or protest some new and nonexistent Bolshevik outrage. Trotsky would sometimes grow angry at the stupidity of the ambassadors; then again he would laughingly offer to write out a bromide prescription to calm their nerves. General Romei of the Italian military mission expressed his disgust with the ambassadors in stronger terms than Trotsky. After returning with Lockhart from one trip to Vologda, he exclaimed, "If we had put all the Allied representatives there in a cauldron and stirred them up, not one drop of common sense would have come out of the whole boiling."[123] Because of the proximity of the Germans, the Bolsheviks began in the early part of March to shift the government from Petrograd to the Kremlin in Moscow, the historic site of Russia's capital up to the time of Peter the Great more than two centuries before. Trotsky, who took up his duties as Commissar of War during this period, left Petrograd with Lockhart and other members of the British mission just as the All-Russian Congress of Soviets met in Moscow to decide for peace or war by its decision to ratify or reject the Brest-Litovsk treaty.

Lockhart's failure to secure a guarantee or even a vague promise from his government of help to Russia had not discouraged Robins or Sadoul from their persistent efforts toward the same end. Sadoul had no better luck with Noulens and received no answer to his appeal to Paris for military assistance. He made a special trip to Vologda to see Francis and obtained from him a pledge of aid which his own ambassador had refused.[124] Robins had left Petrograd with the embassy but returned and saw Trotsky on the fifth. Robins was asked if he still wanted to prevent the peace from being ratified, and when the expected reply was forthcoming, Trotsky told him that the time had come for a definite promise of

[122] *Ibid.*, p. 259.
[123] Lockhart, p. 247.
[124] Sadoul, p. 254.

help from the American government. If he could produce it, Trotsky promised to go to Moscow and defeat ratification. But Robins knew that Trotsky had always been against the peace. "What about Lenin?" he inquired.

"Lenin agrees," said Trotsky.

"Will he say so?"

"He will."

"In writing?"

Trotsky hesitated but finally promised that both would sign a written statement if he would come back that afternoon. Robins returned for the appointment with his secretary and interpreter, Alexander Gumberg, who translated into English the document which Trotsky and Lenin had prepared. It posed two main questions in the event of a new rupture with Germany: (1) What kind of support the Allies, and specifically the United States, would furnish; (2) what steps the Allies, particularly the United States, would take to prevent a Japanese landing in Siberia.[125] After the English version had been read aloud, Robins asked Lenin, "Does the translation give your understanding of the meaning of the document?"

"Yes," said Lenin.

Then, pursued Robins, "If the United States government answers this document affirmatively, will you oppose the ratification of the Peace of Brest-Litovsk at the All-Russian Congress of Soviets at Moscow?"

"Yes," said Lenin again.[126]

The message was immediately coded and sent to Vologda for transmission to Washington. By an unfortunate mischance, the only American officer familiar with the code had just left Vologda, and it was not until Robins himself arrived three days later that the vital dispatch was forwarded to the State Department. Meanwhile the message had been sent to the War Department from Petrograd. Francis cabled his own interpretation of the events in terms that indicated approval of Robins's efforts. "I cannot too strongly urge the folly of an invasion by the Japanese now," he

---

[125] Hard, pp. 134-35 and 138-39.   [126] *Ibid.*, p. 138.

declared in a second cable. "It is possible that the Congress at Moscow may ratify the peace, but if I receive assurance from you that the Japanese peril is baseless, I am of the opinion that the Congress will reject this humiliating peace. The Soviet government is the only power which is able to offer resistance to the German advance and consequently should be assisted if it is sincerely antagonistic to Germany." The ambassador then repeated his belief that Lenin and Trotsky were German agents, an action which certainly seemed likely to chill any favorable consideration of the Soviet offer.[127] Robins, confident that the State Department would respond with a satisfactory answer, begged Lenin to postpone the Soviet meeting, scheduled for the twelfth, for at least forty-eight hours. Lenin was noncommittal, but it was announced in *Izvestia* the next day that the Congress would meet on the fourteenth at Lenin's request.[128]

From every corner of Russia delegates to the fourth Congress of Soviets—about twelve hundred in all—gathered to render the final verdict on the peace terms. Before the first session opened Lenin asked Robins what he had heard from his government.

"Nothing," said Robins.

"What has Lockhart heard?"

"Exactly the same thing." He ventured to ask if the debate might be prolonged, but Lenin said it would have to take its course.[129]

During the evening of the fourteenth, shortly after the assembly had been brought to order, the chairman read a brief message from President Wilson which had been sent at the suggestion of Colonel House.[130] It expressed sympathy for the Russian people "at this moment when the German power has been thrust in to interrupt and turn back the whole struggle for freedom" yet avoided a more concrete demonstration of sympathy with the words, "The

---

[127] Francis to Lansing, March 9, 1917 (861.00/1264), National Archives; incomplete text in *Bolshevik Propaganda*, p. 1012. The version Francis gave Robins omitted the third paragraph containing the "German agent" charge. See Schuman, *American Policy toward Russia*, p. 76, and Paul Harper, pp. 112-13.

[128] *Bolshevik Propaganda*, p. 805. [129] *Ibid.*; Hard, pp. 148-49.

[130] House to Wilson, March 10, 1918, Wilson Papers; Seymour, III, 399 (text on p. 420).

Government of the United States is, unhappily, not now in a position to render the direct and effective aid it would wish to render." The statement was received with applause, but so was the resolution adopted by the Soviet executive committee which replied in terms that could hardly have been considered friendly by the President. Although gratitude was expressed for Wilson's kindly sentiments, "all peoples perishing and suffering from the imperialistic war" were given the "warm sympathy" of the Congress of Soviets in the "firm belief that the happy time is not far distant when the laboring masses of all countries will throw off the yoke of capitalism and will establish a socialistic state of society."[131]

Debate on the treaty began the next morning, continued all day, and resumed on the sixteenth. Most of the speakers opposed ratification, but from the applause which greeted the proponents of both views, it was difficult to judge which side would win out. Lenin did not speak until late in the evening of the last session. Robins was sitting on the steps leading to the platform, and Lenin motioned for him to come over. "What have you heard from your government?" he asked.

"Nothing. What has Lockhart heard from London?"

"Nothing," said Lenin. "I shall now speak for the peace. It will be ratified."[132]

For an hour and twenty minutes Lenin spoke in his quiet, compelling voice, demonstrating with unanswerable logic the futility of further resistance. He called the treaty a "Tilsit peace," in reference to the peace which Prussia had been forced to sign with Napoleon in 1807, and just as the German people had had their vengeance, so would the Russian people, Lenin implied, be able to overthrow the settlement. He was the last speaker. The vote was taken: for ratification, 784; against, 261; not voting, 115.

Two days later the prime ministers and foreign ministers of the Allies—the United States abstaining—issued a joint declaration refusing to acknowledge the treaty because it was the incarnation of the "political crimes, which, under the name of a German peace, have been committed against the Russian people." Germany was

---

[131] *Foreign Relations,* I, 399-400.   [132] Hard, pp. 151-52.

denounced as a "destroyer of national independence, the implacable enemy of the rights of man and the dignity of civilized nations," and it was against "this policy of plunder and to establish in its place the peaceful reign of organized justice" that the Allies were resolved to continue the fight.[133]

A little less than eight months after this statement was made the fortunes of war brought victory to the Allies, and with it, an end to the "Tilsit peace." By the armistice signed on November 11, 1918, Germany was forced to renounce the Treaty of Brest-Litovsk, and on the thirteenth the Soviet government, threatened by White armies supplied with Allied guns and supported with Allied money, declared the treaty null and void.

When the Treaty of Versailles was signed on June 28, 1919, by the pale and nervous German delegates, perhaps General Hoffmann recalled the prophetic words of the irrepressible Karl Radek, the little hunchbacked Bolshevik who had taken such delight in blowing vile black cigar smoke into his face at the peace conference. "In the end," he had told the Germans, "the Allies will put a Brest-Litovsk treaty on you."[134]

[133] Foreign Relations, I, 438-39.
[134] Hard, p. 125; Lockhart, p. 252.

Bibliography

PRIMARY SOURCES
MANUSCRIPTS

I. OFFICIAL

National Archives, Washington, D. C. The extensive diplomatic correspondence relating to revolutionary Russia is open without restrictions, chiefly under file numbers 861.00 and 763.72.

U. S. Consulate Reports. Petrograd, March-July, 1917. Hoover Library, Stanford University. Contains the detailed reports of North Winship, American consul in Petrograd.

U. S. Department of State. "Periodical Report on Matters Relating to Russia" (September, 1917–March, 1918). Hoover Library, Stanford University. A biweekly summary of political and diplomatic events.

II. PRIVATE PAPERS

Darling, William F. Hoover Library, Stanford University. A member of the railway mission to Russia, Darling kept a detailed diary of his experiences in 1917.

Golder, Frank A. Hoover Library, Stanford University. Professor Golder's correspondence and reports of conversations with prominent Russian émigrés furnishes some interesting sidelights on the events of 1917.

Harper, Samuel N. University of Chicago Library. Professor Harper, a pioneer in Russian studies, was an adviser to the American ambassador in 1917, but his papers contain little of significance on that important year aside from "human interest" material.

House, Edward M. Yale University Library. Colonel House, President Wilson's confidant, has preserved an extensive correspondence and a diary dealing only incidentally with Russia. The most significant material has been published in Seymour's *Intimate Papers.*

Judson, William V. Newberry Library, Chicago. General Judson was chief of the American military mission to Russia in 1917. His papers, though they relate chiefly to military matters, are of importance concerning political events.

Lansing, Robert. Library of Congress. With some exceptions the Secretary of State's diplomatic reports and correspondence have been printed in the State Department's *Lansing Papers*.

Polk, Frank L. Yale University Library. Polk was counsellor of the Department of State. His papers, a part of the House Collection, contain no significant revelations but help to complete the American-Russian diplomatic picture.

Root, Elihu. Library of Congress. Root headed the American diplomatic mission to Russia in 1917. His diary, personal letters, and reports furnish a detailed account of the mission's work.

Russell, Charles Edward. Library of Congress. A leading American socialist, Russell was a member of the Root mission. His diary and correspondence is unusually informative on the less official aspects of the journey.

Scott, Hugh L. Library of Congress. General Scott, another member of the Root mission, furnishes added details on the work accomplished, much of it relating to the military situation.

Stevens, John F. Hoover Library, Stanford University. Stevens headed the railway mission to Russia. His papers give a comprehensive picture of Russia's transportation difficulties and the remedies provided, including the second phase of the mission's work during the intervention period.

Thompson, William Boyce. Library of Congress. As head of the American Red Cross mission, Thompson played a leading role in some of the political events of 1917. The material in this collection was assembled by Hermann Hagedorn for his official biography of Thompson.

Wilson, Woodrow. Library of Congress. The President's papers, voluminous on Russia alone, include a good deal of routine correspondence. Those of significance have, with some exceptions, been printed in Baker's *Life and Letters* and the State Department's *Foreign Relations* series.

Wiseman, William. Yale University Library. Sir William was the chief of British military intelligence in Washington. His papers, a part of the House Collection, furnish some incidental information on Allied-Russian relations.

III. OTHER

Milyukov, Paul. "From Nicholas II to Stalin (Half-a-Century of

Foreign Politics)." Typewritten manuscript, *circa* 1941. Hoover Library, Stanford University.

———— and Semyenov, Eugene P. Typewritten English translation of a series of articles entitled "German Money to Lenin" from the *Poslyedny Novosti* [*Latest News*] (Paris), April 3-8, 1921. Hoover Library, Stanford University.

OFFICIAL DOCUMENTS

Adamov, E. A. (ed.). *Konstantinopl i Prolivi: Po Sekretnim Dokumentam B. Ministerstva Inostrannikh Del* [*Constantinople and the Straits: From the Secret Documents of the Former Ministry of Foreign Affairs*]. Moscow: Litizdat NKID, 1925-26.

Complete Report of the Chairman of the Committee on Public Information: 1917, 1918, 1919. Washington: Government Printing Office, 1920.

France, Chambre des Députes. *Débats parlementaires.* Session ordinaire de 1917. Paris, 1917-18.

The German-Bolshevik Conspiracy. Washington: Committee on Public Information, 1918. The official text of the famous "Sisson documents."

Great Britain, House of Commons. *Parliamentary Debates.* Fifth series. London: H. M. Stationery Office, 1917-18.

U. S. Congress. *Congressional Record.* Sixty-fifth Congress, first and second sessions. Washington: Government Printing Office, 1917-18.

U. S. Congress, Senate. Committee on the Judiciary. *Bolshevik Propaganda.* Sixty-fifth Congress, third session. Washington: Government Printing Office, 1919. A bulky volume of testimony by various eyewitnesses to the events of 1917-18. The account of Raymond Robins is particularly useful.

U. S. Department of State. *Papers Relating to the Foreign Relations of the United States: The Lansing Papers, 1914-1920.* 2 vols. Washington: Government Printing Office, 1939-40.

U. S. Department of State. *Papers Relating to the Foreign Relations of the United States: Russia, 1918.* 3 vols. Washington: Government Printing Office, 1931-32. Volumes I and II deal with diplomatic relations, 1917-18; Volume III with economic relations. The documents represent only a selection from a much larger collection now in the National Archives. With a few exceptions, the edition includes all the documents of more than routine interest.

U. S. Department of State. *Papers Relating to the Foreign Relations of the United States: The World War, 1917, Supplement 2.* 2 vols. Washington: Government Printing Office, 1932.

U. S. Department of State. *Proceedings of the Brest-Litovsk Conference.* Washington: Government Printing Office, 1918.

U. S. Department of State. *Texts of the Finland "Peace."* Washington: Government Printing Office, 1918.

U. S. Department of State. *Texts of the Russian "Peace."* Washington: Government Printing Office, 1918.

UNOFFICIAL DOCUMENTS

America's Message to the Russian People: Addresses by the Members of the Special Mission of the United States to Russia in the Year 1917. Boston: Marshall Jones, 1918.

Baker, Ray Stannard. *Woodrow Wilson: Life and Letters.* 8 vols. New York: Doubleday, Doran, 1927-39.

————, and Dodd, William E. (eds.). *The Public Papers of Woodrow Wilson.* 6 vols. New York and London: Harper & Brothers, 1925-27.

Balch, Emily Greene. *Approaches to the Great Settlement.* New York: B. W. Huebsch, 1918.

Bunyan, James. *Intervention, Civil War, and Communism in Russia, April–December 1918: Documents and Materials.* Baltimore: Johns Hopkins Press, 1936.

————, and Fisher, H. H. *The Bolshevik Revolution, 1917-1918: Documents and Materials.* Stanford University, California: Stanford University Press, 1934.

Cocks, F. Seymour (ed.). *The Secret Treaties and Understandings: Text of the Available Documents.* London: Union of Democratic Control, 1918.

Comité Organisateur de la Conférence Socialiste Internationale de Stockholm. *Stockholm.* Stockholm: Tidens Förlag, 1918.

Cumming, C. K., and Pettit, Walter W. (eds.). *Russian-American Relations, March, 1917–March, 1920: Documents and Papers.* New York: Harcourt, Brace and Howe, 1920.

Degras, Jane (ed.). *Soviet Documents on Foreign Policy.* Vol. I, 1917-1924. New York and London: Oxford University Press, 1951.

Gankin, Olga Hess, and Fisher, H. H. *The Bolsheviks and the World War: The Origin of the Third International.* Stanford University, California: Stanford University Press, 1940.

Krasny Arkhiv [*Red Archives*]. 108 vols. Moscow, 1922-41. A Russian historical journal, from which the following collections of documents have been used:

Berzin, Y. "Dnevnik P. N. Milyukova" ["The Diary of P. N. Milyukov"], LIV-LV (1932), 3-48.

Gelis, I. "Romanovy i Soyuzniki v Pervye Dni Revolyutsii"

["The Romanovs and the Allies during the First Days of the Revolution"], XVI (1926), 44-52.

Martynov, E. "Konferentsia Soyuznikov v Petrograde 1917 Godu" ["The Conference of the Allies in Petrograd in 1917"], XX (1927), 39-55.

"Nakanune Peremiria" ["On the Eve of the Armistice"], XXIII (1927), 195-249.

Popov, A. "Diplomaty Vremennovo Pravitelstva v Borbe s Revolyutsiey" ["The Diplomats of the Provisional Government in Its Struggle against the Revolution"], XX (1927), 3-38.

————. "Inostrannye Diplomaty o Revolyutsii 1917 g." ["Foreign Diplomats on the Revolution of 1917"], XXIV (1927), 108-63.

————. "Vokrug Poyezdki Viviani i Albera Toma" ["Concerning the Visit of Viviani and Albert Thomas"], XV (1926), 223-29.

Shlyapnikov, A. "Fevralskaya Revolyutsia i Evropeyskie Sotsialisty" ["The February Revolution and the European Socialists"], XV (1926), 61-85, and XVI (1926), 25-43.

Zakharov, Meyer G. "Vosstanie Russkikh Soldat vo Frantsii v 1917 g." ["The Revolt of the Russian Soldiers in France in 1917"], XCIX (1940), 52-71.

Lazarevski, Vladimir (ed.). Archives secrètes de l'Empereur Nicholas II. Paris: Payot, 1928.

Magnes, Judah L. Russia and Germany at Brest-Litovsk: A Documentary History of the Peace Negotiations. New York: Rand School of Social Science, 1919.

Manteyer, G. de (ed.). Austria's Peace Offer, 1916-1917. London: Constable, 1921.

Oldenbourg, Serge (ed.). Le Coup d'état bolcheviste: 20 octobre-3 décembre 1917. Paris: Payot, 1929.

Le Parti socialiste, la guerre et la paix: Toutes les résolutions et tous les documents du parti socialiste, de juillet 1914 à fin 1917. Paris: Libraire de l'Humanite, 1918.

Popov, I. (ed.). "Perepiska Milyukova i Tereshchenko s Poslami Vremennovo Pravitelstva" ["The Correspondence of Milyukov and Tereshchenko with the Ambassadors of the Provisional Government"], Borba Klassov [Class Struggle], No. 5 (1931), 84-88.

Report of the Seventeenth Annual Conference of the Labour Party. London: Labour Party, [1918].

Report of the Twenty-Sixth Annual Conference. London: Independent Labour Party, 1918.

Root, Elihu. The United States and the War; The Mission to Russia; *Political Addresses.* Cambridge, Mass.: Harvard University Press, 1918.

Russia and Her Allies: Extracts from the Verbatim Report of the Imperial Duma. Fourth session, sixteenth sitting. London: Burrup, Mathieson & Sprague, 1917.

Sack, A. J. *The Birth of the Russian Democracy.* New York: Russian Information Bureau, 1918.

Scott, James Brown (ed.). *Official Statements of War Aims and Peace Proposals: December 1916 to November 1918.* Washington: Carnegie Endowment for International Peace, 1921.

Seymour, Charles. *The Intimate Papers of Colonel House.* 4 vols. Boston and New York: Houghton Mifflin, 1928.

The Soviet Union and Peace: The Most Important of the Documents Issued by the Government of the U.S.S.R. Concerning Peace and Disarmament from 1917 to 1929. With an Introduction by Henri Barbusse. New York: International Publishers, n.d.

Varneck, Elena, and Fisher, H. H. (eds.). *The Testimony of Kolchak and Other Siberian Materials.* Stanford University, California: Stanford University Press, 1935. Gives the admiral's account of his visit to the United States in 1917.

BOOKS AND PAMPHLETS

Addison, Rt. Hon. Christopher. *Four and a Half Years: A Personal Diary from June 1914 to January 1919.* 2 vols. London: Hutchinson, 1934. Scattered material on Britain's Russian policy by the Minister of Munitions.

——————. *Politics from Within, 1911-18.* 2 vols. London: Herbert Jenkins, 1924. Supplements the above work. Includes extracts from reports on Russia sent to the British War Office.

Aldrovandi Marescotti, L. *Guerra diplomatica: Ricordi e frammenti di diario.* Milan: A. Mondadori, 1936. Gives some information on the Allied conference at Petrograd in early February, 1917. The author was a member of the Italian delegation.

Anet, Claude. *La Révolution russe.* 4 vols. Paris: Payot, 1918-19. An impressionistic study (March, 1917–June, 1918) by the Petrograd correspondent of the *Petit parisien.* A literary *tour de force* but marred by lengthy rhetorical passages and a pervasive conservative bias.

[Anonymous]. *The Russian Diary of an Englishman: Petrograd, 1915-1917.* New York: Robert M. McBride, 1919. The author was apparently connected with the British embassy in an official capacity. Unfortunately his diary is devoted more to petty gossip than to significant revelations.

Astrov, W., *et al.* (eds.). *An Illustrated History of the Russian Revolution.* 2 vols. New York: International Publishers, 1928. A semiofficial history, written mainly by leading Bolsheviks who took part in the events described. Many documents printed in full.

Baden, Prince Max of. See Maximilian.

Balabanoff, Angelica. *My Life as a Rebel.* New York and London: Harper & Brothers, 1938. Memoirs of a revolutionary socialist who collaborated with the Bolsheviks at the time of the Revolution. Useful for details on the return of Russian émigrés and the Stockholm conference.

Barnes, Rt. Hon. George N. *From Workshop to War Cabinet.* New York: D. Appleton, 1924. Recollections of a British Labor party leader. Chapter X concerns the Stockholm conference and the Henderson affair, an account which is surprisingly misinformed in some respects.

Beatty, Bessie. *The Red Heart of Russia.* New York: Century Co., 1918. Impressions of revolutionary Russia by an American correspondent. Contains incidental information on the Root and Red Cross missions.

Blair, Dorian, and Dand, C. H. *Russian Hazard: The Adventures of a British Secret Service Agent in Russia.* London: Robert Hale, 1937.

Bryant, Louise. *Six Red Months in Russia: An Observer's Account of Russia before and during the Proletarian Dictatorship.* New York: George H. Doran, 1918. By an American newspaper woman, the wife of John Reed.

Buchanan, Sir George. *My Mission to Russia and Other Diplomatic Memories.* 2 vols. Boston: Little, Brown, 1923. Memoirs of exceptional value by the British ambassador, a conservative but intelligent diplomat of the old school.

Buchanan, Meriel. *The City of Trouble.* New York: Charles Scribner's, 1918.

————. *Diplomacy and Foreign Courts.* London: Hutchinson, n.d.

————. *The Dissolution of an Empire.* London: John Murray, 1932. The three works above are the memoirs of the British ambassador's daughter, often repetitious on Russian events and permeated with a fiery Tory bias. Though filled with petty details, some of the material regarding her father's activities is useful.

Bullard, Arthur. *The Russian Pendulum: Autocracy-Democracy-Bolshevism.* New York: Macmillan, 1919. A journalistic account of the Revolution arranged by subject. Some information, though usually of a general nature, on Allied diplomacy. The author did propaganda work with the American Committee on Public Information.

Callwell, Major-General Sir C. E. *Field-Marshal Sir Henry Wilson: His Life and Diaries.* 2 vols. New York: Charles Scribner's, 1927. One chapter is devoted to the Milner mission to Russia, of which Wilson was a member.

Cantacuzène, Princess. *Revolutionary Days: Recollections of Romanoffs and Bolsheviki, 1914-1917.* London: Chapman & Hall, 1920. Personal trivia and some superficial commentary by the granddaughter of President Grant.

Chicherin, George. *Two Years of Foreign Policy.* New York: Russian Soviet Government Bureau, 1920. A brief but vigorous defense of Soviet foreign policy by the Commissar for Foreign Affairs at the time.

Churchill, Winston S. *The Aftermath.* New York: Charles Scribner's, 1929.

Cianci de Sanseverino, Manfredi. *In Russia durante la rivoluzione.* [Naples: Napoli mondana, 1926]. Memoirs of a member of the Italian military mission, April, 1917–April, 1918. Not particularly informative on diplomatic matters.

Coleman, Frederic. *Japan or Germany: The Inside Story of the Struggle in Siberia.* New York: George H. Doran, 1918. A journalistic treatment of Japan and Siberia in 1917 and a plea for Japanese intervention.

Colton, Ethan T. *Forty Years with Russians.* New York: Association Press, 1940.

Creel, George. *How We Advertised America.* New York and London: Harper & Brothers, 1920. A report on the wartime activities of the Committee on Public Information, including a chapter on its accomplishments in Russia.

————. *Rebel at Large: Recollections of Fifty Crowded Years.* New York: G. P. Putnam's, 1947. Contains a chapter in defense of the "Sisson documents."

Crosley, Pauline S. *Intimate Letters from Petrograd.* New York: E. P. Dutton, 1920. The author was the wife of the American naval attaché. Mostly personal details but some information on political matters.

Czernin, Count Ottokar. *In the World War.* New York and London: Harper & Brothers, 1920. Memoirs of the Austrian Foreign Minister. Useful for his diary on the Brest-Litovsk negotiations.

Daniels, Josephus. *The Wilson Era: Years of War and After, 1917-*

1923. Chapel Hill, N. C.: University of North Carolina Press, 1946. The author, Secretary of the Navy during the war, includes some new material on the Root mission to Russia.

Davis, Malcolm W. *Open Gates to Russia.* New York and London: Harper & Brothers, 1920.

Davison, Henry P. *The American Red Cross in the Great War.* New York: Macmillan, 1919.

De Man, Henry. *The Remaking of a Mind: A Soldier's Thoughts on War and Reconstruction.* New York: Charles Scribner's, 1919. By a Belgian officer and prominent socialist who accompanied the Vandervelde mission to Russia. Some limited information on the visit.

Denikin, General A. I. *Ocherki Russkoy Smuty* [*Sketches of the Russian Turmoil*]. 5 vols. Paris: J. Povolzky, n.d.; Berlin: Knigoizdatelstvo "Slovo," 1924-26. Memoirs of a prominent "White" leader in the civil war, though useful also for the political events of 1917.

Destrée, Jules. *Les Fondeurs de neige: Notes sur la révolution bolchévique a Pétrograd pendant l'hiver 1917-1918.* Brussels and Paris: G. Van Oest, 1920. Memoirs of the Belgian ambassador (October, 1917–February, 1918). Verbose but adds little that is new.

Dorr, Rheta Childe. *Inside the Russian Revolution.* New York: Macmillan, 1917.

Dosch-Fleurot, Arno. *Through War to Revolution: Being the Experiences of a Newspaper Correspondent in War and Revolution, 1914-1920.* London: John Lane, 1931. One of the better journalistic efforts, occasionally informative on diplomatic incidents.

Fedotoff White, D. *Survival through War and Revolution in Russia.* Philadelphia: University of Pennsylvania Press, 1939. The author, a Russian naval officer, was attached to the Root mission and has some interesting material on its work in Russia.

Flint, Charles R. *Memories of an Active Life.* New York and London: G. P. Putnam's, 1923. Autobiography of a leading businessman. Includes a chapter on American relations with the Provisional Government.

Francis, David R. *Russia from the American Embassy: April, 1916–November, 1918.* New York: Charles Scribner's, 1921. A rambling and disappointing narrative by the American ambassador, though necessarily of value for Allied policy toward Russia.

Goldman, Emma. *Living My Life.* 2 vols. New York: Alfred A. Knopf, 1931.

Gompers, Samuel. *Seventy Years of Life and Labor: An Auto-*

biography. 2 vols. New York: E. P. Dutton, 1925. By the long-time president of the American Federation of Labor. Contains a chapter on the Stockholm conference and various aspects of American policy toward Russia.

Gourko, General Basil. *War and Revolution in Russia, 1914-1917.* New York: Macmillan, 1919. Memoirs of a tsarist general. Of some pertinence on diplomatic aspects of the Revolution.

Hanbury-Williams, Major-General Sir John. *The Emperor Nicholas II as I Knew Him.* London: Arthur L. Humphreys, 1922. By the British military attaché at Russian headquarters, 1914-17. His diary and letters concerning the March Revolution are of interest, though not of the first importance.

Hard, William. *Raymond Robins' Own Story.* New York and London: Harper & Brothers, 1920. A popularly written but valuable account of Robins's activities in Russia as head of the American Red Cross mission and unofficial liaison between the American ambassador and the Bolshevik government.

Hardinge, Lord (of Penshurst). *Old Diplomacy.* London: John Murray, 1947. Reveals nothing new on Britain's Russian policy.

Harper, Florence Macleod. *Runaway Russia.* New York: Century Co., 1918. Reminiscences of the Revolution by an American journalist. Largely personal but some passing information on the Root mission.

Harper, Paul V. (ed.) *The Russia I Believe In: The Memoirs of Samuel N. Harper, 1902-1941.* Chicago: University of Chicago Press, 1945. Samuel Harper was for many years perhaps the leading American authority on Russia. He acted as adviser to Ambassador Francis during the summer of 1917.

Herval, René. *Huit mois de révolution russe (juin 1917–janvier 1918).* Paris: Librairie Hachette, 1918.

Hill, Captain George A. *Go Spy the Land: Being the Adventures of I.K.8 of the British Secret Service.* London: Cassell, 1932. A popularly written narrative by a British agent in Russia (August, 1917–October, 1918). Some important material included along with trivia of a personal nature.

Hillquit, Morris. *Loose Leaves from a Busy Life.* New York: Macmillan, 1934.

Hoare, Rt. Hon. Sir Samuel. *The Fourth Seal: The End of a Russian Chapter.* London: William Heinemann, 1930. By a member of the British secret service in Russia in 1916. Useful for his experiences but often misinformed on the political situation.

Hoffmann, Major-General Max. *War Diaries and Other Papers.* 2

vols. London: Martin Secker, 1929. Mainly useful for the chapters on the Brest-Litovsk negotiations in the second volume.

Howard, Lord Esme (of Penrith). *Theatre of Life.* 2 vols. London: Hodder and Stoughton, 1936.

Hyndman, Rosalind Travers. *The Last Years of H. M. Hyndman.* New York: Brentano's, 1924.

Kalpaschnikoff, Andrew. *A Prisoner of Trotsky's.* Garden City, N. Y.: Doubleday, Page, 1920. A lengthy, and of course partisan, version of the "Kalpashnikov affair." Buttressed with a foreword by Ambassador Francis.

Kerensky, Alexander F. *The Catastrophe: Kerensky's Own Story of the Russian Revolution.* New York and London: D. Appleton, 1927.

————. *The Crucifixion of Liberty.* New York: John Day, 1934. The two works above by the head of the Provisional Government are important historical documents but often tend to become sermons against his political foes of both Left and Right rather than memoirs in the ordinary sense. Interesting revelations on Allied policy.

————. *The Prelude to Bolshevism: The Kornilov Rising.* New York: Dodd, Mead, 1919. The text of Kerensky's statement before the commission of inquiry on the Kornilov affair, with supplementary comments by Kerensky.

————. *La Révolution russe, 1917.* Paris: Payot, 1928. Substantially like the English edition *(The Catastrophe)* except for an additional chapter on Albert Thomas and Paléologue. The former wins Kerensky's praise, while the latter fares rather badly.

————. "The Road to the Tragedy," in Kerensky and Captain Paul Bulygin, *The Murder of the Romanovs.* London: Hutchinson, 1935. Includes some hitherto undisclosed details on the withdrawal of the invitation for the projected flight of the royal family to England.

————. *La Vérité sur la massacre des Romanov.* Paris: Payot, 1936. An expanded version of "The Road to the Tragedy."

Knox, Major-General Sir Alfred. *With the Russian Army, 1914–1917: Being Chiefly Extracts from the Diary of a Military Attaché.* 2 vols. London: Hutchinson, 1921. Chiefly valuable to the military historian but not without importance on political and diplomatic matters during the Revolution.

Korostovetz, Vladimir. *Seed and Harvest.* London: Faber and Faber, 1931. Memoirs of a government official, secretary to Milyukov in the early days of the Revolution. Lacks the significance one might anticipate from the author's position.

Kühlmann, Richard von. *Erinnerungen.* Heidelberg: Lambert Schneider, 1948. By the German Foreign Minister and delegate at Brest-Litovsk. Adds little that is new on the negotiations.

Labry, Raoul. *Autour du bolchevisme.* Paris: Privately printed, 1921. The author maintained close relations with the French embassy in Petrograd during the Revolution but has chosen to give mainly a tract on the evils of Bolshevism.

Lansing, Robert. *War Memoirs.* Indianapolis and New York: Bobbs-Merrill, 1935. By President Wilson's Secretary of State. Includes a chapter on relations with Russia.

Legras, Jules. *Mémoires de Russie.* Paris: Payot, 1921. By a member of the French military mission to Russia before and during the Revolution. His book is concerned largely with military rather than political events.

Lenin, V. I. *Collected Works.* 6 vols. New York: International Publishers, 1927-32. An unfinished English edition of the official Russian edition. Lenin's writings are virtually complete, however, on the Revolution (Vols. XX and XXI, each in two books).

Lennox, Lady Algernon Gordon (ed.). *The Diary of Lord Bertie of Thame, 1914-1918.* 2 vols. London: Hodder and Stoughton, 1924. Lord Bertie was the British ambassador to France. His diary has scattered material on Entente relations with Russia.

Lloyd George, David. *War Memoirs.* 6 vols. Boston: Little, Brown, 1933-37. By the British Prime Minister. An invaluable source for Anglo-Russian relations.

Lockhart, R. H. Bruce. *British Agent.* Garden City, N. Y.: Garden City Publishing Co., 1933. A popular but brilliantly written narrative by Lloyd George's emissary to the Soviet government. An indispensable source.

Long, Robert Crozier. *Russian Revolution Aspects.* New York: E. P. Dutton, 1919. By an American newspaperman. Useful on the Root and Stevens missions.

Louis, George. *Les Carnets.* 2 vols. Paris: F. Rieder, 1926.

Loukomsky, General. *Memoirs of the Russian Revolution.* London: T. Fisher Unwin, 1922.

Ludendorff, Erich von. *Ludendorff's Own Story: August 1914-November 1918.* 2 vols. New York and London: Harper & Brothers, 1919.

Marchand, René. *Why I Support Bolshevism.* London: British Socialist Party, n.d. Brief memoirs in pamphlet form of a French correspondent in revolutionary Russia, at the time a supporter of Kerensky. Some information on the activities of the Allied embassies.

Maximilian Alexander Friedrich Wilhelm [Prince Max of Baden]. *Memoirs.* 2 vols. London: Constable, 1928. Useful chiefly for the Brest-Litovsk negotiations.

Miliukov, Paul. *Bolshevism: An International Danger: Its Doctrine and Its Practice through War and Revolution.* London: George Allen & Unwin, 1920. By the former Cadet leader and Minister of Foreign Affairs in the first period of the Provisional Government. Gives a sketchy treatment of his policy but mostly an extended philippic against Bolshevism.

————. *Istoria Vtoroy Russkoy Revolyutsii* [*The History of the Second Russian Revolution*]. Sofia: Rossiisko-Bolgarskoe Knigoizdatelstvo, 1921-24. A comprehensive history of the Revolution intended as a work of scholarship. Its value, however, derives almost wholly from the author's participation in many of the events described.

————. *Russia Today and Tomorrow.* New York: Macmillan, 1922. Scattered information on Allied policy, especially the origins of intervention in early 1918.

Morris, Ira Nelson. *From an American Legation.* New York: Alfred A. Knopf, 1923.

————. *Heritage from My Father: An Autobiography.* New York: privately printed, 1947. The two works above by the American minister to Sweden give minor details on American policy toward the Revolution.

Mott, Colonel T. Bentley. *Twenty Years as Military Attaché.* New York: Oxford University Press, 1937. The author was a member of the Root mission to Russia and includes two chapters on his experiences.

Nabokoff, Constantin. *The Ordeal of a Diplomat.* London: Duckworth, 1921. Memoirs of the Russian chargé d'affaires in London during the Revolution. An excellent source. Strongly anti-Bolshevik.

Nekludoff, A. *Diplomatic Reminiscences before and during the World War, 1911-1917.* London: John Murray, 1920. Memoirs of a Russian diplomat, of only minor importance for the revolutionary period.

Niessel, General. *Le Triomphe des bolchéviks et la paix de Brest-Litovsk: Souvenirs, 1917-1918.* Paris: Librarie Plon, 1940. By the head of the French military mission in Petrograd. Its value would have been greatly enhanced with more on his personal experiences and less material already well known.

Nikitine, Colonel B. V. *The Fatal Years: Fresh Revelations on a Chapter of Underground History.* London: William Hodge,

1938. Memoirs of a Russian officer, head of the Counter-Espionage Bureau from March to July, 1917. Some details on Allied activity in Russia, though the bulk of the space is devoted to "proofs" of Bolshevik subservience to German gold.

Noulens, Joseph. *Mon ambassade en Russie soviétique, 1917-1919.* 2 vols. Paris: Libraire Plon, 1933. Memoirs of Paléologue's successor as French ambassador. A valuable source, though padded with irrelevant and already well-known material. Noulens displays an unusually strong conservative bias.

Obshchestvo Bivsh. Rossiiskikh Soldati vo Frantsii i na Balkanakh. *Oktyabr za Rubezhom (Sbornik Vospominanii)* [*October Abroad (A Collection of Memoirs)*]. Moscow: Gosudarstvennoe Izdatelstvo. n.d. Personal experiences of Russian soldiers who fought in France and the Balkans.

Oudendyk, William J. *Ways and By-Ways in Diplomacy.* London: Peter Davies, 1939. By the Dutch ambassador to Petrograd in late 1917 and early 1918. Adds little to other diplomatic accounts.

Painlevé, Paul. *Comment j'ai nommé Foch et Pétain: La Politique de guerre de 1917; le commandement unique interallié.* Paris: Libraire Felix Alçon, 1924.

Paléologue, Maurice. *An Ambassador's Memoirs.* 3 vols. London: Hutchinson, 1923-25. The voluminous diary of the French ambassador to Russia during the war. Of considerable literary merit but obviously "touched up" after the events described. It is nonetheless perhaps the best source on Allied-Russian relations until his recall in May, 1917.

Paley, Princess. *Memories of Russia, 1916-1919.* London: Herbert Jenkins, 1924. A pro-tsarist account of the Revolution. Largely concerned with personal details but pertinent for its absurd attack on the British ambassador.

Pankhurst, E. Sylvia. *The Life of Emmeline Pankhurst: The Suffragette Struggle for Women's Citizenship.* London: T. Werner Laurie, 1935.

Pares, Bernard. *My Russian Memoirs.* London: Jonathan Cape, 1931. The late Professor Pares was a leading British authority on Russia. He enjoyed close personal contacts with the leaders of the Provisional Government and worked with the British embassy during the summer of 1917.

Paton, John. *Never Say Die: An Autobiography.* New York: Longmans, Green, 1936. Some fresh details on the abortive MacDonald mission to Russia.

Persky, Serge. *De Nicolas II à Lénine (1917-1918).* Paris: Payot,

1919. A fiercely anti-Bolshevik history of the Revolution composed of dispatches which originally appeared in Swiss newspapers.

Poincaré, Raymond. *Au service de la France: Neuf annees de souvenirs.* 10 vols. Paris: Librairie Plon, 1926-33. Memoirs of the President of France. Vol. IX on 1917 is occasionally informative on the Russian policy of the Allies.

Pollock, John. *The Bolshevik Adventure.* London: Constable, 1919.

Price, M. Philips. *My Reminiscences of the Russian Revolution.* London: George Allen & Unwin, 1921. By the Manchester *Guardian's* correspondent during the revolutionary years. Pro-Bolshevik but without Marxian orthodoxy, the book is one of the few good accounts by a journalist.

Reed, John. *Ten Days That Shook the World.* New York: Modern Library, 1934. A classic on the November Revolution by an American journalist of Bolshevik sympathies. Brilliant impressionistic writing but contains some factual errors.

Ribot, Alexandre. *Journal et correspondances inédites, 1914-1922.* Paris: Librairie Plon, 1936.

————. *Lettres à un ami: Souvenirs de ma vie politique.* Paris: Editions Bossard, 1924. The author of the two works above was the French Premier and Foreign Minister in 1917. He gives more than passing attention to Franco-Russian relations, especially in the *Lettres.*

Rodzianko, M. V. *The Reign of Rasputin: An Empire's Collapse.* London: A. M. Philpot, 1927. Memoirs of the last president of the Duma.

Rosen, Baron. *Forty Years of Diplomacy.* 2 vols. London: George Allen & Unwin, 1922. The author, an experienced Russian diplomat of the old regime, devotes several very critical chapters to the foreign policy of the Provisional Government and his vain endeavors to change it.

Russell, Charles Edward. *Bare Hands and Stone Walls: Some Recollections of a Side-Line Reformer.* New York: Charles Scribner's, 1933. Memoirs of an American socialist. He accompanied the Root mission to Russia but has managed to convey little of importance about the work of the mission in his chapter on the subject.

Sadoul, Captain Jacques. *Notes sur la révolution bolchevique.* Paris: Editions de la Sirène, 1919. By a member of the French military mission to Russia in close contact with Lenin and Trotsky. An invaluable source. Highly critical of Allied policy.

Salyer, Oliver M. *Russia White or Red.* Boston: Little, Brown, 1919.

Shulgin, V. V. *Dni [Days].* Leningrad: Rabochee Izdatelstvo "Priboi," 1926. A dramatic and brilliantly written account of the March Revolution by a conservative nationalist leader in the Duma.

Sisson, Edgar. *One Hundred Red Days: A Personal Chronicle of the Bolshevik Revolution.* New Haven, Conn.: Yale University Press, 1931. By the representative in Russia (late 1917 and early 1918) of Creel's Committee on Public Information. A valuable if verbose record but so badly organized and written that its appeal to the nonspecialist in the period would probably be nil.

Snowden, Viscount Philip. *An Autobiography.* 2 vols. London: Ivor Nicholson and Watson, 1934. By a British socialist, a leader of the Independent Labor party during the war. Contains two informative chapters on British labor and the Russian Revolution.

Stebbing, E. P. *From Czar to Bolshevik.* London: John Lane, 1918. Memoirs in diary form of an Englishman in Petrograd during the period of the Provisional Government. Conservative and patriotic in tone but more informative than most of the early accounts. Scattered material on Allied-Russian relations.

Steffens, Lincoln. *Autobiography.* New York: Harcourt, Brace, 1931. The famous American "muckraker" visited Russia soon after the March Revolution and returned to convey a message from Kerensky to Wilson.

Sukhanov, Nikolai. *Zapiski o Revolyutsii [Notes on the Revolution].* 7 vols. Berlin, St. Petersburg, and Moscow: Z. I. Grzhebin, 1922-23. Voluminous memoirs of a nonpartisan Left socialist, a member of the executive committee of the Petrograd Soviet. Very valuable for all phases of the Revolution.

Thompson, Donald C. *Donald Thompson in Russia.* New York: Century Co., 1918.

Thorne, Will. *My Life's Battles.* London: George Newnes, n.d. The author accompanied the Anglo-French socialist mission to Russia but describes the visit very superficially.

Trotsky, Leon. *From October to Brest-Litovsk.* New York: Socialist Publication Society, 1919.

————. *The History of the Russian Revolution to Brest-Litovsk.* London: George Allen & Unwin, 1919.

————. *Lenin.* New York: Minton, Balch, 1925.

————————. *My Life: An Attempt at an Autobiography.* New York: Charles Scribner's, 1930. The above works by Trotsky all contain useful material on the Revolution. His memoirs are by far the most valuable.

Tyrkóva-Williams, Ariadna. *Cheerful Giver: The Life of Harold Williams.* London: Peter Davies, 1935.

————————. *From Liberty to Brest-Litovsk: The First Year of the Russian Revolution.* London: Macmillan, 1919. A substantial account of the Revolution by a Cadet sympathizer, the Russian wife of Harold Williams, a prominent British journalist and authority on Russia.

Vandervelde, Emile. *Souvenirs d'un militant socialiste.* Paris: Éditions Denoël, 1939. By a prominent Belgian socialist.

————————. *Three Aspects of the Russian Revolution.* London: George Allen & Unwin, 1918. Largely concerns conditions in Russia as seen during the author's visit as a member of the Belgian socialist mission.

Viroubova, Anna. *Memories of the Russian Court.* New York: Macmillan, 1923. By the Empress's confidante, a woman of superstitious nature and low intelligence.

Waters, Brigadier-General W. H.-H. *"Secret and Confidential": The Experiences of a Military Attaché.* New York: Frederick A. Stokes, 1926.

Wightman, Orrin Sage. *The Diary of an American Physician in the Russian Revolution.* Brooklyn, N. Y.: *Brooklyn Daily Eagle,* 1928. Some information on the American Red Cross mission but mostly concerned with picturesque travel details.

Wilcox, E. H. *Russia's Ruin.* London: Chapman & Hall, 1919. A strongly anti-Bolshevik interpretation by the correspondent of the London *Daily Telegraph.* Goes little beyond the Kornilov affair but has a particularly full account of the Milyukov foreign policy crisis.

Williams, Albert Rhys. *Through the Russian Revolution.* New York: Boni and Liveright, 1921. A pro-Bolshevik account by an American journalist.

Williams, Francis. *Fifty Years' March: The Rise of the Labour Party.* London: Odhams Press, 1949. One chapter concerns the impact of the Russian Revolution on the British Labor Party.

Wilton, Robert. *Russia's Agony.* New York: Longmans, Green, 1918. By the correspondent of the London *Times.* Similar in tone to the Wilcox work but less informative. Also concludes with the Kornilov affair.

Winogradsky, General. *La Guerre sur le front oriental: En Russie—en Roumanie.* Paris: Charles-Lavauzelle, 1926.
Yakhontoff, Victor A. *Over the Divide: Impersonal Record of Personal Experiences.* New York: Coward-McCann, 1939.

ARTICLES

Buchanan, Meriel. " 'The Foulest Crime in History'—The Truth," *Saturday Review,* CLIX (May 18, 1935), 616-17.
Cordonnier, Emile. "Auprès du tsarisme agonisant: Souvenirs d'une mission française en 1917," *Revue,* CXX (Aug., 1917), 240-61.
Edward, Duke of Windsor. "A Prince at War," *Life,* XXIII (Dec. 22, 1947), 81-97.
Lissovsky, Yuri. "Lager Lya-Kurtin (Russkaya Revolyutsia vo Frantsii)" ["The Camp of La Courtine (The Russian Revolution in France)"], *Arkhiv Russkoy Revolyutsii,* XVII (1926), 256-79.
Marsengo, Maurizio. "Russia 1915-1917 (dal diario di unaddetto militare)," *Nuova antologia,* CCCLXXIX (May 1 and 6, 1935), 12-37 and 208-40.
[Milner, Lord Alfred]. "Before Russia Went West," *National Review,* CXV (Nov., 1940), 653-64.
[————]. "Lord Milner in Russia," *National Review,* CXVII (Nov., 1941), 526-31.
Obey, André. "Camarades rouski (aout-septembre 1917)," *Revue de Paris,* XXVII (Dec., 1920), 527-54.
Paley, Princess. Response à Sir George Buchanan," *Revue de Paris,* XXX (April, 1923), 689-90.
Reed, John. "How Soviet Russia Conquered Imperial Germany," *Liberator,* II (Jan., 1919), 16-26.
Remond, Général Adrien. "Quelques souvenirs de deux missions en Russie: 1916, 1917," *Bulletin de la Société Nivernaise des lettres, sciences et arts,* XXVII (1929), 525-75.
Routsky, Pierre. "A Page from the Past," *Russian Review,* VII (Spring, 1948), 69-75.
Schatzky, B. E. "La Révolution russe de fevrier 1917 et les États-Unis d'Amérique: Notes et souvenirs," *Monde slave,* V (Sept., 1928), 353-76.
Sers, Lieutenant Louis. "Un Parc d'aviation française en Russie bolcheviste, mars 1917–mars 1918," *Revue des deux mondes,* XLVI (Aug. 15, 1918), 764-98.

NEWSPAPERS

Daily Telegraph (London).
Evening Transcript (Boston).

Excelsior (Paris).
Figaro (Paris).
Guardian (Manchester).
Herald (New York).
Izvestia (Petrograd).
Journal des débats (Paris).
Labour Leader (Manchester).
Matin (Paris).
Morning Post (London).
Petite république (Paris).
Pravda (Petrograd).
Le Temps (Paris).
The Times (London).
Times (New York).

PERIODICALS

Current History (New York).
Current Opinion (New York).
Independent (New York).
International Conciliation (New York).
Literary Digest (New York).
Nation (London).
New Age (London).
New Republic (New York).
Opinion (Paris).
Revue (Paris).
Revue bleue (Paris).
Saturday Review (London).
Spectator (London).

SECONDARY SOURCES

BOOKS AND PAMPHLETS

Albert-Petit, A. *La France de la guerre.* 3 vols. Paris: Éditions Bossard, 1918-19.

Antonelli, Etienne. *Bolshevik Russia.* New York: Alfred A. Knopf, 1920. A topical survey by a French scholar of pronounced anti-Bolshevik views. Chapter VI summarizes Allied-Russian relations from the November Revolution to the beginnings of intervention.

Arthur, Sir George. *Life of Lord Kitchener.* 3 vols. New York: Macmillan, 1920. An authorized biography. Two chapters are devoted to Kitchener's ill-fated mission to Russia.

Bailey, Thomas A. *America Faces Russia: Russian-American Relations from the Earliest Times to Our Day.* Ithaca, N. Y.: Cornell University Press, 1950. Very brief on the revolutionary period.

Berëzkin, A. *SShA—Aktivny Organizator i Uchastnik Voennoi Interventsii protiv Sovetskoi Rossii (1918-1920 gg.)* [*The U.S.A.— Active Organizer and Participant in the Military Intervention against Soviet Russia (1918-1920)*]. Moscow: Gospolitizdat, 1949. A "cold war" product revising the traditional interpretation of American intervention.

Bilainkin, George. *Maisky: Ten Years Ambassador*. London: George Allen & Unwin, 1944.

Brand, Carl F. *British Labour's Rise to Power: Eight Studies*. Stanford University, California: Stanford University Press, 1941. Three of the studies concern (in part) British labor and the Russian Revolution.

Brockway, Fenner. *Socialism over Sixty Years: The Life of Jowett of Bradford (1864-1944)*. London: George Allen & Unwin, 1946. Includes a section on the abortive MacDonald mission to Russia, of which Jowett was a member.

Bruntz, George G. *Allied Propaganda and the Collapse of the German Empire in 1918*. Stanford University, California: Stanford University Press, 1938.

Carr, Edward Hallett. *The Bolshevik Revolution, 1917-1923*. 2 vols. New York: Macmillan, 1935. A scholarly and objective, account. A third volume dealing with foreign affairs is forthcoming.

Chamberlin, William Henry. *The Russian Revolution, 1917-1921*. 2 vols. New York: Macmillan, 1935. A scholarly and objective, if somewhat colorless, work by an American journalist many years resident in Russia. Some attention devoted to foreign affairs.

Chambers, Frank P. *The War behind the War, 1914-1918: A History of the Political and Civilian Fronts*. London: Faber and Faber, 1939. An excellent work. Proportionate space given to Russian events.

Chernov, Victor. *The Great Russian Revolution*. New Haven, Conn.: Yale University Press, 1936. A first-rate history of the Revolution by the former Socialist Revolutionary leader. Goes to the eve of the Bolshevik Revolution. Two chapters are specifically devoted to the foreign policy of the Provisional Government, of which Chernov is very critical.

Cruttwell, C. R. M. F. *A History of the Great War, 1914-1918*. Oxford: Clarendon Press, 1934.

Cudahy, John ("A Chronicler"). *Archangel: The American War with Russia.* Chicago: A. C. McClurg, 1924. Covers some details of Russo-American relations prior to intervention.

Danilov, Yu. N. *Russkie Otryady na Frantsuzskom i Makedonskom Frontakh 1916-1918 gg.* [*Russian Troops on the French and Macedonian Fronts, 1916-1918*]. Paris: Soyuza Ofitserov Uchastnikov Voiny na Frantsuzskom Front, 1933. By a former Russian general. Primarily a military history; based in large part on the archives of the French war ministry.

Dennis, Alfred L. P. *The Foreign Policies of Soviet Russia.* New York: E. P. Dutton, 1924. A pioneer work by an American scholar on the 1917-23 period, generally anti-Soviet in interpretation. Now badly dated.

Dugdale, Blanche E. C. *Arthur James Balfour.* 2 vols. London: Hutchinson, 1936. A biography of Britain's wartime Foreign Minister by his niece. Devotes some attention to Russian matters.

Dulles, Foster Rhea. *The Road to Teheran: The Story of Russia and America, 1781-1943.* Princeton, N. J.: Princeton University Press, 1944. A concise and ably written account. Two chapters are devoted to the revolutionary period.

Elton, Lord. *The Life of James Ramsay MacDonald (1866-1919).* London: Collins, 1939. MacDonald was a leader of the British Independent Labor party during the war. A section of Chapter IX is devoted to his abortive Russian mission and the Stockholm conference.

Fainsod, Merle. *International Socialism and the World War.* Cambridge, Mass.: Harvard University Press, 1935. A scholarly monograph containing the best secondary account of the Stockholm conference, as well as other pertinent matter on the Russian Revolution and the international socialist movement.

Farbman, Michael S. *Russia and the Struggle for Peace.* London: George Allen & Unwin, [1918]. A brief topical treatment of the Revolution (through the summer of 1917), with emphasis on the peace question. Severely critical of Allied policy toward Russia.

Fayle, C. Ernest. *Seaborne Trade.* 3 vols. London: John Murray, 1920-24.

Fischer, Louis. *The Soviets in World Affairs: A History of Relations between the Soviet Union and the Rest of the World.* 2 vols. London: Jonathan Cape, 1930. An ably written study covering the 1918-29 period. Pro-Soviet in tone but not uncritical. Only the first few chapters of the first volume are pertinent to the present study.

————. *Why Recognize Russia? The Arguments for and*

against the Recognition of the Soviet Government by the United States. New York: Jonathan Cape & Harrison Smith, 1931. Gives a summary of American-Russian relations during the Revolution.

Fiske, Harvey E. *The Inter-Ally Debts: An Analysis of War and Post-War Public Finance, 1914-1923.* New York–Paris: Bankers Trust Company, 1924.

Florinsky, Michael T. *The End of the Russian Empire.* New Haven, Conn.: Yale University Press, 1931. A topical survey of the tsarist regime on the eve of the Revolution. Though inadequate in many respects, it has not yet been superseded.

Forster, Kent. *The Failures of Peace: The Search for a Negotiated Peace during the First World War.* Washington: American Council on Public Affairs, 1941. A scholarly monograph, one chapter of which deals with the Stockholm conference.

Fox, Ralph. *The Class Struggle in Britain in the Epoch of Imperialism.* London: Martin Lawrence, 1932. The author, a British Communist, devotes a few pages to British labor and the Russian Revolution.

Genkin, I. I. *Soedinennye Shtati Ameriki i SSSR: Ikh Politicheskie i Ekonomicheskie Vzaimo Otnoshenia* [*The United States of America and the USSR: Their Political and Economic Relations*]. Moscow and Leningrad: Gosudarstvennoe Sotsialno-Ekonomicheskoe Izdatelstvo, 1934. A brief section is devoted to their relations during the Revolution.

Giraud, Victor. *Le Général de Castelnau.* Paris: Editions G. Crés, 1921. A short biography containing a chapter on the general's visit to Russia with the Milner mission.

Gordon, Alban. *Russian Civil War: A Sketch for a History.* London: Cassell, 1937.

——————. *Russian Year: A Calendar of Revolution.* London: Cassell, 1935. The two works above give a popular account of the revolutionary years with some attention to diplomacy.

Gorky, M., et al. (eds.). *The History of the Civil War in the U.S.S.R.* Vol. I, *The Prelude of the Great Proletarian Revolution* (New York: International Publishers, n.d.). Vol. II, *The Great Proletarian Revolution* (Moscow: Foreign Languages Publishing House, 1946). The official history of the Revolution, of which two volumes have thus far appeared. Factually accurate and based on an impressive amount of archival and other source material but committed to an orthodoxy peculiar to official histories, in this instance accentuated by the Trotsky-Stalin controversy of the postrevolutionary period.

Graves, William S. *America's Siberian Adventure, 1918-1920.* New York: Jonathan Cape & Harrison Smith, 1931. Includes a summary of Allied-Russian relations prior to intervention.

Gukovsky, A. I. *Antanta i Oktyabrskaya Revolyutsia [The Entente and the October Revolution].* Moscow and Leningrad: Gosudarstvennoe Sotsialno-Ekonomischeskoe Izdatelstvo, 1931. A brief study of a semipopular nature covering the period from the March Revolution to the summer of 1918. Not always well organized and apparently based on a limited number of sources.

Hagedorn, Hermann. *The Magnate: William Boyce Thompson and His Time.* New York: John Day, 1935. A readable authorized biography, almost a third of which concerns Thompson, Robins, and their propaganda work with the Red Cross mission in Russia.

Hamilton, Mary Agnes. *Arthur Henderson: A Biography.* London: William Heinemann, 1938. An uncritical but useful biography of the prominent British Labor leader, a member of the war cabinet. A lengthy chapter is devoted to his Russian mission, the Stockholm conference, and the attendant cabinet crisis.

Hart-Davis, Rupert. *Hugh Walpole: A Biography.* New York: Macmillan, 1952. Walpole headed a British propaganda bureau in Russia.

Hicks, Granville. *John Reed: The Making of a Revolutionary.* New York: Macmillan, 1936.

Ioffe, Ya. *Organizatsia Interventsia i Blokady Sovetskoy Respubliki 1918-1920 [The Organization of the Intervention and Blockade of the Soviet Republic, 1918-1920].* Moscow and Leningrad: Gosudarstvennoe Izdatelstvo, 1930. The first chapter concerns the diplomatic background following the November Revolution. Adds nothing new.

Jacoby, Jean. *Le Tsar Nicolas II et la révolution.* Paris: Arthème Fayard, 1931. A pro-tsarist account, interesting for its perpetuation of the legend of the British ambassador's implication in the March Revolution.

Jenkins, Edwin A. *From Foundry to Foreign Office: The Romantic Life-Story of the Rt. Hon. Arthur Henderson, M.P.* London: Grayson & Grayson, 1933. Relevant on the Stockholm conference and Henderson's Russian mission but superseded by the Hamilton biography.

Jessup, Philip C. *Elihu Root.* 2 vols. New York: Dodd, Mead, 1938. A scholarly authorized biography but not entirely uncritical. Gives a full account of the Root mission to Russia.

Kellogg, Paul U., and Gleason, Arthur. *British Labor and the*

War: Reconstructors for a New World. New York: Boni and Liveright, 1919. A detailed documented study, mainly useful for the material on British labor's attitude toward revolutionary Russia.

Kerjentzev, V. *Les Alliés et la Russie.* Moscow: Edition du Groupe Communiste Français, 1919. A brief pro-Bolshevik interpretation of Allied-Russian relations during the Revolution and intervention. Unduly polemical in tone and of doubtful accuracy on some controversial points.

King, Joseph. *The Russian Revolution: The First Year.* London: Union of Democratic Control, 1918. A popular brochure, severely critical of Allied policy toward the Revolution.

Kiritzesco, Constantin. *La Roumanie dans la guerre mondiale (1916-1919).* Paris: Payot, 1934.

Lafue, Pierre. *Gaston Doumergue: Sa vie et son destin.* Paris: Librarie Plon, 1933. A popular biography containing a brief account of Doumergue's mission to Russia.

Laserson, Max M. *The American Impact on Russia: Diplomatic and Ideological, 1784-1917.* New York: Macmillan, 1950. Contains a concluding chapter on American relations with the Provisional Government.

Lasswell, Harold D. *Propaganda Technique in the World War.* New York: Alfred A. Knopf, 1927. Gives passing treatment of American propaganda in revolutionary Russia.

Lenz, J. *The Rise and Fall of the Second International.* New York: International Publishers, 1932. Presents the Communist view of the Stockholm conference.

Levidov, Mikh. *K Istorii Soyuznoi Interventsii v Rossii [Towards a History of Allied Intervention in Russia].* Leningrad: Rabochee Izdatelstvo "Priboi," 1925. The first volume of a projected history of the intervention (apparently never completed). Deals with the diplomatic background of 1917-18. A scholarly study, based largely upon Allied newspapers but an incomplete selection of other primary sources.

Loth, David. *Woodrow Wilson: The Fifteenth Point.* Philadelphia and New York: J. B. Lippincott, 1941.

Louis, Paul. *Histoire du socialisme en France depuis la révolution jusqu'a nos jours.* Paris: Libraire des Sciences Politiques et Sociales, 1925.

Lovenstein, Meno. *American Opinion of Soviet Russia.* Washington: American Council on Public Affairs, 1941. A useful study of public opinion as reflected in newspapers, magazines, and books. Begins with the March Revolution.

Maddox, William P. *Foreign Relations in British Labour Politics: A Study of the Formation of Party Attitudes on Foreign Affairs and the Application of Political Pressure Designed to Influence Government Policy, 1900-1924.* Cambridge, Mass.: Harvard University Press, 1934. Deals summarily with the Labor party and the Stockholm conference.

Maisky, I. *Vneshnaya Politika R.S.F.S.R., 1917-1922* [*The Foreign Policy of the R.S.F.S.R., 1917-1922*]. Moscow: Izdatelstvo "Krasnaya Nov," 1923. A brief study by a Soviet diplomat. Begins with the Brest-Litovsk negotiations.

Makeev, Nicholas, and O'Hara, Valentine. *Russia.* London: Ernest Benn, 1925. Includes a section on the foreign policy of the Provisional Government.

Manning, Clarence A. *The Siberian Fiasco.* New York: Library Publishers, 1952. A popular account of American intervention.

Marriott, Sir J. A. R. *Anglo-Russian Relations, 1689-1943.* London: Methuen, 1944.

Mathews, Basil. *John R. Mott: World Citizen.* New York and London: Harper & Brothers, 1934. Mott was a member of the Root mission.

Maurras, Charles. *Les Chefs socialistes pendant la guerre.* Paris: Nouvelle Librairie Nationale, 1918.

Mavor, James. *The Russian Revolution.* New York: Macmillan, 1928. An early attempt at a scholarly history by an acknowledged authority on Russia. Has not stood the test of time.

Maynard, John. *Russia in Flux: Before October.* London: Victor Gollancz, 1941.

Michelson, Alexander, *et al. Russian Public Finance during the War.* New Haven, Conn.: Yale University Press, 1928.

Michon, Georges. *The Franco-Russian Alliance, 1891-1917.* London: George Allen & Unwin, 1929. An interpretative history. Very critical of French policy, especially during the period of the Russian Revolution.

Middleton, K. W. B. *Britain and Russia: An Historical Essay.* London: Hutchinson, 1947.

Millard, Thomas F. *Democracy and the Eastern Question.* New York: Century Co., 1919. Interesting materials on the origin of Japanese intervention in Siberia.

Mock, James R., and Larson, Cedric. *Words That Won the War: The Story of the Committee on Public Information, 1917-1919.* Princeton, N. J.: Princeton University Press, 1939. An excellent history of the wartime "Creel committee," of which one chapter is devoted to its activities in Russia under Edgar Sisson's direction.

Mowat, R. B. *A History of European Diplomacy, 1914-1925.* New York: Longmans, Green, 1927.

Nolde, Baron Boris E. *Russia in the Economic War.* New Haven, Conn.: Yale University Press, 1928.

Norton, Henry Kittredge. *The Far Eastern Republic of Siberia.* London: George Allen and Unwin, 1923.

Novitzky, V. *Russia and the Allies in the Great War.* London: Kniga, 1924.

Pares, Bernard. *The Fall of the Russian Monarchy: A Study of the Evidence.* New York: Alfred A. Knopf, 1939. An important work, but suffers from lack of organization and an excessive emphasis upon personalities. The fall of the dynasty is related in a socioeconomic vacuum.

Pingaud, Albert. *Histoire diplomatique de la France pendant la grande guerre.* 3 vols. Paris: Editions "Alsatia," 1938-40. Covers some aspects of French relations with revolutionary Russia in the third volume, notably the Thomas and Noulens missions.

Poitevin, Pierre. *Une Bataille au centre de la France en 1917: La Révolte des armées russes au camp de La Courtine.* Limoges: Société des Journaux et Publications, 1934. A brochure superseded by the book below.

——————. *La Mutinerie de La Courtine: Les Régiments russes révoltés en 1917 au centre de la France.* Paris: Payot, 1938. A monograph based on the few printed sources available and interviews with witnesses. Presented in the form of a documentary narrative.

Potemkin, V. P. (ed.). *Istoria Diplomatii* [*History of Diplomacy*]. 3 vols. Moscow and Leningrad: Gosudarstvennoe Izdatelstvo Politicheskoi Literatury, 1941-45. A Soviet interpretation of diplomatic history from ancient times to the present. Several chapters in the second volume on the diplomacy of the Revolution.

Pokrovsky, M. N. *Imperialistskaya Voina: Sbornik Statei* [*The Imperialist War: Collected Articles*]. Moscow: Gosudarstvennoe Sotsialno-Ekonomicheskoe Izdatelstvo, 1934. By Soviet Russia's foremost historian until the repudiation of the "Pokrovsky school" in 1935. Some of the essays concern the diplomacy of the Revolution. Includes a reprint of his *Vneshnaya Politika* (below).

——————. (ed.). *Ocherki po Istorii Oktyabrskoy Revolyutsii* [*Studies on the History of the October Revolution*]. 2 vols. Moscow and Leningrad: Gosudarstvennoe Izdatelstvo, 1927. A collection of scholarly monographs by various Soviet historians. N. L. Rubinstein's study of the foreign policy of the Provisional

Government is the most definitive treatment of the subject by a Soviet writer.

————. *Oktyabrskaya Revolyutsia i Antanta* [*The October Revolution and the Entente*]. Moscow and Leningrad: Gosudarstvennoe Izdatelstvo, 1927. A popular outline. Gives an account of the negotiations of Sadoul and Robins with the Soviet government preceding the Brest peace.

————. *Vneshnaya Politika Rossii v XX Veke* [*Russian Foreign Policy in the Twentieth Century*]. Moscow: Kommunistichovo Universiteta, 1926. A brief study presented in the form of four lectures. Covers Kerensky's foreign policy, the Brest peace, and Allied intervention in summary fashion.

Pope, Arthur Upham. *Maxim Litvinoff*. New York: L. B. Fischer, 1943.

Postgate, R. W. *The International during the War*. London: The Herald, 1918. Includes a good brief account of the Stockholm conference and the Henderson affair.

Pratt, Julius W. "Robert Lansing," in Samuel Flagg Bemis (ed.), *The American Secretaries of State and Their Diplomacy,* Vol. X. New York: Alfred A. Knopf, 1929.

Radek, Karl. *Vneshnaya Politika Sovetskoi Rossii* [*The Foreign Policy of Soviet Russia*]. Moscow and Leningrad: Gosudarstvennoe Izdatelstvo, 1923. An interpretative survey from the Bolshevik Revolution to 1922. Still the best Soviet account of these years.

Reid, Edith Gittings. *The Life and Convictions of William Sydney Thayer*. New York and London: Oxford University Press, 1936.

Ross, Edward Alsworth. *The Russian Bolshevik Revolution*. New York: Century Co., 1921. By an American sociologist who traveled in Revolutionary Russia. One of the few early accounts that bear some resemblance to reality.

————. *The Russian Soviet Republic*. New York and London: Century Co., 1923. Begins with an account of the Brest negotiations in chronological continuation of the above work.

Sadoul, Jacques. *Naissance de l'U.R.S.S.* Paris: Charlot, 1946.

Sayers, Michael, and Kahn, Albert E. *The Great Conspiracy: The Secret War against Soviet Russia*. Boston: Little, Brown, 1946. A Communist interpretation of the internal and external opposition to the Soviet regime, the first two chapters being relevant to the present study. Some factual errors and an overly sensationalized treatment but based on considerable research.

Schuman, Frederick Lewis. *American Policy toward Russia since 1917: A Study of Diplomatic History, International Law, and*

Public Opinion. New York: International Publishers, 1928. A scholarly, well written study, still valuable despite the publication of new material since 1928. Critical of American policy.

—————. *Soviet Politics at Home and Abroad.* New York: Alfred A. Knopf, 1946.

Serge, Victor. *L'An I de la révolution russe: Les Débuts de la dictature du proletariat (1917-1918).* Paris: Libraire du Travail, 1930.

Shub, David. *Lenin: A Biography.* Garden City, N. Y.: Doubleday, 1948. Easily the best biography of Lenin but not without numerous weaknesses. Particularly full on the revolutionary period.

Slovès, H. *La France et l'union soviétique.* Paris: Les Éditions Rieder, 1935. A competent, scholarly work. Begins with two chapters on the Revolution, Brest-Litovsk, and intervention as it concerned France.

Strakhovsky, Leonid I. *The Origins of American Intervention in North Russia (1918).* Princeton, N. J.: Princeton University Press, 1937. A scholarly but badly written monograph by a Russian who played a part in the events described. The first chapter is devoted to Brest-Litovsk and the background of intervention.

Suarez, Georges. *Briand: Sa vie—son oeuvre.* 5 vols. Paris: Librairie Plon, 1938-41. An exhaustive biography by a conservative French writer. The fourth volume devotes considerable attention to Franco-Russian relations in 1917.

Tanin, M. *10 Let Vneshnei Politiki S.S.S.R. (1917-1927) [Ten Years of the Foreign Policy of the U.S.S.R.].* Moscow and Leningrad: Gosudarstvennoe Izdatelstvo, 1927. A general survey, of which the first two chapters cover Brest-Litovsk and the origins of intervention.

Taracouzio, T. A. *War and Peace in Soviet Diplomacy.* New York: Macmillan, 1940.

Temperley, H. W. V. (ed.). *A History of the Peace Conference of Paris.* 6 vols. London: Henry Frowde, Hodder & Stoughton, 1920-24. A semiofficial history. Gives the diplomatic background in the first volume.

Terrail, Gabriel ("Mermeix"). *Les Négociations secrètes et les quatre armistices avec pièces justificatives.* Paris: Libraire Ollendorff, 1921. Includes an account of the Stockholm conference, interesting for its Germanophobic interpretation.

—————. *Nivelle et Painlevé: La Deuxième crise du commandement (decembre 1916–mai 1917).* Paris: Libraire Paul Ollendorff, 1919. Has a chapter on the mutiny of the Russian soldiers in France.

Tompkins, Pauline. *American-Russian Relations in the Far East.* New York: Macmillan, 1949.

Trotsky, Leon. *The History of the Russian Revolution.* 3 vols. New York: Simon and Schuster, 1932. A brilliant interpretative work with some attention to diplomacy. Must be used with caution, particularly in dealing with Stalin.

————. *Stalin: An Appraisal of the Man and His Influence.* New York: Harper & Brothers, 1946. A lengthy political tract disguised as a work of scholarship. Unfinished at Trotsky's death.

Van Der Slice, Austin. *International Labor, Diplomacy, and Peace, 1914-1919.* Philadelphia: University of Pennsylvania Press, 1941. A scholarly monograph, not always as well organized as it might be, but with a good deal of information on Allied labor and socialist groups and their attitude toward the Russian Revolution.

Vernadsky, George. *Lenin: Red Dictator.* New Haven, Conn.: Yale University Press, 1931. A political biography, rather hostile in interpretation.

Viereck, George Sylvester. *The Strangest Friendship in History: Woodrow Wilson and Colonel House.* New York: Liveright, 1932.

Walsh, Edmund A. *The Fall of the Russian Empire: The Story of the Last of the Romanovs and the Coming of the Bolsheviki.* Boston: Little, Brown, 1928. A popular account by a conservative writer. Since superseded by more substantial works.

Wheeler-Bennett, John W. *The Forgotten Peace: Brest-Litovsk, March 1918.* New York: William Morrow, 1939. A definitive, scholarly work, extremely well written. Considerable attention given to Allied diplomacy.

————. *Hindenburg: The Wooden Titan.* London: Macmillan, 1936.

White, John Albert. *The Siberian Intervention.* Princeton, N. J.: Princeton University Press, 1950.

Williams, William Appleman. *American Russian Relations, 1781-1947.* New York: Rinehart, 1952. A revised and considerably enlarged version of the author's doctoral dissertation (see below).

Yakhontoff, Victor A. *USSR Foreign Policy.* New York: Coward-McCann, 1945.

Zilliacus, K. *Mirror of the Past: A History of Secret Diplomacy.* New York: A. A. Wyn, 1946. A left-wing interpretation of diplomatic history (*ca.* 1914-28), particularly critical of Allied policy toward Russia.

THESES AND DISSERTATIONS

I. STUDIES OF AMERICAN AND ALLIED INTERVENTION

(Note: The following contain pertinent material relating to the present work though their major emphasis is on the period after the Brest-Litovsk peace.)

Berutti, John Morris. "Woodrow Wilson's Policy toward Russia." Typewritten master's thesis, Department of History, Stanford University, 1949.

Bock, Benjamin. "The Origins of the Inter-Allied Intervention in Eastern Asia, 1918-1920." Typewritten Ph.D. dissertation, Department of Political Science, Stanford University, 1940.

Bogart, Mildred Marshall. "Allied Policies of Intervention in Russia." Typewritten master's thesis, Department of History, Stanford University, 1938.

Brandenburg, William A., Jr. "The Origins of American Military Intervention in Russia, 1918-1920." Typewritten Ph.D. dissertation, Department of History, University of Colorado, 1946.

Cagan, Leo David. "Administration of American Intervention in Russia, 1918-1920: A Study in Policy Conflict." Typewritten master's thesis, Department of International Relations, University of Chicago, 1947.

Colligan, William J. "Some Factors in the Development of American Intervention in Siberia, March 1917–August 1918." Typewritten honors thesis in History, Harvard University, 1948.

Connally, Patricia. "The Preliminaries to Allied Intervention in Siberia, 1917-1918: A Study of the Diplomatic Negotiations and of the Motives Involved." Typewritten master's thesis in history, Graduate School, Syracuse University, 1948.

Fike, Claude Edwin, Jr. "A Study of Russian-American Relations during the Ominous Years, 1917-1921." Typewritten Ph.D. dissertation, Graduate College, University of Illinois, 1950.

Frisbee, W. H., Jr. "American Intervention in Russia, 1918-1920." Typewritten honors thesis in History, Harvard University, 1935.

Kaston, Howard. "American Intervention, Diplomatic and Military, in Soviet Russia, 1918-1922." Typewritten master's thesis, Department of History, University of California, 1932.

Levine, Allan Lewis. "American Intervention in Siberia, 1918-1920." Typewritten honors thesis in History, Harvard University, 1942.

McGowan, Thomson Cook. "A Study of the Effects of American Foreign Policy on Soviet Foreign Policy from November 1917 to August 1920." Typewritten honors thesis in Government, Harvard University, 1947.

Newlin, Michael H. "United States Policy toward Russia, 1917-1920." Typewritten honors thesis in Government, Harvard University, 1949.

Pelzel, Sophia Rogoski. "American Intervention in Siberia, 1918-1920." Lithographed Ph.D. dissertation, Department of Political Science, University of Pennsylvania, 1946.

Priest, Lyman William. "The French Intervention in South Russia, 1918-19." Typewritten master's thesis, Department of History, Stanford University, 1947.

Unterberger, Betty Miller. "America's Siberian Expedition, 1918-1920: A Study of National Policy." Typewritten Ph.D. dissertation, Graduate School of Arts and Sciences, Duke University, 1950.

Varkala, Joseph C. "Allied Intervention in Siberia, 1918-1920." Typewritten master's thesis, Department of International Relations, University of Chicago, 1936.

II. OTHER

Anderson, Paul H. "The Attitude of the American Leftist Leaders toward the Russian Revolution (1917-1923)." Lithographed Ph.D. dissertation, Notre Dame University, 1942. An ill-assorted and awkward compilation but useful within the limits defined.

Belk, Norvell Carlton. "The War Aims and Peace Proposals of the British Labor Party, 1914-1918." Typewritten master's thesis, Department of History, Stanford University, 1929. Contains material on British labor and the Stockholm conference.

Benjamin, Alfred. "The Great Dilemma: The Foreign Policy of the Russian Provisional Government, March–May 1917." Typewritten Ph.D. dissertation, Faculty of Political Science, Columbia University, 1950. An exhaustive and impartial study of the Provisional Government's foreign policy under Milyukov.

Caukin, Esther. "The Peace Proposals of Germany and Austria-Hungary, 1914-1918." Typewritten Ph.D. dissertation, Department of History, Stanford University, 1927. Contains a chapter on separate peace negotiations with Russia.

Davis, Betty Jane. "The Diplomacy of the Straits, 1914-1946." Typewritten master's thesis, Department of Political Science, Stanford University, 1946.

DeYoung, Charles Daniel. "David Rowland Francis: American in Russia." Typewritten master's thesis, University of Wisconsin, 1949. A critical appraisal of Francis's career as ambassador to Russia.

Finnegan, Edward H., S.J. "The United States Policy towards Russia, March 1917–March 1918." Typewritten Ph.D. dissertation, Department of History, Fordham University, 1947. A very detailed study, painstakingly impartial. Based upon printed material in English and some manuscript sources. Emphasizes public opinion.

Gasiorowski, Zugmunt Jerzy. "The Secret Straits Agreement of 1915." Typewritten master's thesis, Department of History, University of California, 1947. Brings the story up to 1917.

Holmes, Wanda-Lee. "Russians in the Opinion of American Diplomats, 1781-1917." Typewritten master's thesis, Department of History, Stanford University, 1949. Indicates, as do virtually all secondary sources, that Ambassador Francis's ability left much to be desired.

Lichman, Jacob. "Early American Relations with Bolshevik Russia, November 1917–March 1918." Typewritten honors thesis in History, Harvard University, 1937. A competent summary, superseded in scope by Finnegan's dissertation (above).

Morony, Jean. "Trends in Russian Foreign Policy, 1895-1928." Typewritten master's thesis, Department of Political Science, Stanford University, 1933.

Papouktchieva, Maria. "La Politique de la Russie a l'égard des détroits." Printed Ph.D. dissertation, University of Geneva, 1944.

Reitzer, Ladislas F. "United States–Russian Economic Relations, 1917-1920." Typewritten Ph.D. dissertation, Department of International Relations, University of Chicago, 1950. A detailed study beginning with the March Revolution.

Sacks, Benjamin. "The Independent Labor Party during the World War." Typewritten Ph.D. dissertation, Department of History, Stanford University, 1934. Includes material on the I.L.P., Russia, and the Stockholm conference.

Smith, Francis Hartley. "Relations between the British Labour Party and the Independent Labour Party during the World War." Typewritten master's thesis, Department of History, University of Chicago, 1935. Relates the orientation of both parties to the Russian Revolution and the Stockholm conference.

Steading, Alma Davis. "The United States and Kerensky: A Study of Relations with Russia, March–November 1917." Typewritten master's thesis, Department of History, University of South Carolina, 1948. A brief summary, rather superficial in detail.

Treat, Margaret. "United States Press Opinion Regarding the First Phase of the Russian Revolution, March–November 1917." Typewritten master's thesis, Department of History, Stanford University, 1949. An excellent summary of editorial opinion in eighteen leading newspapers. Amply documents the misconceptions about the Revolution fostered in the press.

Williams, William Appleman. "Raymond Robins and Russian-American Relations, 1917-1938." Typewritten Ph.D. dissertation, University of Wisconsin, 1950. A well-written study based mainly on manuscript sources and conversations with Robins. Emphasizes late 1917 and 1918. Critical of American policy.

ARTICLES

Davis, Jerome. "One Hundred and Fifty Years of American-Russian Relations, 1777-1927." *The Annals* [of the American Academy of Political and Social Science], CXXXII(July, 1927), 18-31.

Friedland, T. "Frantsuzskaya Pechat ob Oktyabr (Iyul–Dekabr 1917 goda)" ["The French Press on October (July–Dec. 1917)"], *Istorik Marksist* [*Marxist Historian*], V (1927), 71-93.

Girshfeld, A. "O Roli SShA v Organizatsii Antisovetskoi Interventsii v Sibiri i na Dalnem Vostoke" ["The Role of the U.S.A. in the Organization of the Anti-Soviet Intervention in Siberia and the Far East"], *Voprosy Istorii* [*Questions of History*], No. 8 (Aug., 1948), 3-22.

Graham, Malbone W. "Russian-American Relations, 1917-1933: An Interpretation," *American Political Science Review*, XXVIII (June, 1934), 387-409.

Guliga, A. "Nachalny Period Antisovetskoi Interventsii SShA (1917-1918 gg.)" ["The Beginning Period of Anti-Soviet Intervention by the U.S.A. (1917-1918)"], *Voprosy Istorii* [*Questions of History*], No. 3 (March, 1950), 3-25.

Houghton, N. D. "The Policy of the United States and Other Nations with Respect to the Recognition of the Russian Soviet Government, 1917-1929," *International Conciliation*, No. 247 (Feb., 1929), 85-106.

Kazovskaya, A. "Nota Milyukova i Aprelskie Dni" ["Milyukov's Note and the April Days"], *Proletarskaya Revolyutsiya* [*Proletarian Revolution*], No. 63 (April, 1927), 83-100.

Kerner, Robert J. "Russia and the Straits Question, 1915-17," *Slavonic Review*, VIII (March, 1930), 589-600.

Lippmann, Walter, and Merz, Charles. "A Test of the News," *New Republic*, XXIII (Aug. 4, 1920), 1-42 (special supplement).

Lozovskii, A. "Leiboristskaya Partiya i Fevralskaya Revolyutsiya" ["The Labor Party and the February Revolution"], *Voprosy Istorii* [*Questions of History*], No. 2 (Feb., 1948), 70-88.

Maxe, Jean. "Sadoul chez les russes," *La Revue critique des idées et des livres,* XXVII (Jan. 25, 1920), 139-51.

Mirkine-Guetzevitch, B. "La Politique exterieure du gouvernement provisoire russe (la question de la paix en 1917)," *Bulletin de la société d'histoire moderne,* March, 1928, 27-33.

Mohrenschildt, Dimitri von. "The Early American Observers of the Russian Revolution, 1917-1921," *Russian Review,* III (Autumn, 1943), 64-74.

Moore, Harriet. "American Relations with the Russian Empire and the USSR," *American Quarterly on the Soviet Union,* III (Nov., 1940), 3-26.

Pares, Bernard. "Sir George Buchanan in Russia," *Slavonic Review,* III (March, 1925), 576-86.

Pierre, André. "Les États-Unis et la gouvernement des soviets (1917-1918)," *Monde slave,* X (Oct., 1933), 298-313.

—————. "Les États-Unis et la première révolution russe (mars– novembre 1917)," *Revue d'histoire de la guerre mondiale,* XI (Jan., 1933), 1-16.

Pingaud, Albert. "La Mission de M. Doumer en Russie (1915)," *Revue des deux mondes,* IX (June 15, 1932), 865-73.

—————. "La Mission de M. Doumergue en Russie en 1917," *Revue d'histoire de la guerre mondiale,* XV (Oct., 1937), 339-52.

Rain, Pierre. "Nicolas II et sa diplomatie pendant la guerre," *Revue des sciences politiques,* LII (Jan.–March, 1929), 105-27.

Rotshtein, F. "Anglia i Oktyabrskaya Revolyutsia" ["England and the October Revolution"], *Istorik Marksist* [*Marxist Historian*], V (1927), 36-48.

Stevens, Walter B. "Missourians Abroad: David R. Francis, Ambassador Extraordinary and Plentipotentiary to Russia," *Missouri Historical Review,* XIII (April, 1919), 195-225.

Storozhev, Prof. V. N. "Diplomatiya i Revolyutsiya" ["Diplomacy and Revolution"], *Vestnik Narodnovo Komissariata Inostrannikh Del* [*Messenger of the People's Commissariat for Foreign Affairs*], No. 4-5 (June 20, 1920), 69-104.

Strakhovsky, Leonid I. "The Franco-British Plot to Dismember Russia," *Current History,* XXXIII (March, 1931), 839-42.

Index

American Federation of Labor: and Allied labor conference, 215; mentioned, 29; and message to Russia, 139; and Stockholm conference, 79-80; Wilson's speech to, 165-66

American Revolution, 95

Amherst, Trotsky in, 41

Anarchism, 189

Anarchists, 39, 155

Anderson, Colonel Henry, American Red Cross representative, and Kalpashnikov affair, 184-85

Anglo-French convention (Dec. 23, 1917), 190, 193

Anti-Semitism: and Bolsheviks, 163; and Root mission to Russia, 96-97

Archangel, 7, 13, 15

Armenia: as British sphere, 190; Milyukov on, 48-49; Turkish, 150

Asquith, Herbert, British statesman, welcomes Russian mission, 12

Associated Press, 153

Atlantic Ocean, 101, 110, 197

Aurora, Russian cruiser, 155, 160

Austria: and Allied secret treaty, 9; army of, 11, 208; and Brest-Litovsk negotiations, 206-8 (see also Czernin); and negotiations with Allies, 94; Russian offensive against, 10, 112; Vasilchikova in, 12; U. S. declares war on, 178; and the war, 10, 11, 197; war prisoners of, 193; workers of, 227

Austria-Hungary, 206, 207, 224

Bakhmetev, George, Russian (tsarist) ambassador to U. S., 106

Bakhmetev, Professor Boris, Russian (Provisional Government) ambassador to U. S.: and House, 212; mentioned, 141; and mission to U. S., 106-8, 111; on November Revolution, 165

Balfour, Arthur, British Foreign Minister: at Allied conference, 177; and House, 192; and Lockhart, 235, 236-37; mentioned, 81; and Nabokov, 117; and Wilson's address, 212

Balkans, 224

Baltic provinces, Germans occupy, 232

Baltic Sea: mentioned, 103; German expedition in, 152, 153

Bank of Commerce (N. Y.), 146

Bedford, 205

Belgium: mentioned, 69; and socialist mission to Russia, 68-69

Benckendorff, Count Alexander, Russian ambassador to England, 13, 63

Berger, Victor, American socialist, and Stockholm conference, 75-76

Berkman, Alexander, American anarchist, 39

Berlin, 13, 163, 196, 204, 222, 225; see also Germany

Berliner Tageblatt, 130

Berne, 228

Bertron, Samuel R., American banker, and mission to Russia, 97, 101-6

Bessarabia, 187, 190

Billings, Dr. Franklin, American physician, 143

Bismarck, Prince Otto von, 235

Bitsenko, Anastasia, Socialist Revolutionary leader, at Brest-Litovsk, 196

Black Sea, 103, 109

Blackpool, 86

Bolshevik Revolution, 37, 164; see also November Revolution

Bolsheviks: Allied opinion of, 163-66; Allied policy benefits, 65, 88, 132, 149; and Allied propaganda, 181; and Brest-Litovsk negotiations, see Brest-Litovsk; central committee of, 56, 224, 227, 230, 231; and Constituent Assembly, 220-22; Duma representatives arrested, 4; as German agents and spies, 104, 114, 163, 179, 183, 201-4, 217, 233; government of, 100, 170, 237 (see also Soviet government); and Japanese intervention, 236 (see also Japan, intervention in Russia); and Judson, 171-72; and "July Days," 113-15; and Kalpashnikov affair, 184-85; and Kornilov coup, 124, 128, 131, 138; Kornilov on, 119; and Lenin, 44; and May demonstrations, 57; menace of, 188; mentioned, 40, 50, 64, 126, 147, 149, 152, 153, 173, 174, 180, 182, 209, 230, 234; and Moscow State Conference, 120; and November Revolution, 88, 158-66; oppose the war, 4; party conference of, 62-63; peace decree of, 161, 168-69, 206; and Pre-Parliament, 142; prepare for insurrection, 154-55; press of, 155, 199, 200 (see also Izvestia, Pravda); propaganda of, 113, 142, 144,

188, 200-1, 213, 225; return to Russia, 38-40, 42-43; and Russian troops in France, 137; and secret treaties, 9, 20, 161, 168; and Sisson, 201; and Soviet resolution, 60; and Stockholm conference, 67, 77, 83; Trotsky joins, 41; and Wilson's address, 210-13

Bolshevism: and Allies, 175-76, 200, 219; Francis on, 166; German general staff on, 42; Hoffmann on, 230; mentioned, 3, 106, 123, 146, 147, 152, 176, 177, 181, 183, 187, 188, 206; popularity of in army, 113; see also Communism

Bolshoy Theater, 120

Bonar Law, Andrew: in Commons, 151; praises Tsar, 29

Bordeaux, 87

Borgbjerg, Frederick, Danish Social Democrat, 67

Borodin, Michael, Russian radical, 39

Bosphorus, Straits of, see Straits

Boston Evening Transcript, 234

Boston Transcript, 27

Breshkovskaya, Catherine, Russian revolutionary: Pravda on, 181; and Thompson, 144-45

Brest-Litovsk: and Allied press opinion, 234-35; armistice negotiations at, 179, 195-99, 204; negotiations mentioned, 209, 210, 214, 216, 227, 228; peace of, 26, 193-94; peace negotiations at, 206-8, 209, 217-20, 224-26, 233; treaty of, 237

Brusilov, Alexis, Russian general: on Bolsheviks, 113; leads offensive, 10

Buchanan, Lady, wife of Sir George, 129, 160

Buchanan, Meriel, daughter of Sir George, 129

Buchanan, Sir George, British ambassador to Russia: against Russian mission, 11; and Allied conference, 151-52; on Allied policy, 93; 176-77; on Allied protest, 170-71; characterized, 6; complaints to, 84; and Francis, 17; and Kerensky, 118, 152, 154; and Kornilov coup, 124; leaves Russia, 183, 184, 187; on Lenin, 43-44; and March Revolution, 18, 22, 32-33; mentioned, 129; and Nicholas II, 16, 18, 19; protests to Provisional Government, 131-32, 139-41; recall of, 69-71; and recognition of Provisional

Government, 31-32; and Russian armistice, 199-200; speech of, 59; on Stockholm conference, 78; and Tereshchenko, 115, 141, 151, 152; and Trotsky, 41, 167, 175

Bucharest, 151

Buckingham Palace, 132

Buffalo, 166

Bukharin, Nicholas, Bolshevik leader: edits paper, 40; as "Left Communist," 222-23, 231-32; returns to Russia, 39

Bulgaria: and Brest-Litovsk, 206-7; and the war, 15, 197

Burtsev, Vladimir, Socialist Revolutionary leader, 153

Cachin, Marcel, French socialist: and mission to Russia, 51, 52; speech of, 72, 76

Cadets, see Constitutional Democrats

Caporetto, Italian defeat at, 197

Canada, 109

Carter, William, British socialist, and abortive Russian mission, 73-74

Catherine II, Empress of Russia, 102

Caucasus, 190

Cecil, Lord Robert, British minister: on Allied policy, 92; on Bolshevik peace proposal, 169

Central Powers: and armistice with Russia, 179, 196-99; and Bolshevik peace proposal, 161; and Bolshevik propaganda, 200-1; and March Revolution, 26; mentioned, 13, 112, 194, 210, 214, 217; and peace negotiations with Russia, see Brest-Litovsk; socialists of, 75; and the war, 197

Central Rada, see Ukraine, Rada of

Chaikovsky, Nicholas, Russian revolutionary, 145

Chamber of Commerce (U. S.), 139

Chamber of Deputies (France): Pichon in, 209; resolutions on war aims, 92-93; socialists of, 29, 51, 209; and Stockholm conference, 76

Chamber of Deputies (Italy), and debate on Russia, 32

Chernov, Victor, Socialist Revolutionary leader: and Buchanan, 93; and "July Days," 114; on Kerensky, 127; and land program, 116; on Milyukov, 58, 63; resigns from cabinet, 138; returns to Russia, 39; on secret treaties, 45

Judson, General William V., American military attaché in Russia: and Bolsheviks, 171-72; and Francis, 167; mentioned, 148; recalled, 174; on Thompson and Robins, 149; visits Trotsky, 174, 175
"July Days": events of, 113-15; mentioned, 105, 116, 117, 202
Junkers, 155, 157

Kaledin, Alexis, Russian general: and Allies, 185-86, 193, 230; and French officers, 194; and Kalpashnikov affair, 184
Kalpashnikov, Andrew, Russian officer: and Bolshevik government, 184-85; mentioned, 186, 194
Kamenev, Leo, Bolshevik leader: arrested, 115; at Brest-Litovsk, 196, 218; and mission to England, 228-29; opposes insurrection, 154-55; on Stockholm conference, 77
Karakhan, Leo, Bolshevik leader, at Brest-Litovsk, 196, 199, 201, 233
Kemp, Admiral, British officer, 132
Kerensky, Alexander: and Allied conference, 149, 177; Allied message to, 118; Allied protest to, 139-41; and Allied socialist mission, 52-53; on Allies, 147-48; and Belgian mission, 68; and Buchanan, 84, 152, 154; cabinet of, 141-42; escapes to England, 162; and General Scott, 104; government of, 117; and Kolchak mission, 109; and Kornilov, 119, 123, 125-28, 130, 138; mentioned, 26, 108, 148, 157, 163, 165, 171, 182, 220, 234; messages to, 29, 52; and Milyukov, 47, 49, 55-56; as minister of justice, 25; as minister of war, 65; at Moscow State Conference, 119-22; and November Revolution, 158-59; as "persuader-in-chief," 93-95; as potential dictator, 115, 118; at Pre-Parliament, 155-56; as premier, 116; and press interview, 153-54; press reports on, 166; proposes resignation, 61, 156; and Romanovs, 34; and Russian offensive, 111-13; and Russian troops in France, 134; and secret treaties, 45, 111; and Soviet, 50, 62; and Stockholm conference, 82-84; and Tereshchenko, 154; and Thomas, 54; and Thompson, 144-45; and U. S.,

139, 141; and Verkhovsky, 153; and Wilson, 110-11
Kerth, Lieutenant Colonel Monroe, American representative in Russia, 172
Kiel, naval mutiny at, 197
Kienthal conference, 66
Kiev: Allied military missions in, 176; Belgian mission in, 69; Bolsheviks capture, 224; Fitz-Williams in, 224; Ukrainian Rada at, 186
Kitchener, Lord, British minister, 13-14
Knox, Alfred, British military attaché in Russia: advises Provisional Government, 115; and Bolsheviks, 160; and Kornilov, 121, 123, 141; leaves Russia, 183; and pro-war propaganda, 50, 95; and Rodzyanko, 45; on Russian army, 112; on Russian situation, 148-49; and Stockholm conference, 85
Kolchak, Alexander, Russian admiral, and mission to U. S., 109-10
Kollontai, Alexandra, Bolshevik leader, 39, 222
Kommunist, 235
Kornilov, Lavr, Russian general: and Allies, 193-94; and Allied press opinion of, 124-26, 130-31; and attempted coup, 122-30, 132, 138, 139, 141, 155; characterization, 118-19; escape of, 176; and Kerensky, 113; and May demonstrations, 57, 59; mentioned, 65, 148, 166, 234; at Moscow State Conference, 119, 121; resigns, 61.
Kornilov, the National Hero, 121
Krasnov, Peter, Russian general, 162
Kremlin, 200, 237
Kronstadt, 114, 159
Kropotkin, Prince Peter, Russian anarchist, 38
Krylenko, Ensign Nicholas, Bolshevik leader: as commander-in-chief, 170; English offer to, 223; as "German-Jewish spy," 202; and murder of Dukhonin, 176
Krymov, General, Russian officer, 122-23, 130
Kshesinskaya Palace, 114
Kühlmann, Baron Richard von, German Foreign Minister: at Brest-Litovsk, 206-7, 217-19, 222, 225-27; mentioned, 223
Kurdistan, 190

delegation returns to, 208; Democratic Conference in, 141-42; embassies in, 202; garrison of, 155, 157; German threat to, 231-32; Gurko leaves, 132; Henderson in, 69; Henderson leaves, 77; "July Days" in, 113-15, 117; Knox in, 112; Kolchak in, 109; and Kornilov *coup*, 123-24, 127-30; Lenin returns to, 43, 154; Lockhart in, 183; March Revolution in, 22-25; May demonstrations in, 57-59, 60; mentioned, 6, 13, 30, 63, 72, 73, 74, 95, 98, 99, 115, 121, 139, 143, 146, 147, 154, 164, 165, 166, 169, 172, 173, 176, 179, 180, 181, 182, 184, 187, 193, 202, 207, 211, 217, 220, 223, 227, 228, 229, 233; return of political prisoners to, 37; Root mission in, 102-5; Steffens in, 111; Soviet of, 25, 34, 50, 71, 93, 103, 130, 138, 141, 155, 159, 209, 214, 216, 225; strike in, 8, 16, 21, 22; Thompson and Robins in, 144; Trotsky returns to, 41

Petrov, Peter, Bolshevik leader, 175, 228
Petrunkevitch, Alexander, American professor, 99
Philadelphia *Press*, 234
Pichon, Stephen, French minister, 209
Plekhanov, George, Menshevik leader, 4, 38
Poincaré, Raymond, 4, 189
Pokrovsky, Michael, Bolshevik leader, 206, 222
Poland, 207, 232
Pope, 120
Portland *Oregonian*, 126
Pravda: on Bolshevik decree, 189; on Diamandi, 187; on Germans, 216; offices raided, 114; publishes secret treaties, 168; on S.R.'s, 181; and Trotsky, 41; and Wilson's address, 213
Pre-Parliament, *see* Provisional Council of the Russian Republic
Progressive party (U. S.), 143
Protopopov, Alexander, Vice-President of Duma, 12
Provisional Council of the Russian Republic: dissolved, 159; Kerensky at, 155-56; meeting of, 142-43; Tereshchenko at, 151; Verkhovsky at, 153
Provisional Government: and Allied conference, 149-52; and Allied criticism of, 118; and Allied protest to, 139-41; and Allied socialist mission, 52; arrests by, 37, 115; and Bakhmetev mission, 106-9, 111; Bolsheviks on, 44, 56; cabinet changes in, 61-65, 89, 116-17; formation of, 25; foreign policy of, 45-49, 52-56, 58-65, 89-91, 93, 151; and Gurko affair, 132; and "July Days," 113-15; and Kolchak mission, 109-10; and Kornilov *coup*, 122-32, 138; Knox on, 148; manifesto of, 46, 49; mentioned, 29, 32, 43, 48, 106-7, 133, 152, 163, 165, 167, 182, 220; and November Revolution, 158-60; and offensive, 111-13, 118, 124; and peace, 65, 88; recognized by Allies, 31-32; recognized by U. S., 30; and Romanovs, 34-37; and Russian troops in France, 134, 137; and Sazonov, 63; and secret treaties, 45-47, 110-11; and Soviet, 38, 41, 147; and Stockholm conference, 77, 81-85; strength of, 155, 156; threatened, 157; and U. S. missions, 96-106, 108, 109, 111; weakness of, 144

Prussia, 6, 205, 210, 240; *see also* Germany
Pskov, 33, 162
Purishkevich, Vladimir, Russian monarchist, 17

Rada, *see* Ukraine, Rada of
Radek, Karl, Bolshevik leader: at Brest-Litovsk, 217, 241; heads press bureau, 200, 201; as "Left Communist," 222-23; returns to Russia, 42
Rapp, Eugene, representative of Russian war ministry, 133
Rappel, 118
Rasputin, Gregory, Russian religious charlatan: attacked in Duma, 17; and the Empress, 5, 9-10; on Kitchener, 14; mentioned, 13; murdered, 17
Red Army, 227
Red Cross: and Bolsheviks, 182; and Kalpashnikov affair, 184; mentioned, 129, 145; mission to Russia, 143
Red Guard: and Allies, 231; and Constituent Assembly, 221; and German threat, 233; mentioned, 155; and November Revolution, 158, 160
Reed, John, American journalist, 200
Reilly, Sidney, British agent in Russia, and Sisson documents, 203
Reinstein, Boris, American socialist: and

82; war aims of, 44, 92; and war with Japan, 3, 8 (see also Japan, intervention in Russia); and Wilson's address, 212-13; see also Allied Powers, Bolsheviks, Brest-Litovsk, Constituent Assembly, Democratic Conference, Duma, Moscow State Conference, Petrograd, Pre-Parliament, Provisional Government, Soviet government, Soviet of Workers' and Soldiers' Deputies, Stockholm conference

Russian Revolution, 3, 22, 34, 43, 88, 98, 104, 131, 142, 159, 164, 173, 209, 217, 218, 224, 226, 227, 231; see also Bolshevik Revolution, March Revolution, November Revolution

Russian Revolution of 1905, 3, 25

Russkoe Slovo, 165

Russo-Japanese War (1904-5), 3, 8

Sadoul, Captain Jacques, French representative in Russia: and aid to Bolshevik Russia, 216-17, 237; arrives in Russia, 180; and Hoffmann map, 223; mentioned, 182, 193; and Noulens, 235, 237; as unofficial agent, 179, 195

St. Louis, 30

St. Petersburg, see Petrograd

Salonika: mentioned, 15, 132, 134; mutiny of Russian troops in, 137; Russian troops from, 135

Samara, 133

San Francisco, 39, 110

San Francisco *Chronicle*, 126

Sanders, William, British socialist, and mission to Russia, 51

Sarajevo, 3

Saturday Review, 118, 125, 163

Sazonov, Sergé, Russian Foreign Minister: as ambassador, 63; mentioned, 70; resigns, 16; on Russian soldiers, 16

Scotland, 11, 13, 73

Scott, Major-General Hugh L., American chief of staff, and mission to Russia, 98, 101-6

Seamen's and Firemen's Union (Great Britain), 73, 215

Seattle, 101, 107, 111

Sebastopol, 109

Secret treaties: Bolsheviks and, 9, 168, 209; France and, 9, 20, 91; Great Britain and, 9, 20, 92, 210; Keren-

sky and, 45, 111; mentioned, 53, 93; Milyukov and, 46-49; Russia and, 8-9, 45, 161; Tereshchenko and, 90; U. S. and, 111

Semyenov, Eugene P., Russian journalist, and Sisson documents, 203

Semyenov, Gregory, Cossack leader, 193

Senate (France), 14

Senate (U. S.), 107

Serbia, 150-51

Shatov, Bill, Russian radical, 39

Shlyapnikov, Alexander, Bolshevik leader, 53

Shulgin, Basil, Duma deputy, 24-25

Siberia: Allied intervention in, 101, 190-93; Bolsheviks exiled to, 4; Romanovs in, 37; Japanese intervention in, 236, 238; route through, 39

Sisson, Edgar, American representative in Russia: and Bolshevik propaganda, 201; and forged documents, 203-4; and mission to Russia, 146-47, 181-82; and Wilson's address, 211-12, 213

Skobelev, Michael, Soviet deputy: and Buchanan, 93; as conference delegate, 150-51; as minister, 65; resigns from cabinet, 138

Smirnov, E., Soviet delegate, and mission to the West, 78-80, 85, 87

Smolny Institute: Allied ambassadors at, 187; Judson at, 174; Knox at, 160; mentioned, 167, 179, 217, 228, 231; Robins at, 182, 185; Sisson at, 213; Soviet congress at, 160

Snowden, Philip, British socialist, 52, 74, 92

Social Democrats (Russia), 4; see also Bolsheviks, Mensheviks

Socialism, 189, 216

Socialist Labor party (U. S.), 75

Socialist party (France): congress of, 87; defies government, 86-87; on Franco-Russian alliance, 51; and invitation to British socialists, 79; newspaper of, 126; on Stockholm conference, 72, 76; see also Chamber of Deputies, socialists of

Socialist party (Great Britain), 52, 72, 73

Socialist party (Italy), 72

Socialist party (U. S.), 75-76, 86, 97-98

Socialist Revolutionary party (Russia): and Constituent Assembly, 220-21: